SEEDS OF DAUTRINIAS

ILLUSTRATIONS OF ESCU

- VOLUME ONE -

JOHN D. ESCU

SOARING RULEK PUBLISHING

Cover design: rafido.webnode.fr

Cover Illustrations: John D. Escu

Interior illustrations: John D. Escu

Copyedit and Proofreading: courtneyumphress.com

Published by: Soaring Rulek Publishing

Contact: john.d.escu@gmail.com

ISBN:

Paperback: **978-3-9826369-6-2**

eBook: **978-3-9826369-8-6**

FOREWORD

Thank you for your interest in the **Seeds of Dautrinias**!
Before you read this book, I recommend you read and complete **Favors Within Ashes**, book one in the **Sins of Starlight Collapse** series.

ISBN:
Paperback: **978-3-9826369-0-0**
Hardcover: **978-3-9826369-1-7**
eEook: **978-3-9826369-2-4**

Blessed be the Gods!

Thank you for your interest in exploring the origin of Dautrinias!

In this illustration book, you will be presented with the design evolution of the most important characters from the novel *Favors Within Ashes*, book one in the Sins of Starlight Collapse series.

The journey of this world began in the late nineties when, as a mostly solitary child, I explored the forests and hills surrounding my childhood city in Romania.

I would take my father's military hunting knife (which I was not allowed to touch, and got a lot of scolding for doing so—only when I got caught) alongside my trusty spear (an old, rusted walking stick left in the attic by the former Germans who used to live in the house) and commence my adventures.

I imagined I was one of the epic characters from the anime and cartoons I watched, or a superhero I read about in the comic books I could sometimes find at the local newsstands.

My parents were reluctant every time I would beg them to buy comic books, because at that time, they were only translated into the Hungarian or German languages. They could not understand why I would want to have comic books written in words I could not comprehend. I would always tell them I did not need to understand what was written inside and I would just imagine my own stories and apply them to the images within.

Inevitably, I started drawing my own comic books. Mostly anime fanfiction mixed with my own characters. I rarely showed them to anyone. My drawing skills were not that good, and I had no teachers or training. I just had the desire to draw what I imagined.

With the passage of time, I began showing more interest in music, teaching myself how to play guitar and bass, composing and recording music. All thoughts of drawing did not often occur anymore, though my ideas regarding Dautrinias and its characters remained in my head, growing and developing. I would sketch them anytime I got the chance—at school, at work, during work breaks.

I was guided by my parents into focusing on school and studies rather than art. They never forbade me from drawing or playing guitar as long as I did well in school. But even though I didn't do as well as they wanted, I still had the freedom to express my creativity.

I will forever be thankful for that and the fact that my sketchbooks, once believed to be thrown away, were safely kept in our home's basement in Romania. Some of those drawings are present in this book.

Now, for the first time , you will be able to see some of the very first drafts and sketches of Marco, Mara, Dolur, Jerada, Stephano, and all the other characters of importance from the first novel of the Sins of Starlight Collapse series. Alongside these drawings, you can read about my process of creating these characters. Some I had to add to the story to improve the flow of the narrative, while others were split from one entity into more characters.

Most of the characters had other names and changed appearances. If you are expecting high-end, perfect drawings, bear in mind some of these sketches are older than twenty years. In my early days of sketching, I wasn't that good of an artist, but I followed my heart and taught myself to do art, in all its forms, to become the best I could be.

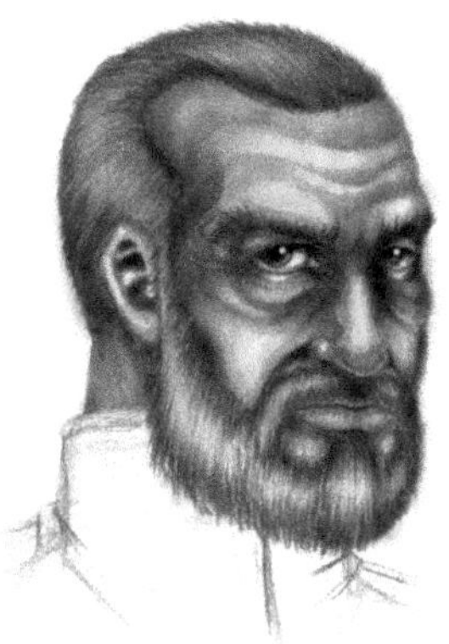

- GENERAL DOLUR LODORT -

One of the first characters I imagined and created, even before thinking of this world and story, was the character I now call the "Trinity of Man."

Created and developed in the late nineties, this one was called "James the Gray Wolf," and he was the very first character I created, belonging to a version of the story that took place in a modern world, largely influenced by the nu metal music scene. The story later moved into a Victorian-style era, but in 2013, I gradually gravitated toward a medieval time and setting.

In 2014, I split this character into three others. One of them was Dolur Lodort.

With Dolur, I wanted to have a character whose morality and honor I would feel proud to speak of. A man who would inspire safety and reliability. One who would not resort to lashing out with his sword when conflicts arose, but rather would try to communicate and search for a peaceful resolution. The classic "wise old man" trope.

A few years after creating him and adding him to the early drafts of *Favors Within Ashes*, I knew I needed to show his experience in battle, but I was not (and still am not) fond of flashback scenes. Thus I added the prosthetics.

I was always bothered by the perfectly healthy veterans who lacked scars (of any sort) in the media I consumed. Dolur needed to represent a more realistic version of someone who had seen battle.

His design was straightforward from the beginning, as I envisioned him as a rugged old man who could still hold his own and imposed leadership and admiration.

I wanted to present and describe him in armor but knew his body would not be able to carry such weight with his prosthetics. In the first designs, the prosthetic arm had three fingers, but inside the book, I added another for usage purposes.

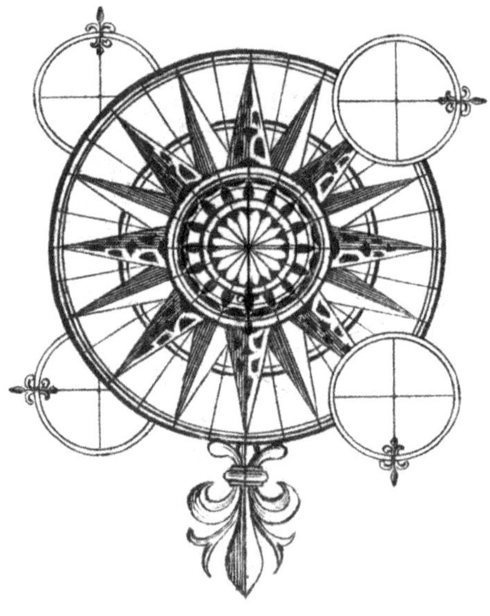

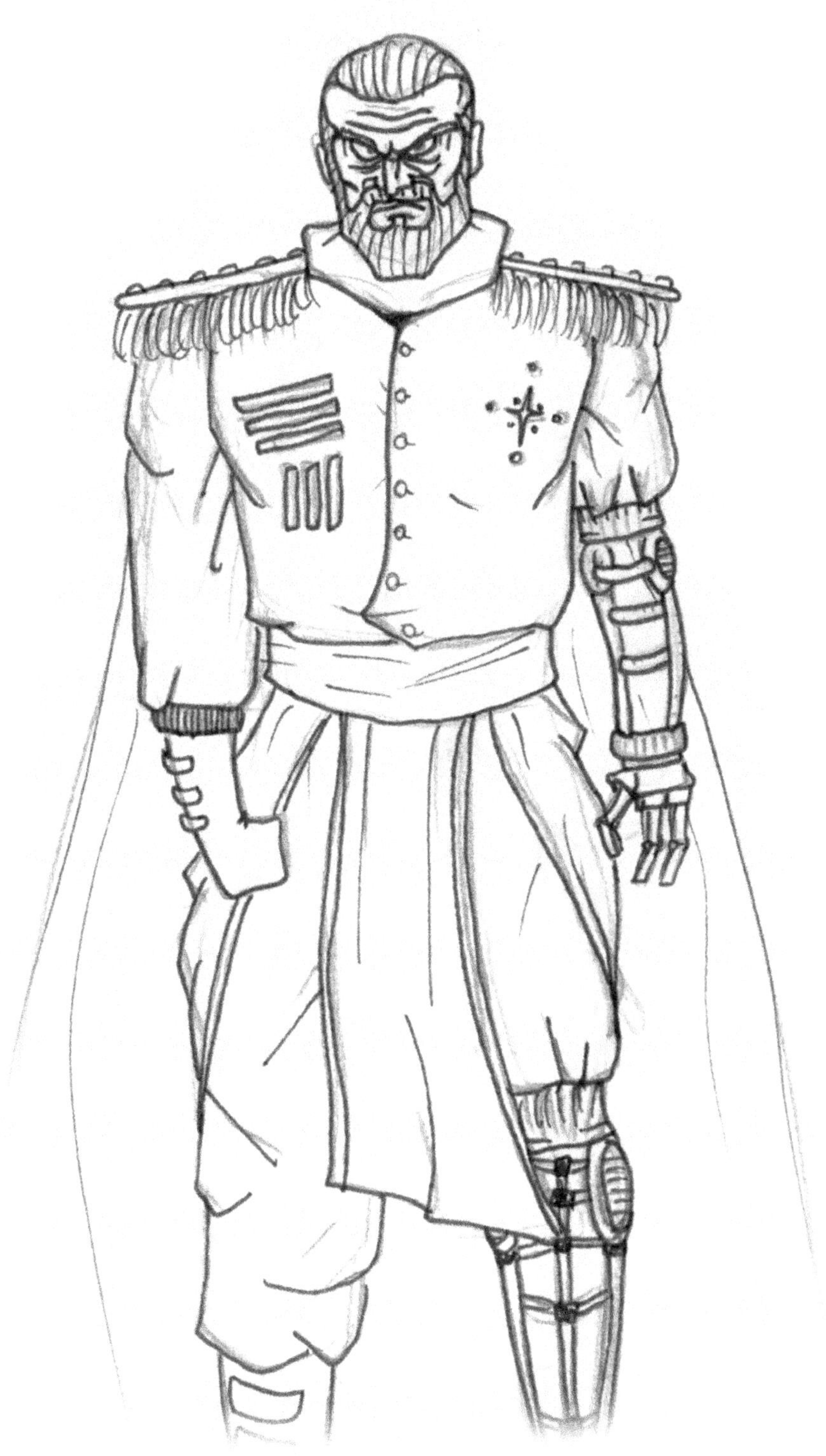

Design: 2019

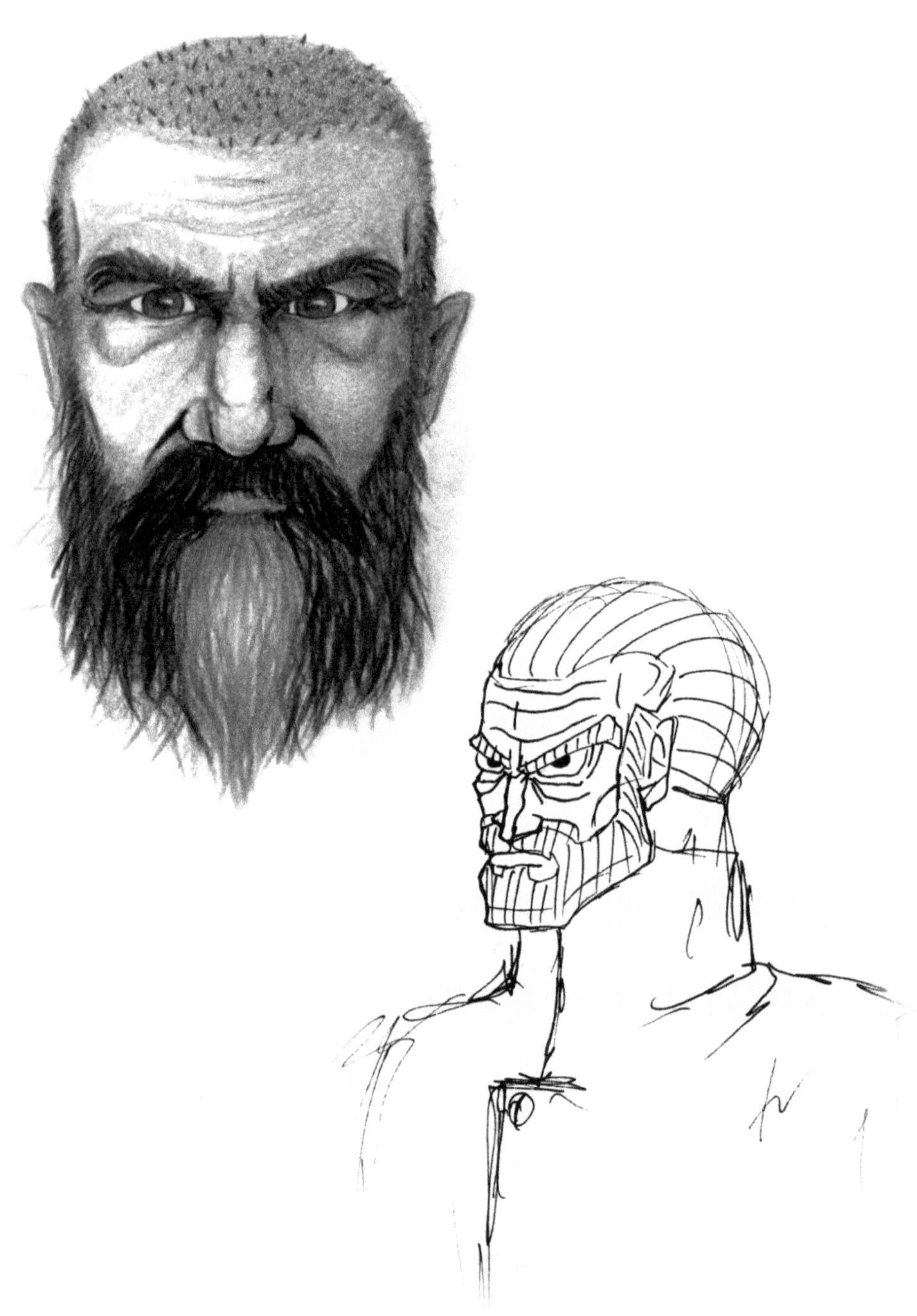

Design: 2020

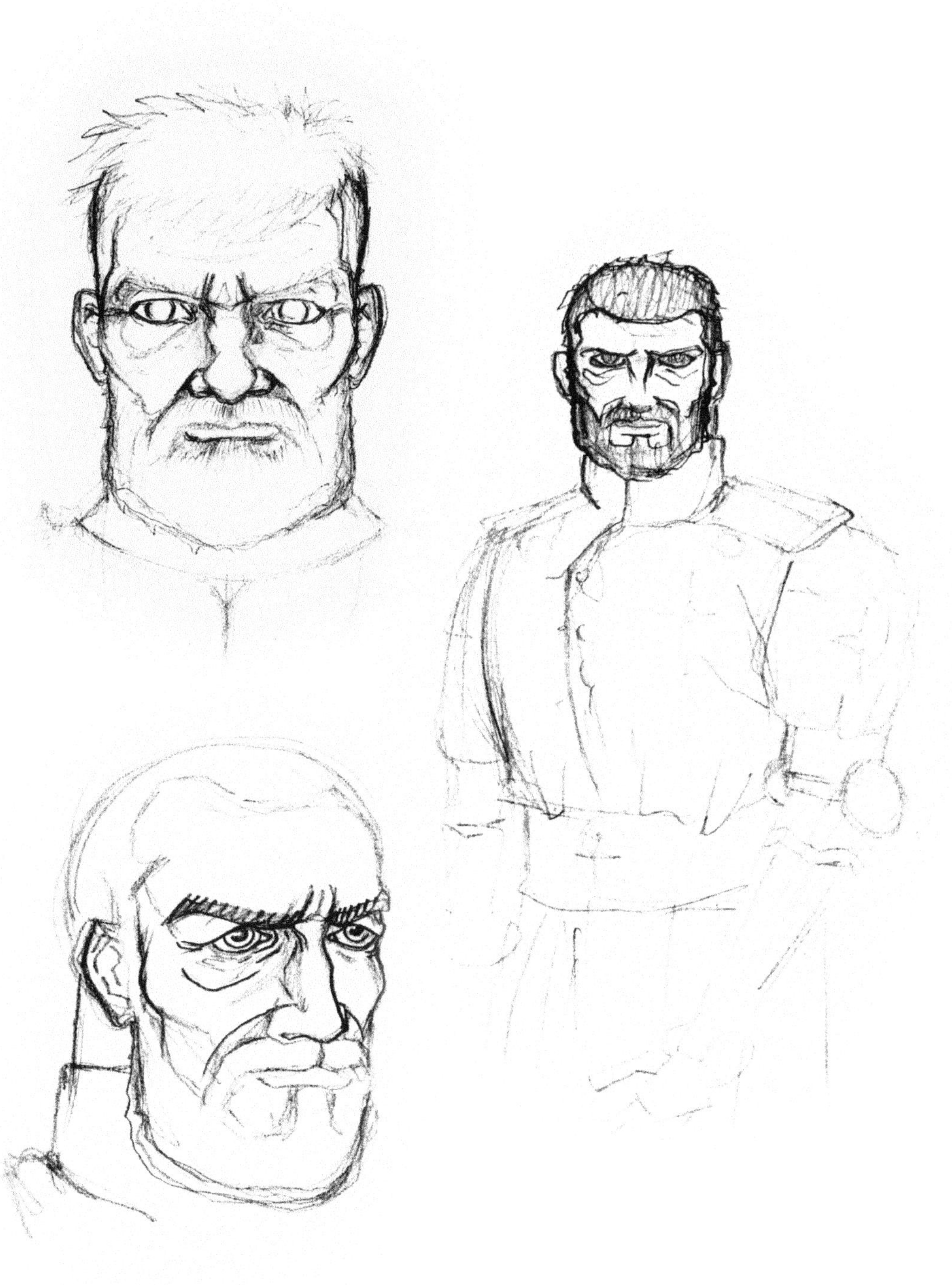

Design: 2022, 2023

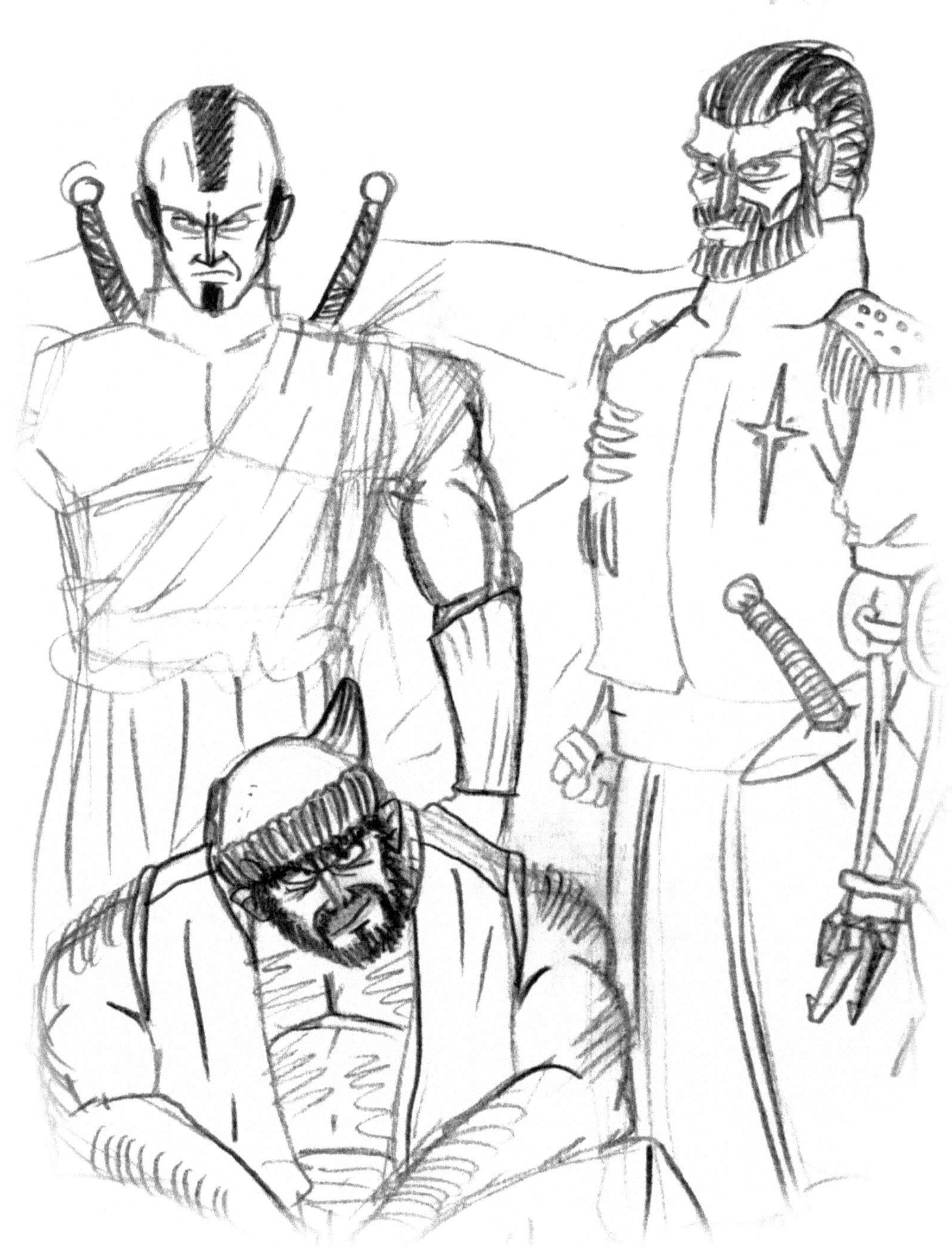

Kristoff, Kilean and Dolur Lodort

Design: 2019

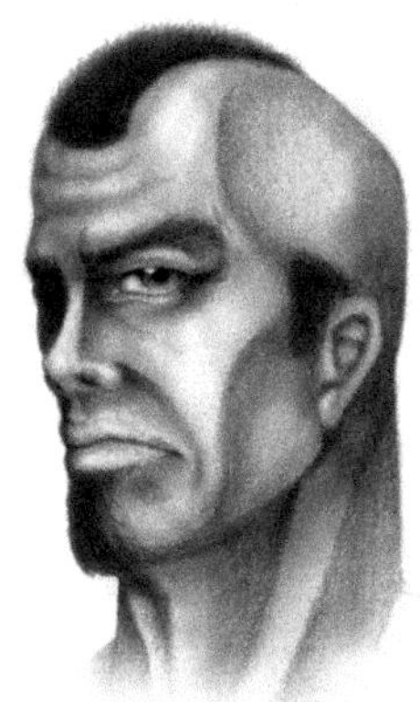

- King Kristoff Lodort -

Created in 2014, Kristoff had to be an efficient-looking man. His character needed to represent pure strength—tall, massive, strong, muscular as a Greek god.

I began to admire the character the more I wrote about him, and I realized that if I attached myself to him, it would be harder to work on his character and flush him out the best I could. Thus I added the ridiculous hairstyle.

At the time, I struggled with making the appearances of the characters as different as possible, through hairstyles, the way they talked, clothing or accessories (hats, weapons, etc.). It did not take long to abandon this concept. After surpassing fifty characters, I stopped trying to make them look so different and instead tried to base their appearances on their surroundings.

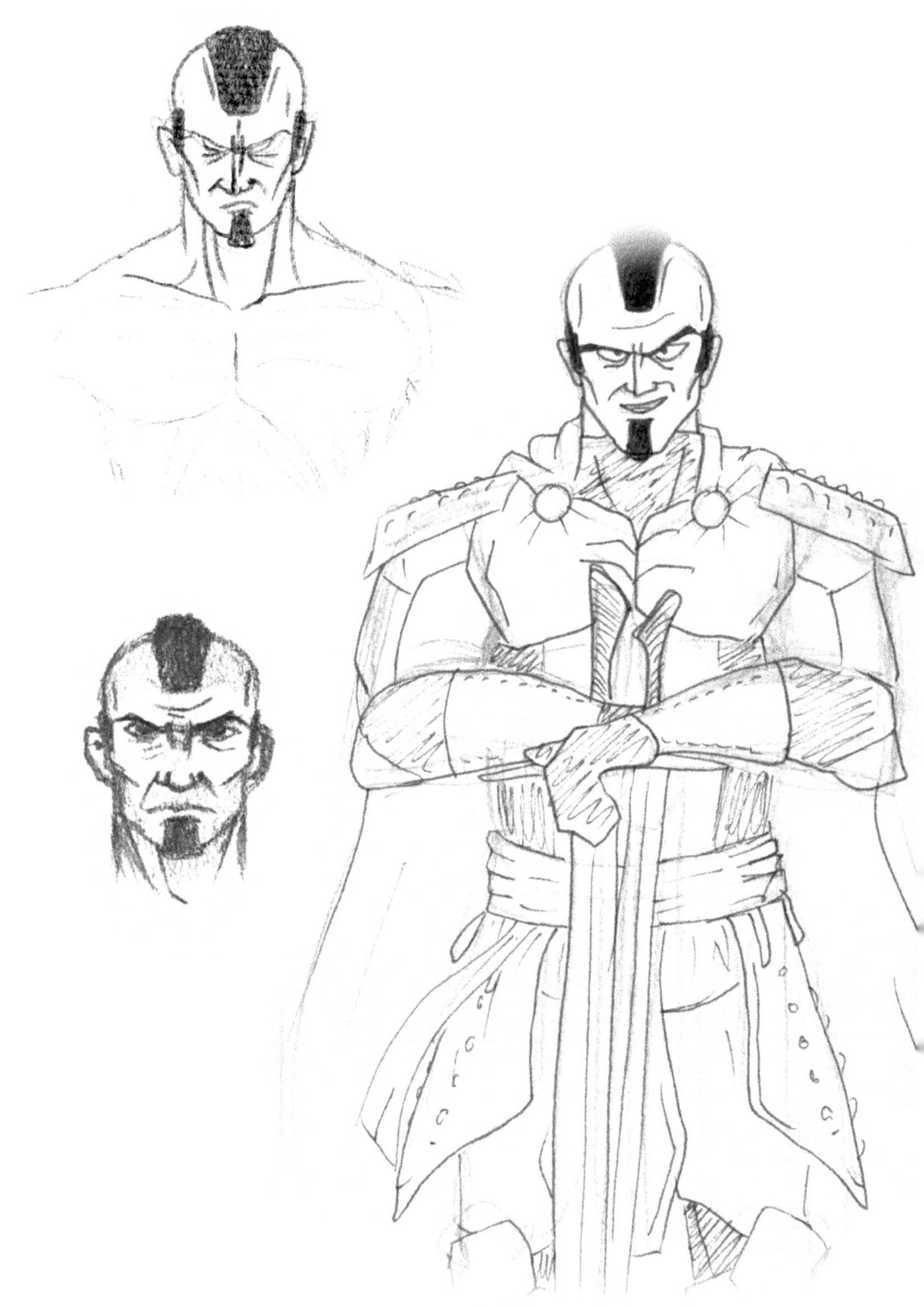

Design: 2019

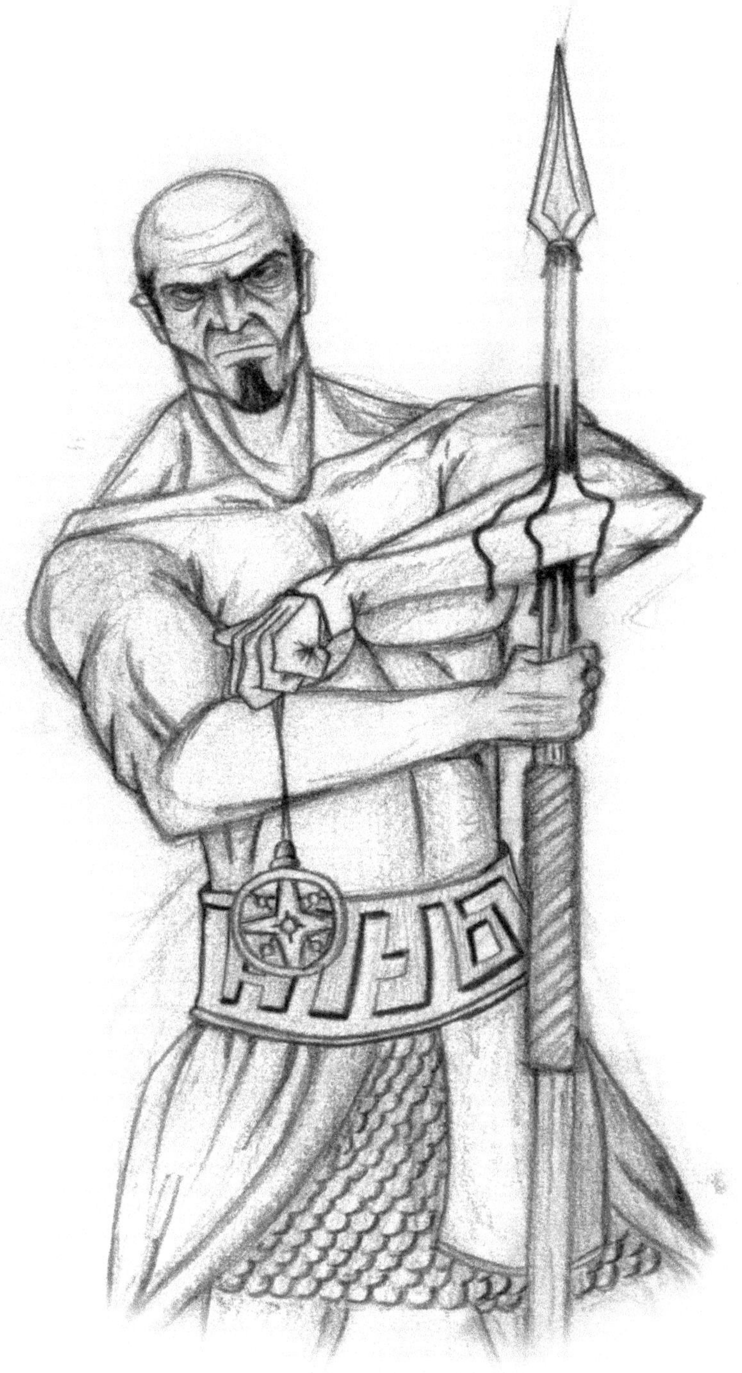

Does not represent events in the story

Design: 2021

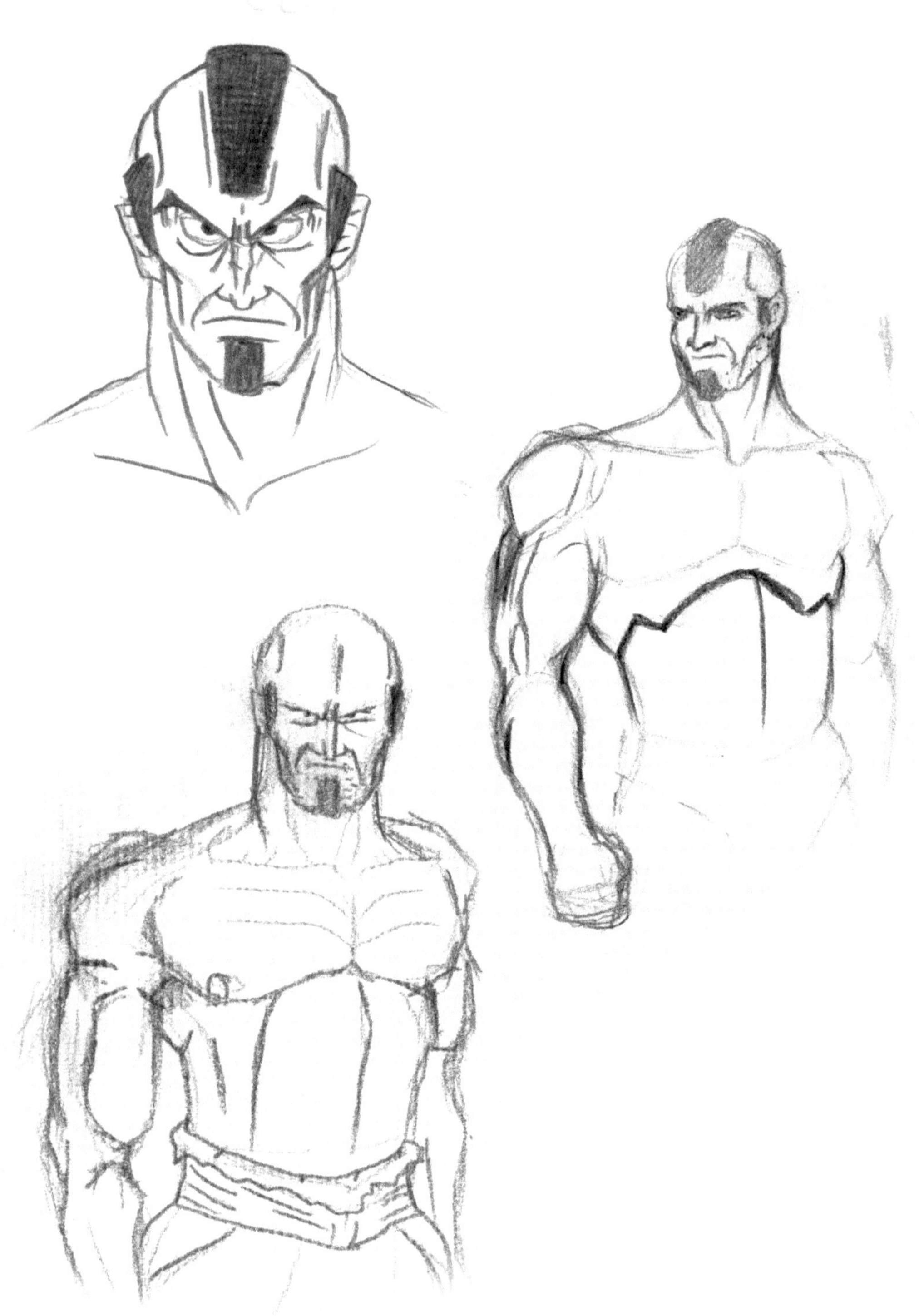

Design: 2019, 2021, 2023

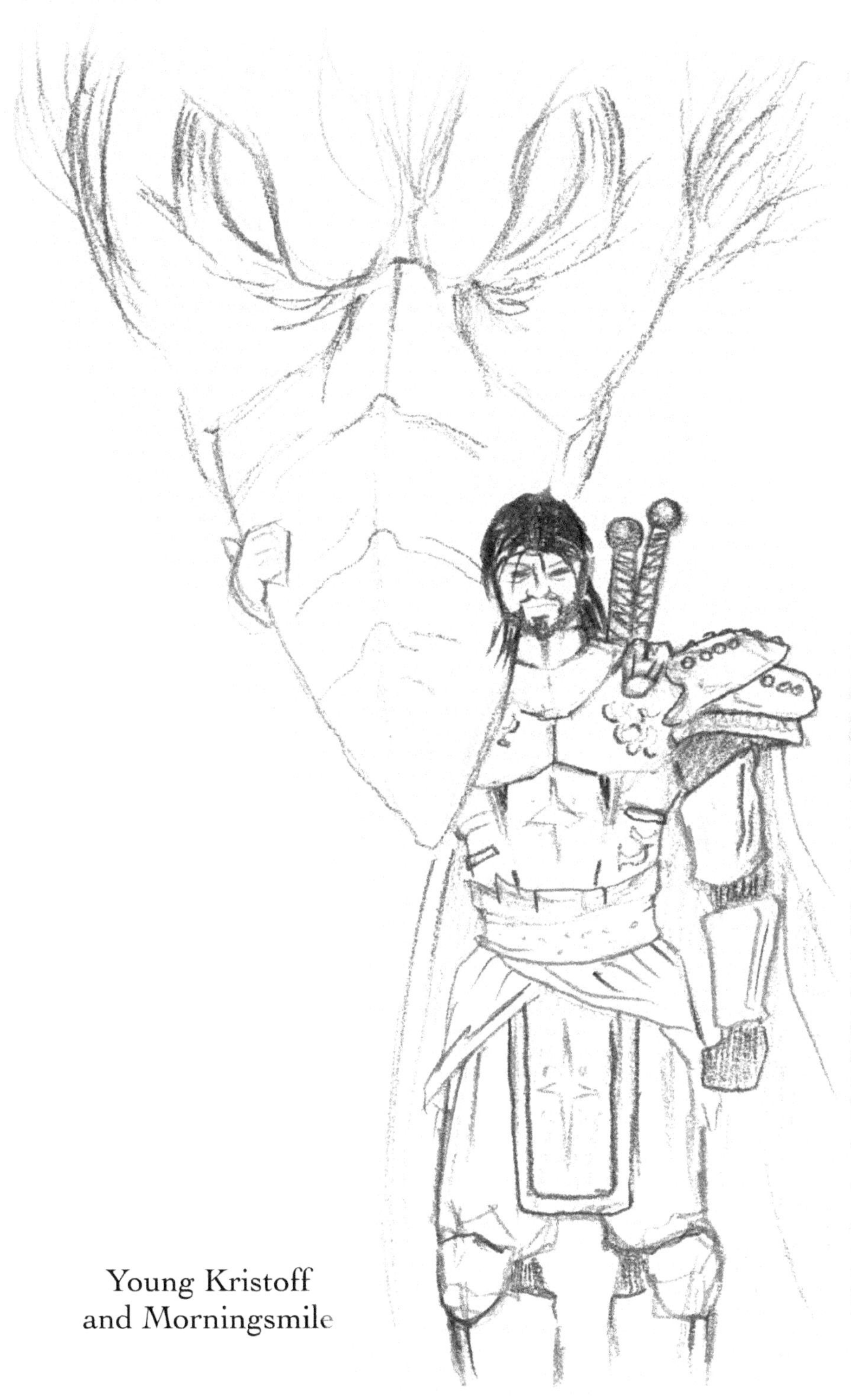

Young Kristoff
and Morningsmile

Design: 2019

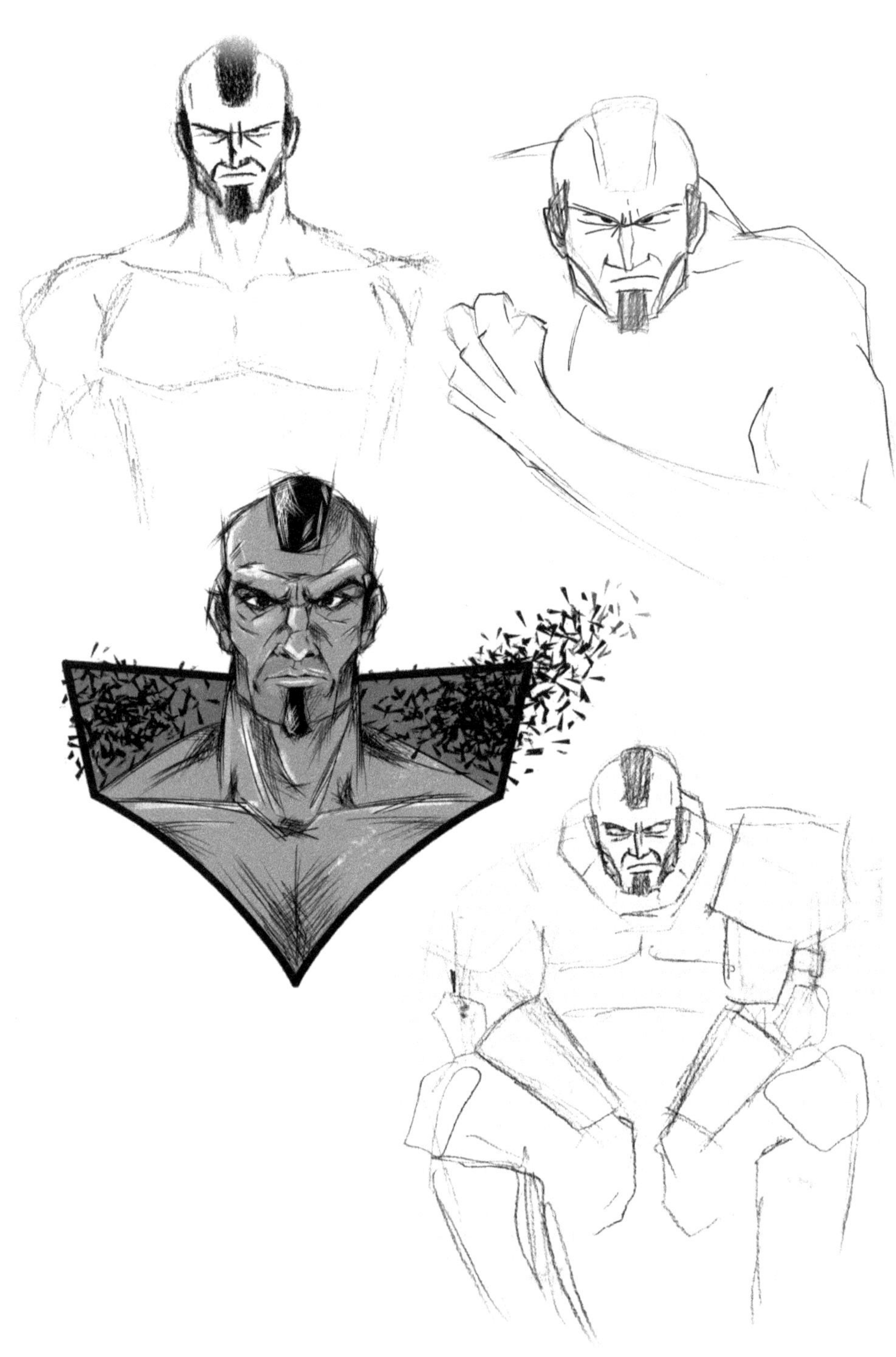

Design: 2019, 2020. Digital: 2022

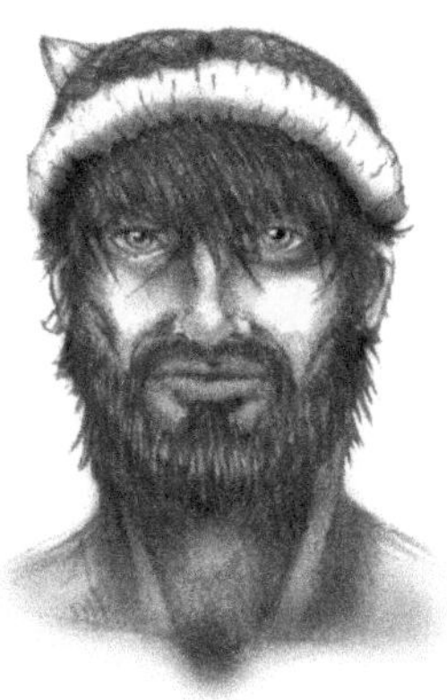

- Kilean Lodort -

Like his younger brother, Kristoff, Kilean needed to look the part. Older but still capable.

As I wanted the brothers to not be too much alike, Kilean's facial design looks more unkempt as opposed to Kristoff.

I always imagined this man as sweaty and tired, in very inhumane conditions. He was originally created as a king whom James the Gray Wolf encountered in a forest. In the scenarios I imagined while I played alone in the wilderness, I used the image of Kilean as the Forest Man who would not allow me to climb trees. A person who seemed concerned with the greater scheme of things rather than whatever issues or problems the commoners would have.

I added his helm during the time when I believed every character needed to have a unique appearance (like Kristoff's facial hair or Dolor's prosthetics).

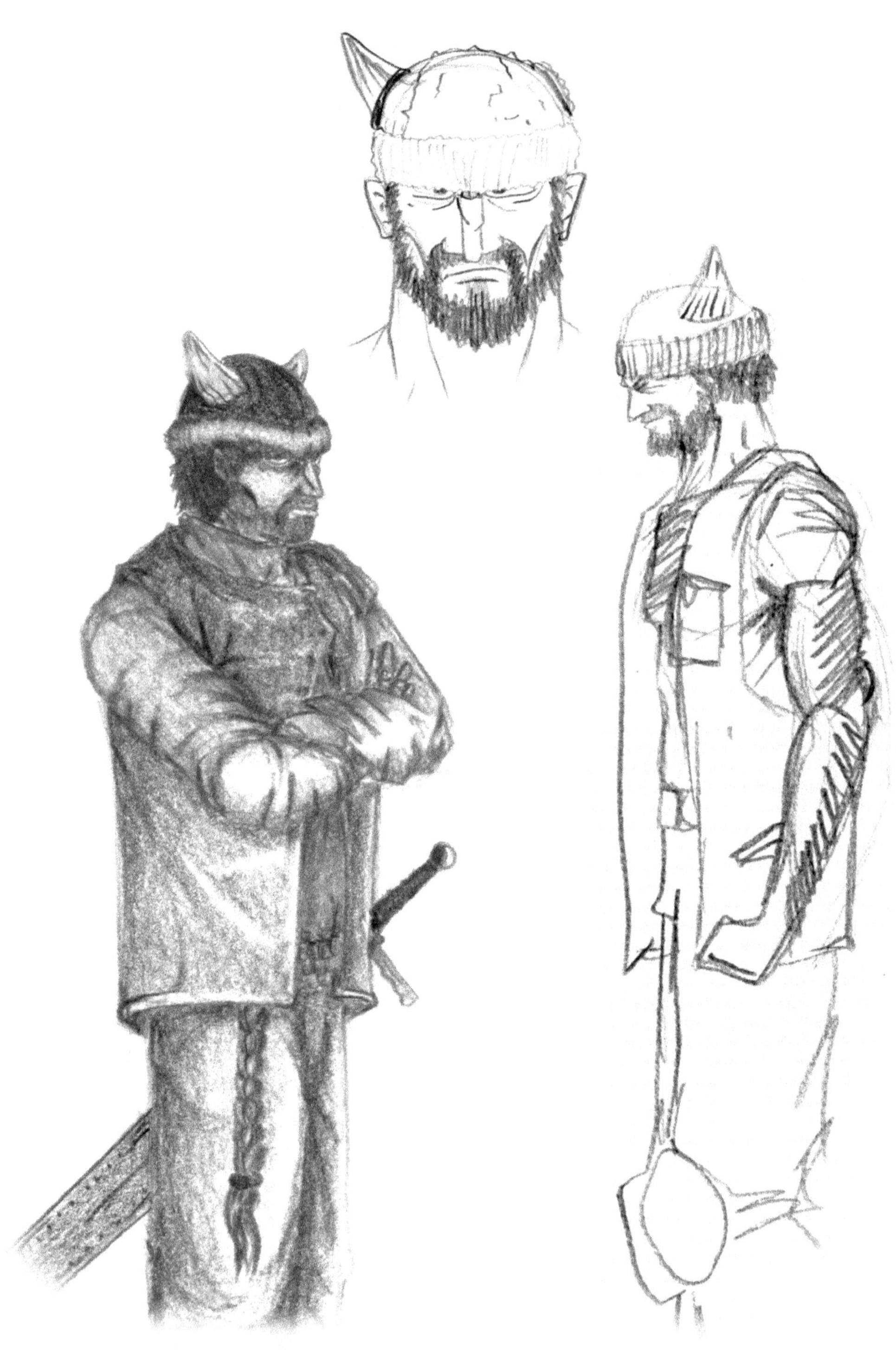

Design: 2019, 2020

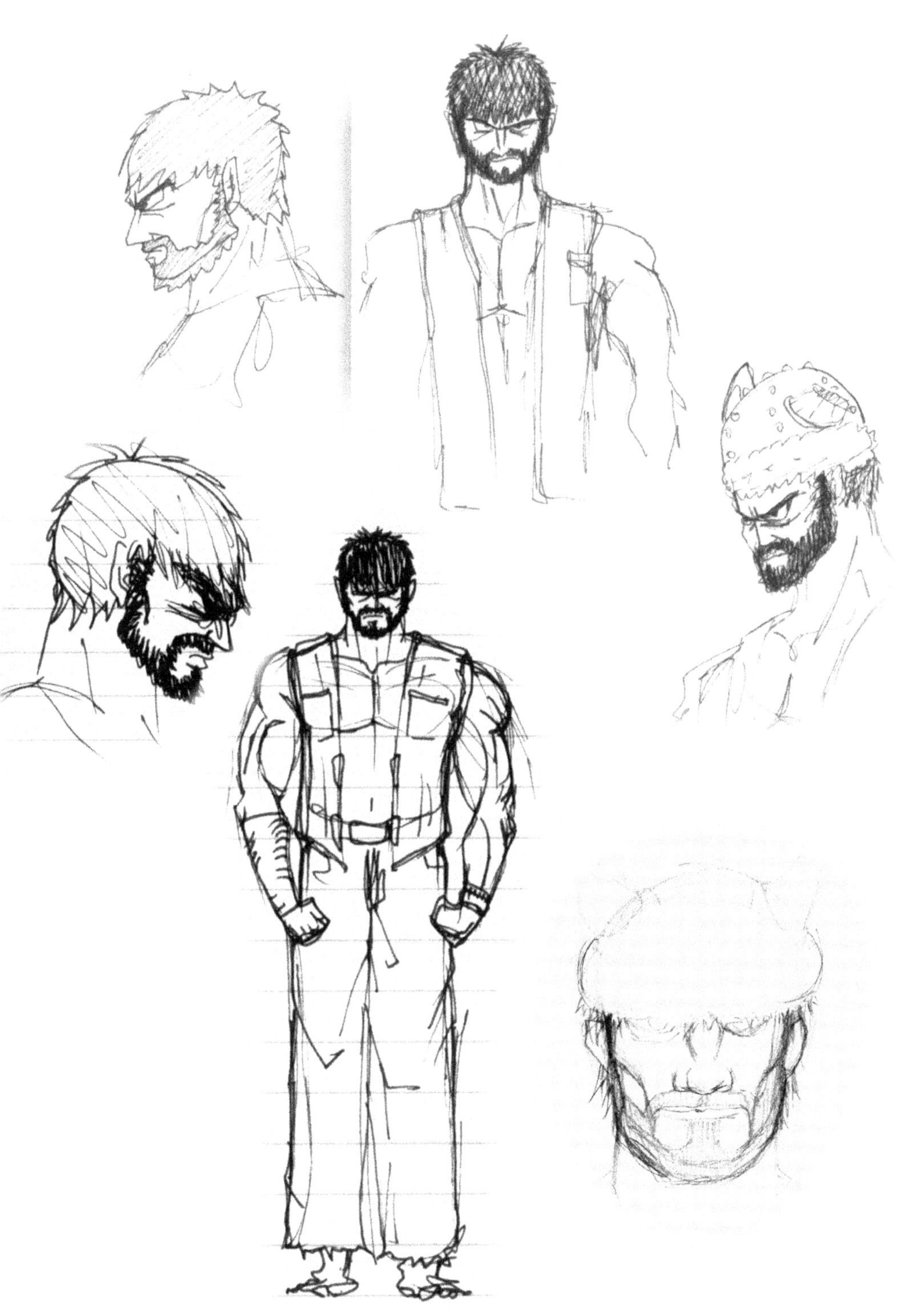

Design: 2018, 2020, 2024

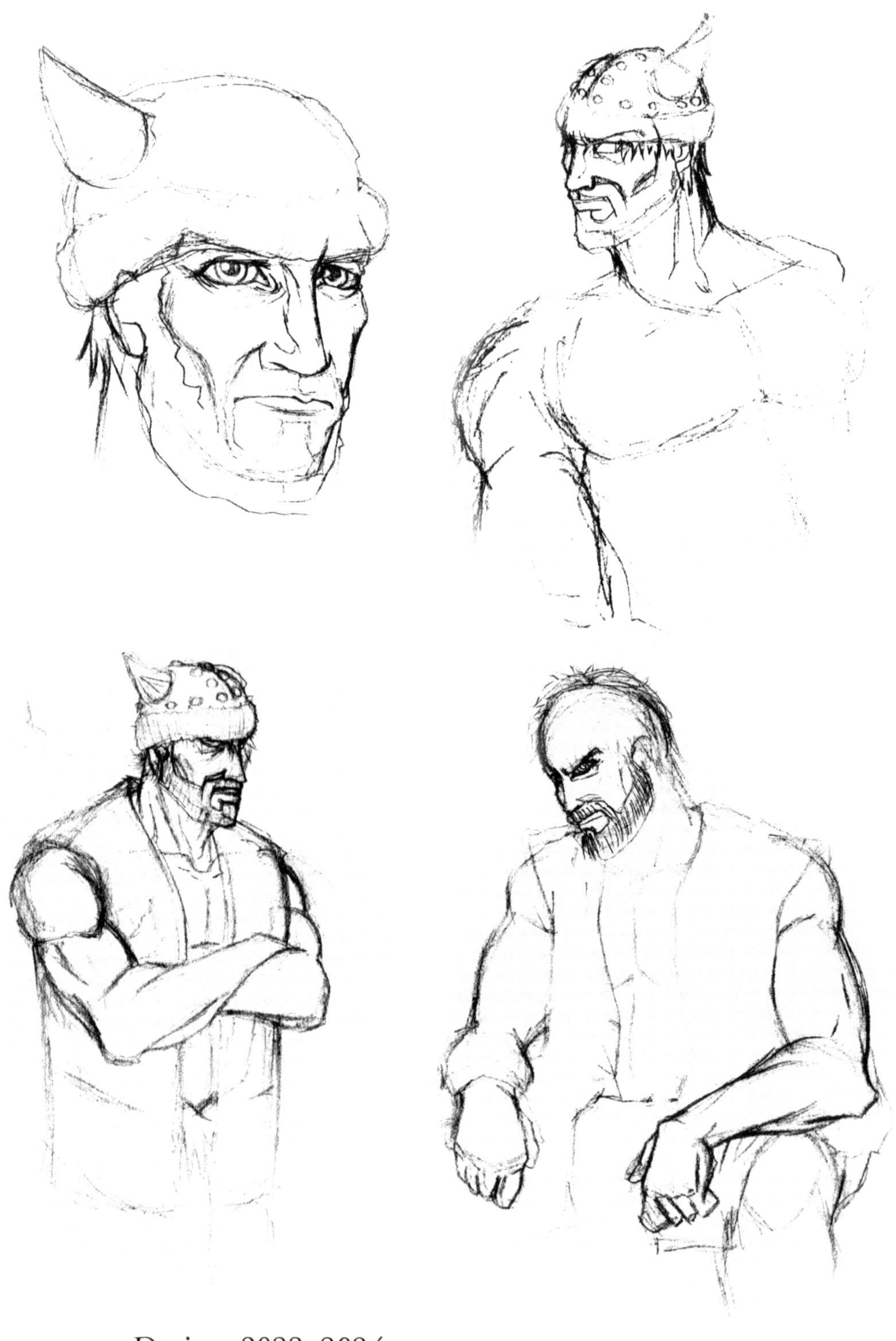

Design: 2022, 2024

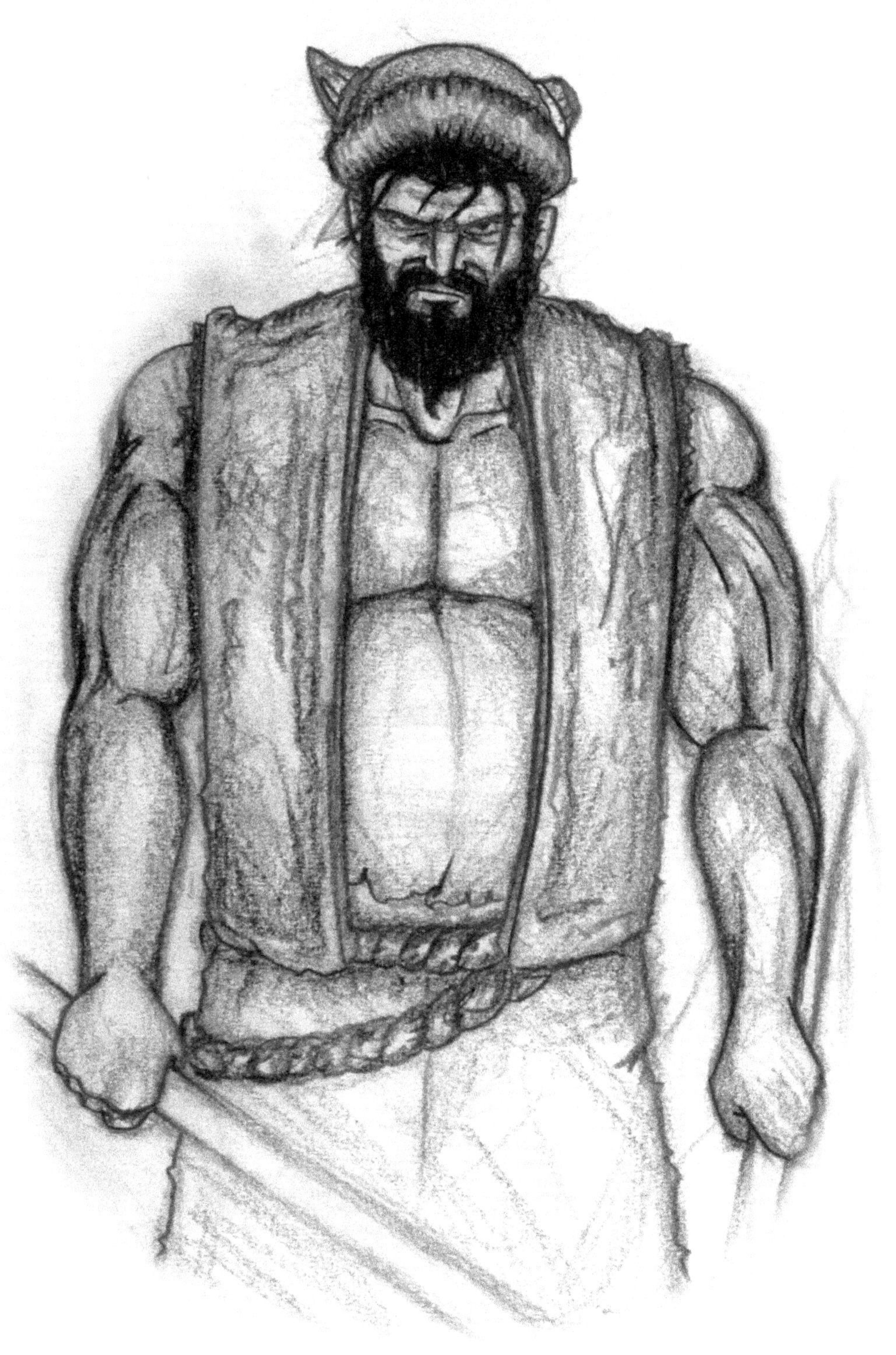

Design: 2022

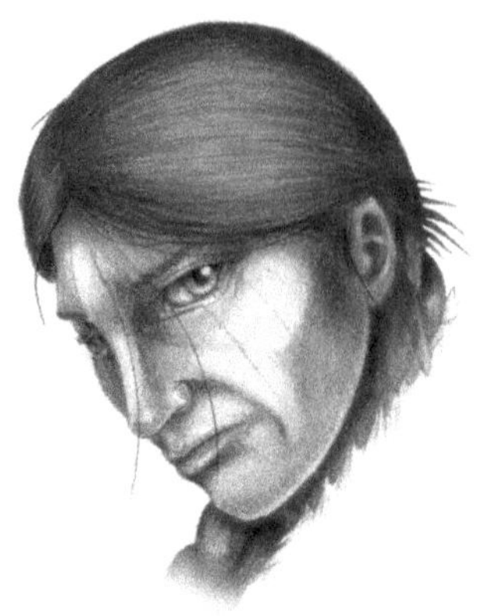

- Jerada Lodort -

It is hard to answer who my favorite character is. I always say my favorite is the one I am currently writing about, but whenever I hear this question, Jerada's concept comes to mind.

Initially named "April" for the month I first drew her in (2005), she needed to be a badass. I wanted her to look like the coolest and baddest woman in the story. At the time when she was created, the story had drifted away from the contemporary "nu metal" scene and toward the steampunk Victorian era. The more I progressed the story and enlarged the cast, the more I realized I would have to go back a few centuries.

The earliest memory I have of Jerada's concept is her meeting James the Gray Wolf in a dark sewer. I don't know why or where, exactly, but their faces approached each other and they both became alert, frightened of one another. That scene evolved into many other variations, and at times it was even abandoned. It later resurfaced when I wrote the "Only One" chapter.

I included the single braid because I had a hard time drawing a woman who did not look manly or angry, so I added a feminine element to her look.

She wielded many weapons (being mostly connected to the Victorian-era style of the story), and I envisioned her as a sharpshooter.

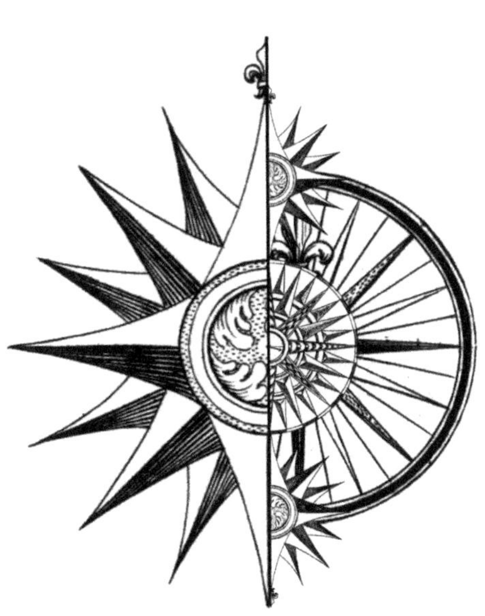

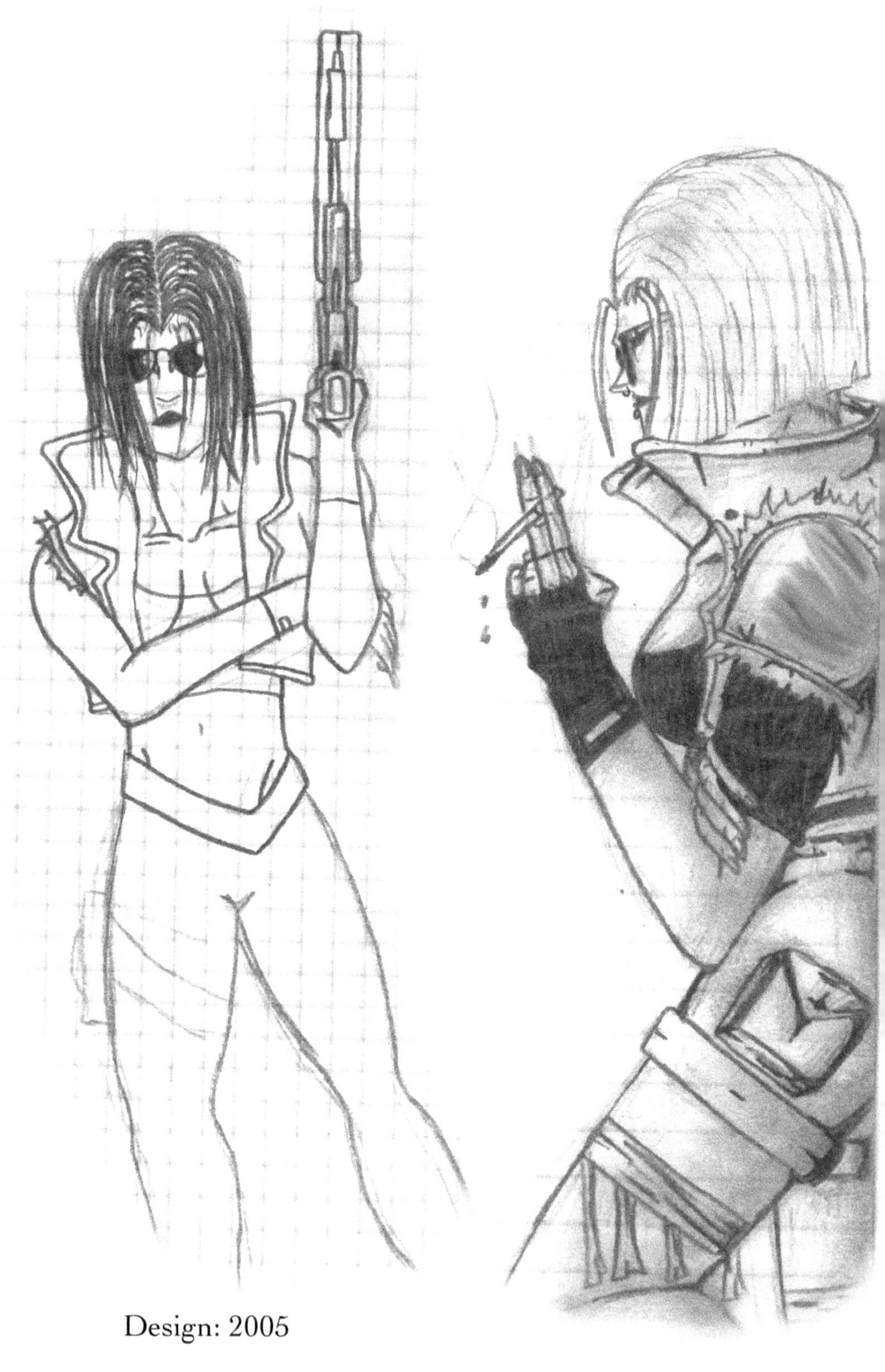

Design: 2005

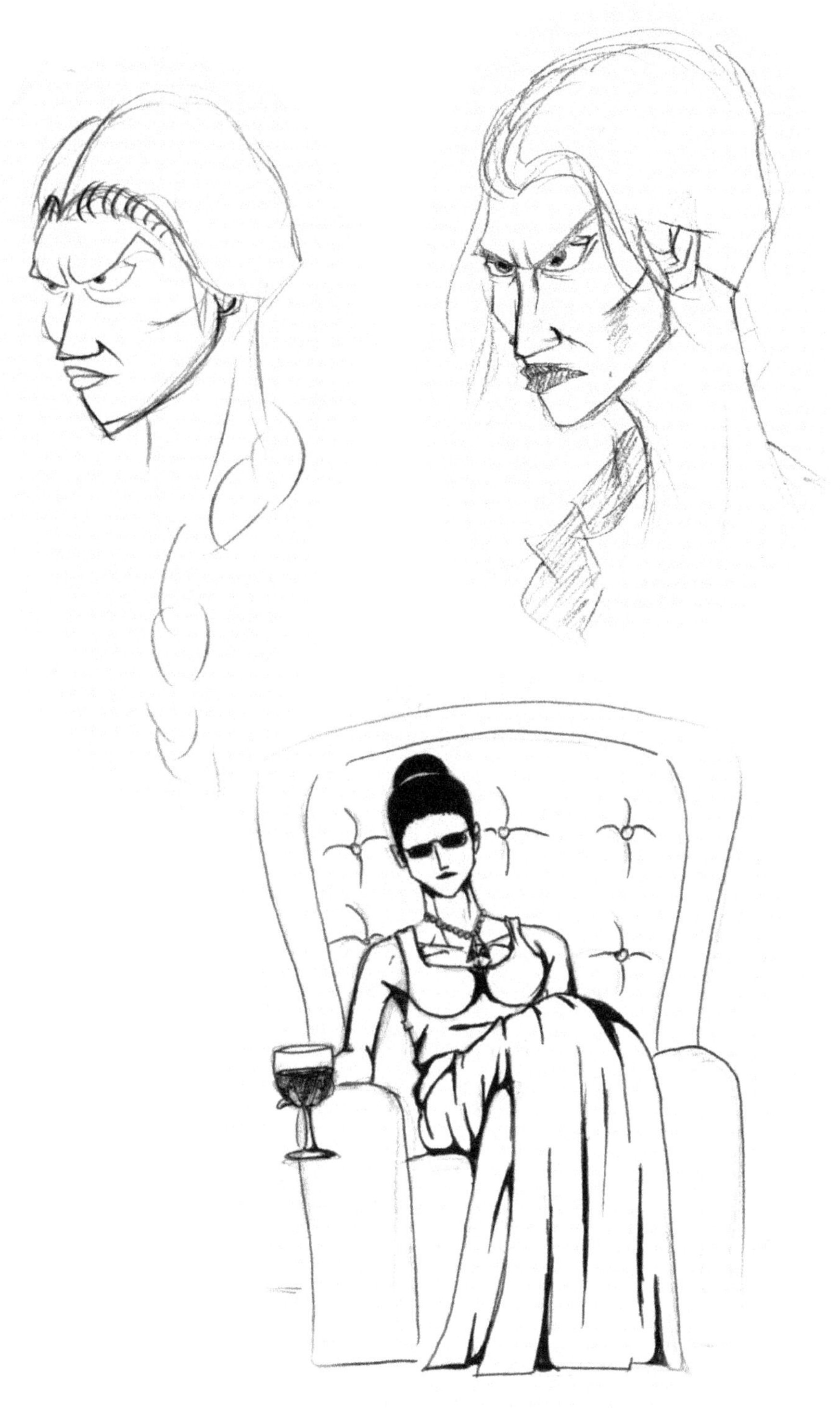

Design: 2010, 2019, 2023

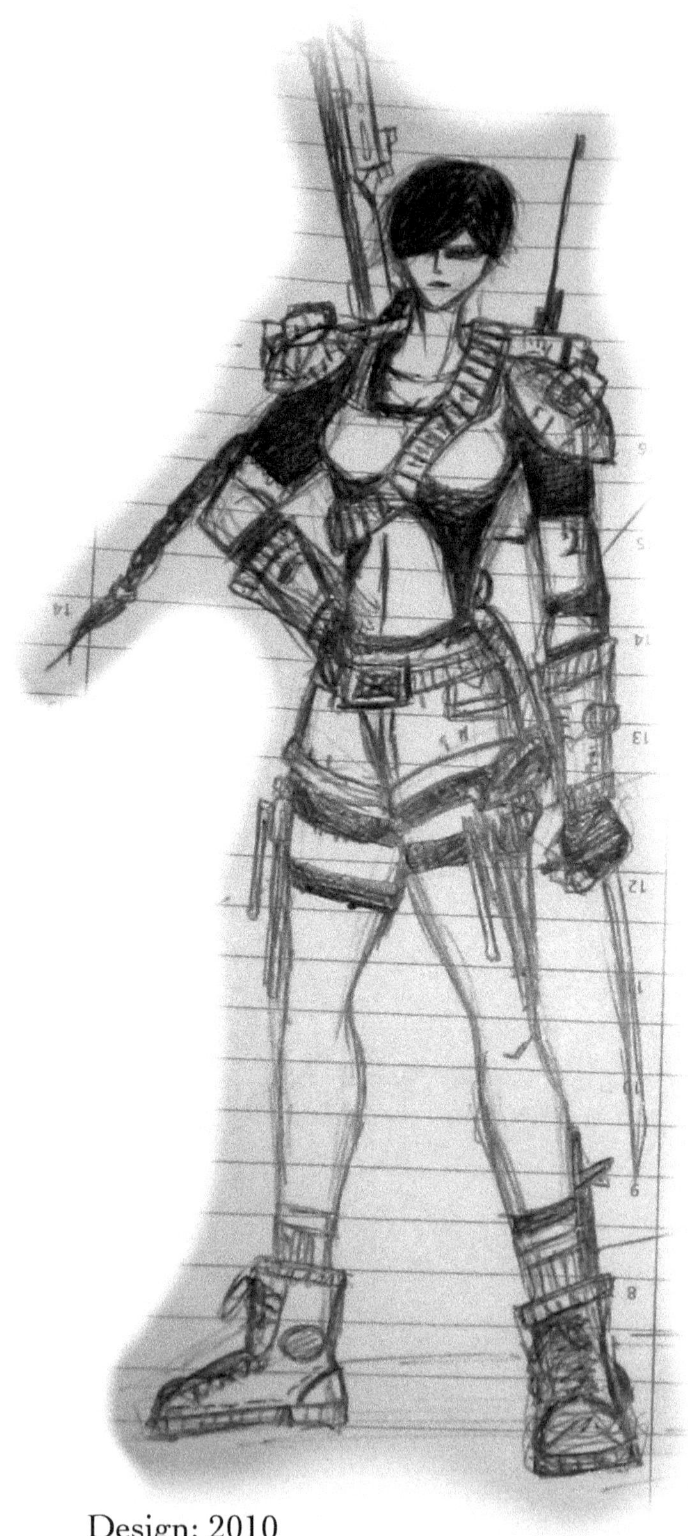

Design: 2010

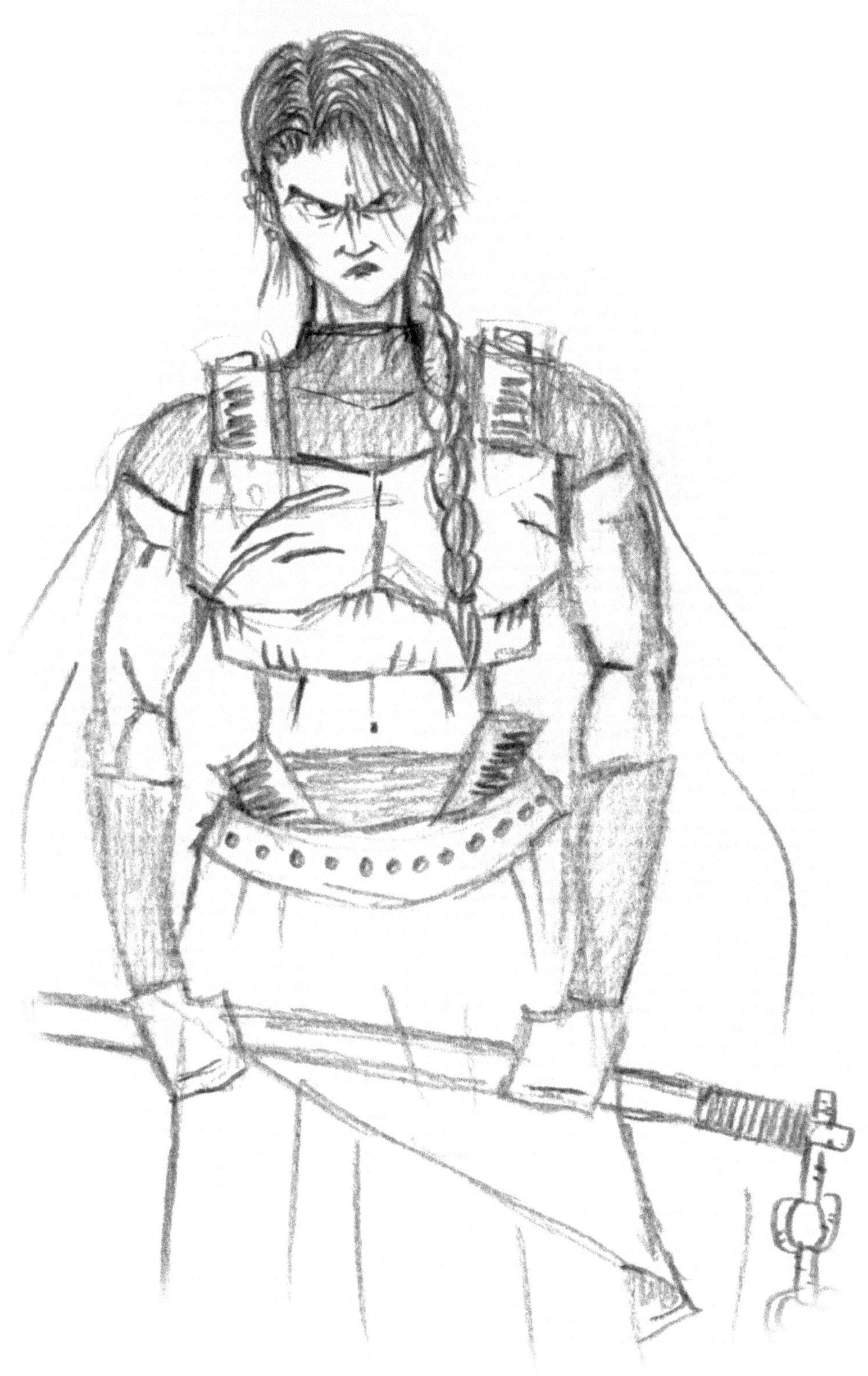

Design: 2019

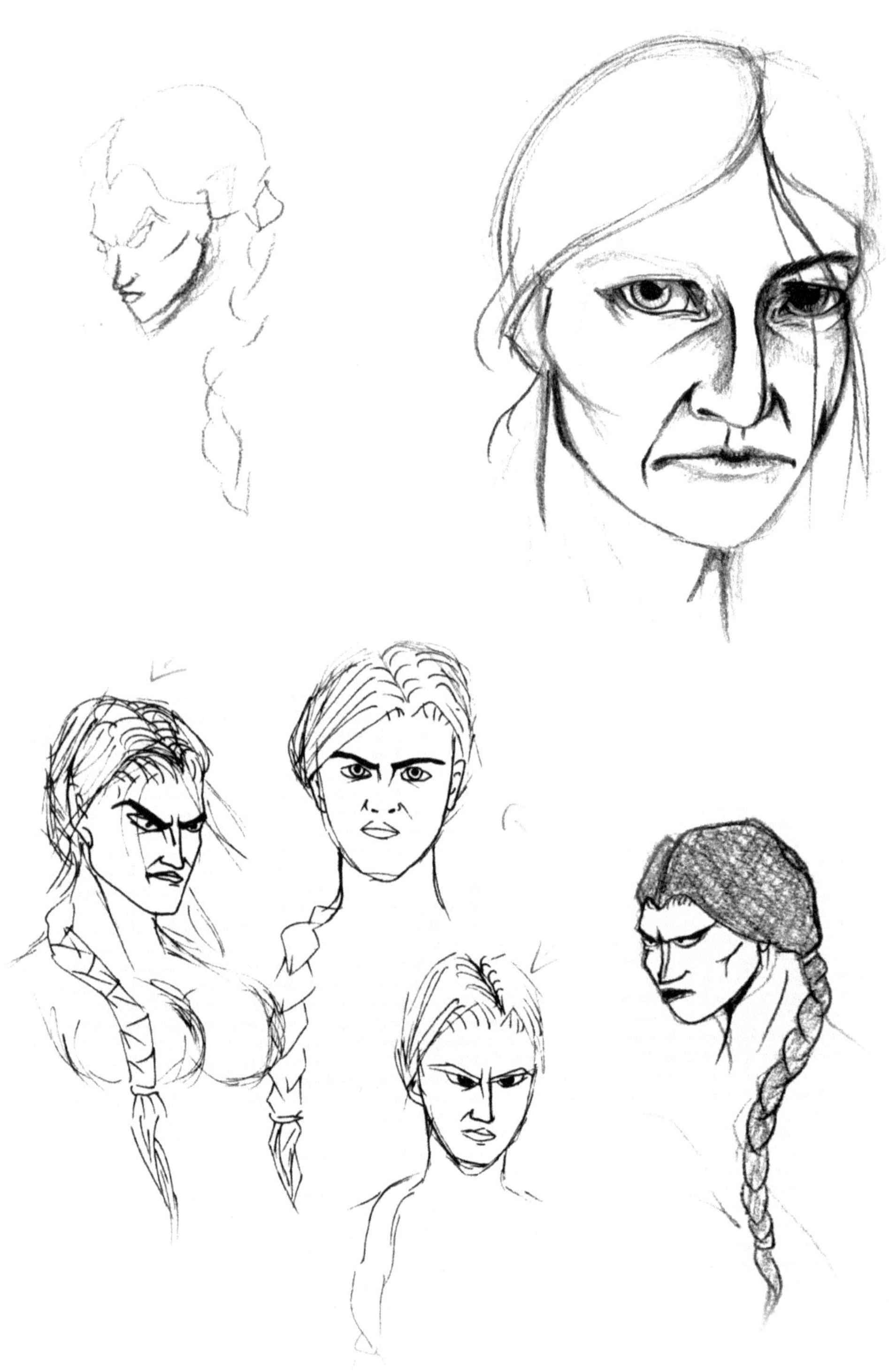

Design: 2018, 2024

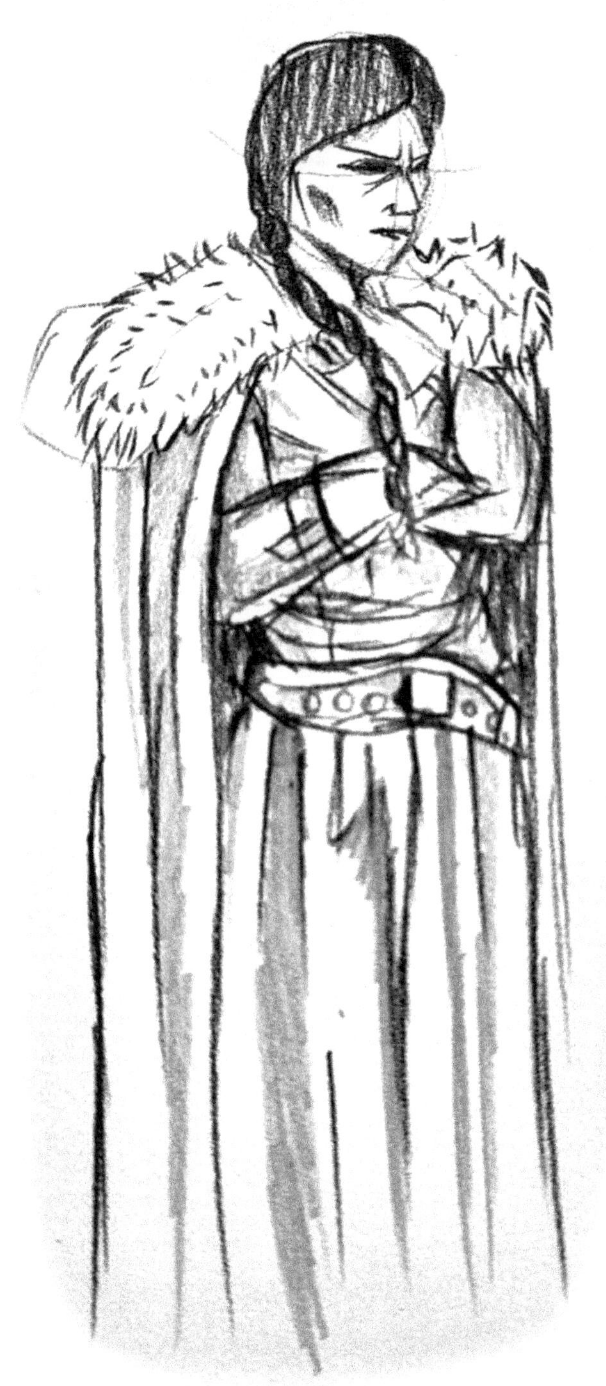

Design: 2020

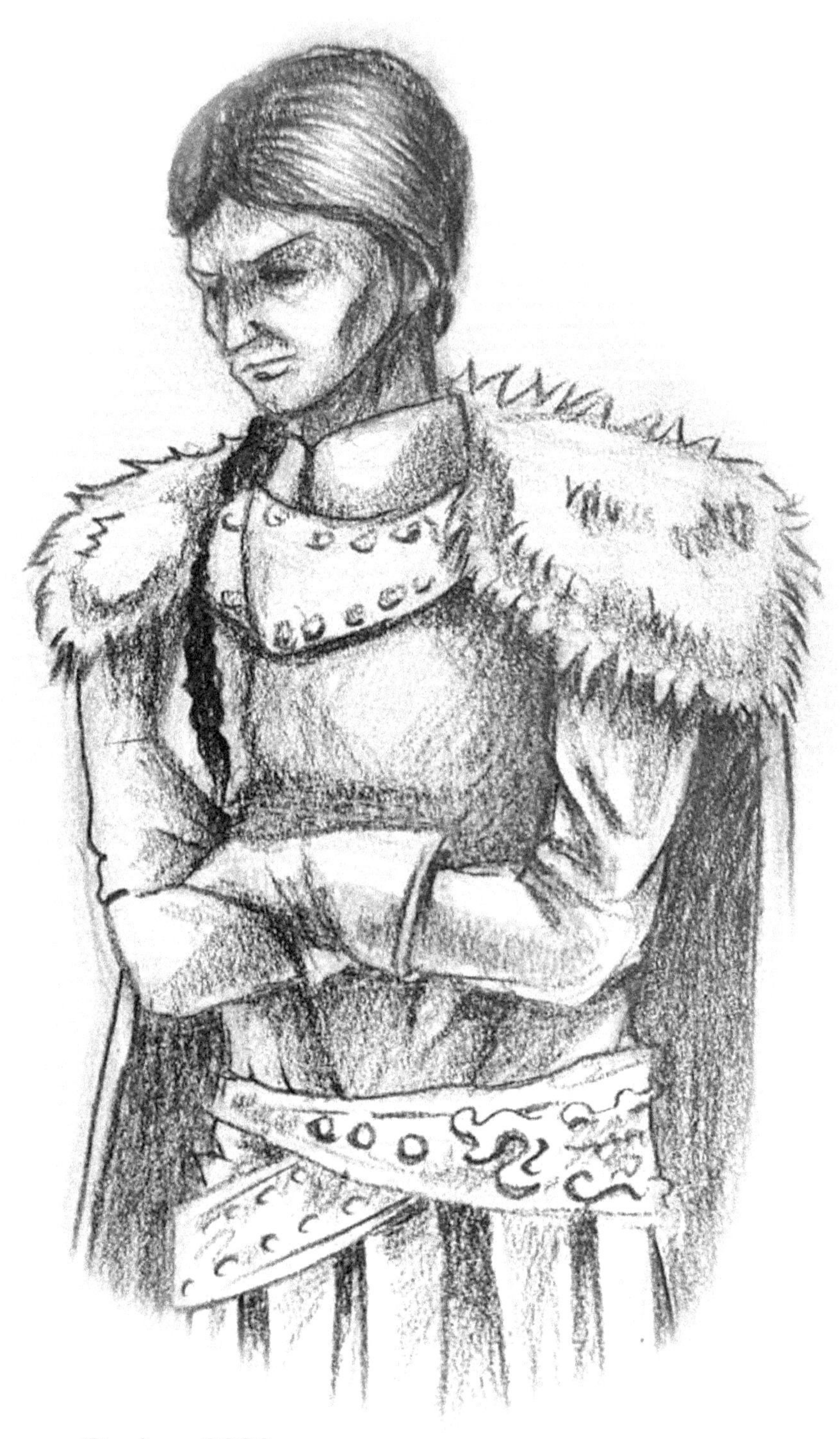

Design: 2020

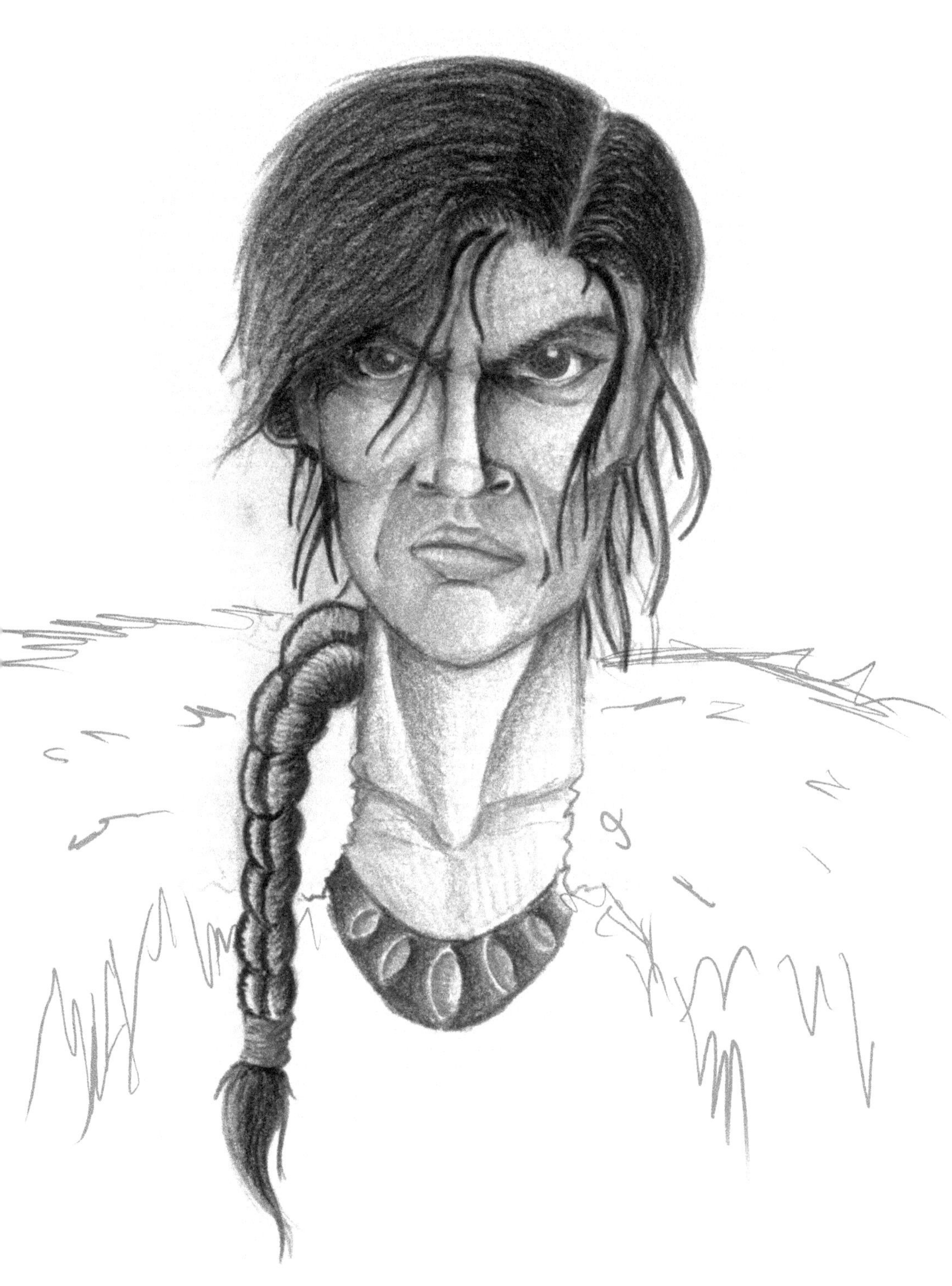

Design: 2021

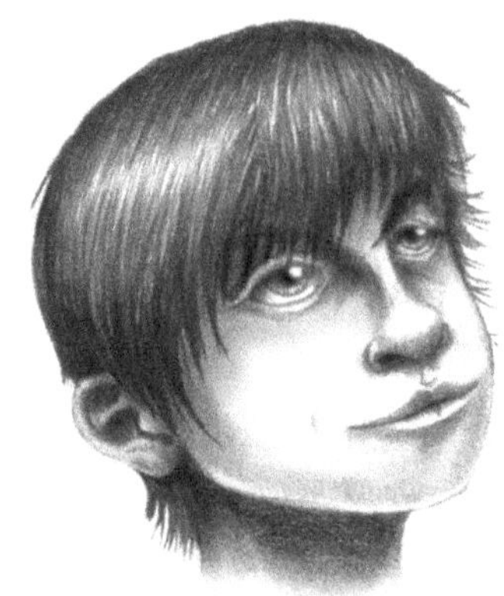

- Corin Lodort -

I created Corin shortly after introducing Dolur to the story. I enjoyed their dynamic and Corin's simplicity and innocence.

He had a twin sister, Nadja. They were together at all times, but although I tried to incorporate her better within the story, I could not come up with a purposeful storyline for her. She would have been mostly with her grandmother Enna, but after reaching over one hundred characters, I decided to remove her completely from the story (along with other characters).

Only after drawing Corin's last version, I decided to include him in *Favors Within Ashes*.

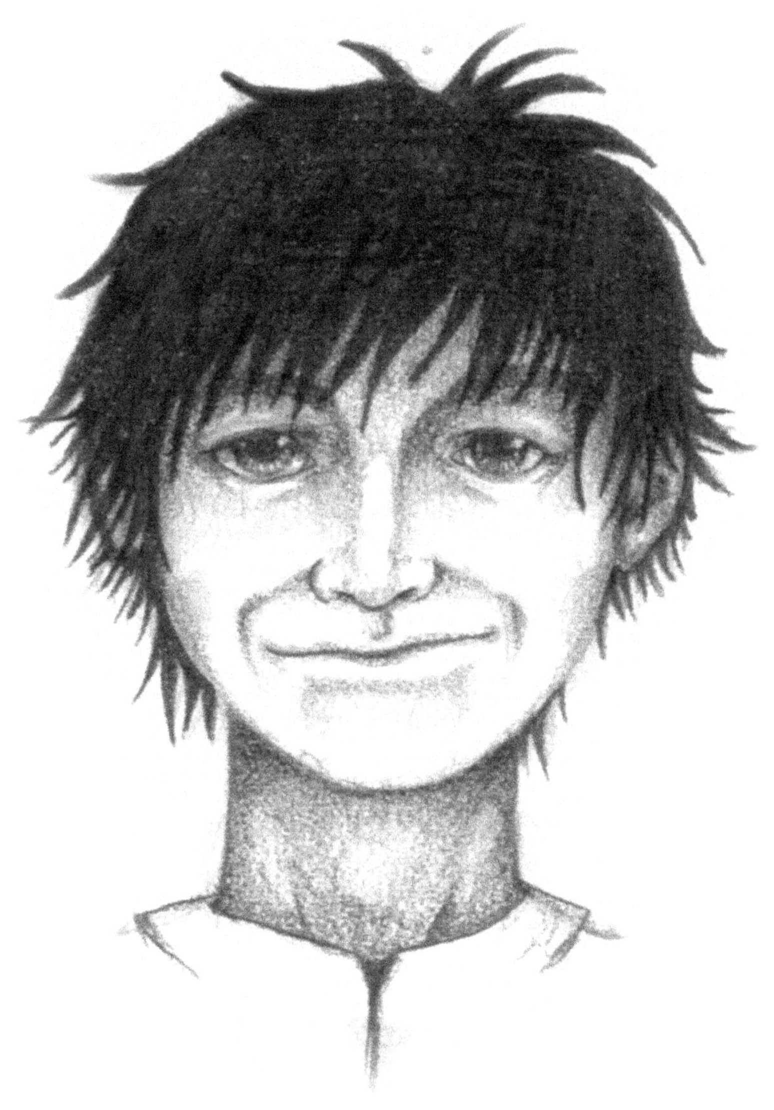

Design: 2023

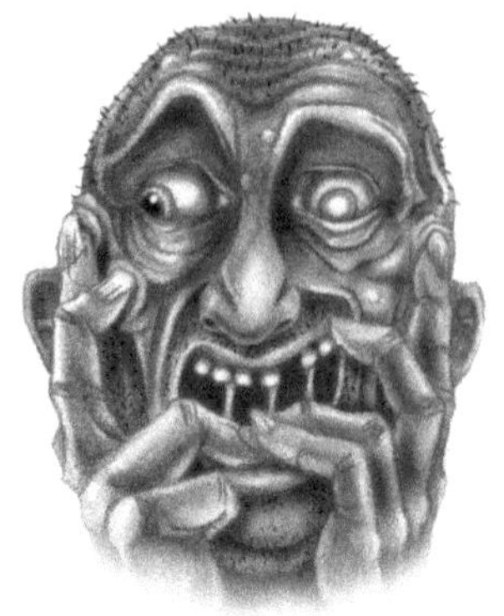

- MOTIA -

My silver coin, oh how it turns,
Inside my belly, it all burns.

Where ryuns fly and ruleks swim,
The blizzard creeps within my skin.

I dream of sand, blood and skin,
Where one rat sleeps and the other is green.

Warming ice and trembling water,
I have not forgotten, have you, father?

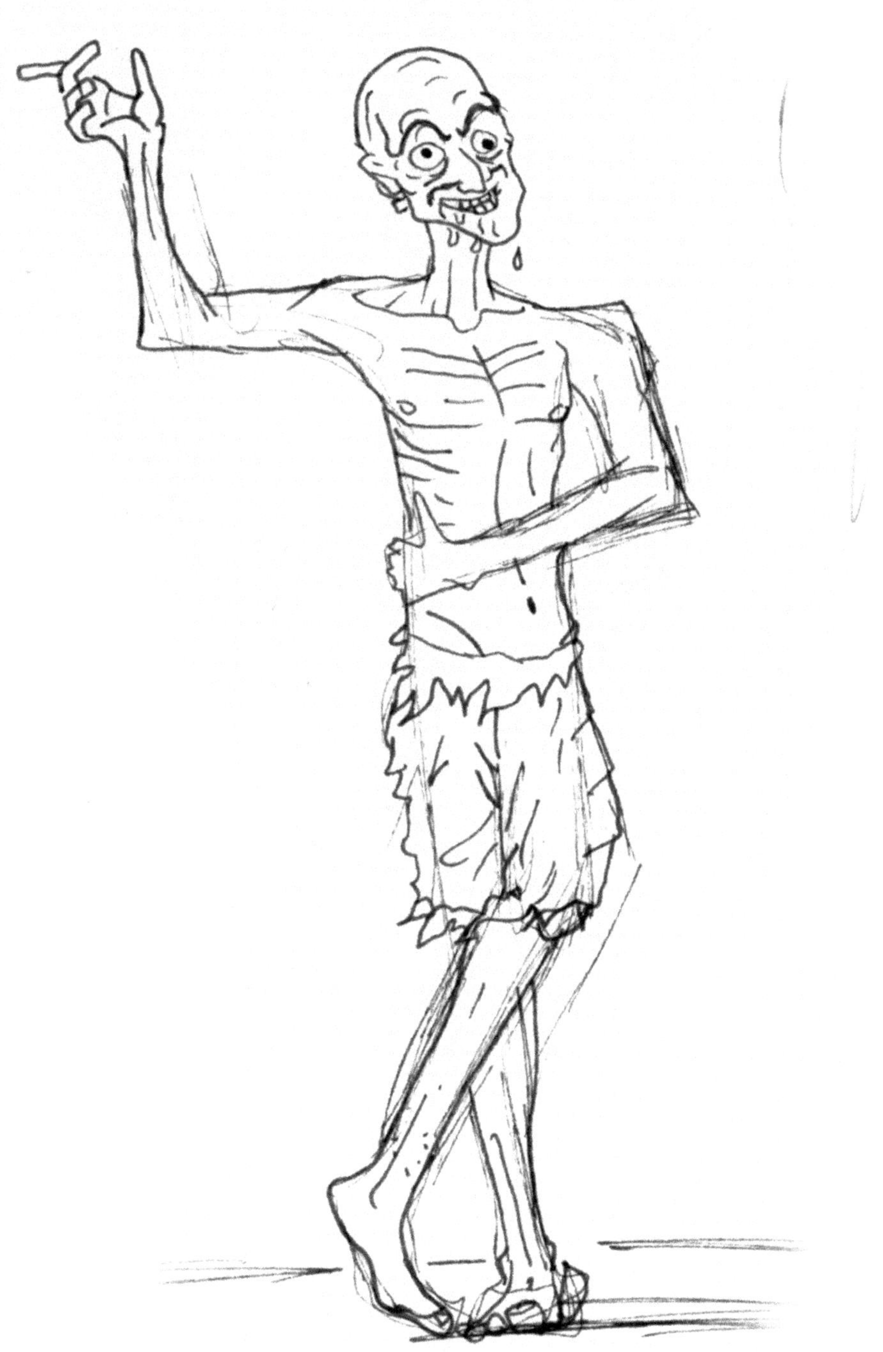

Design: 2019

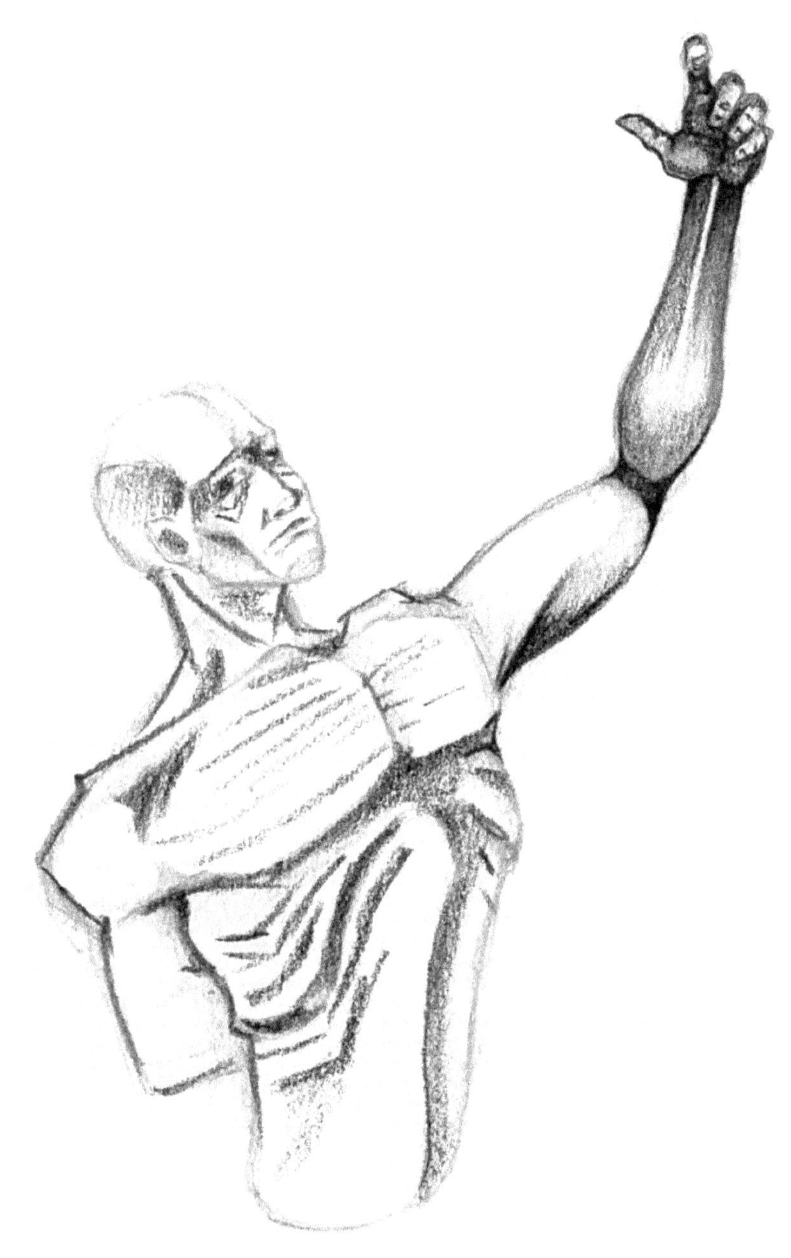

Design: 2024

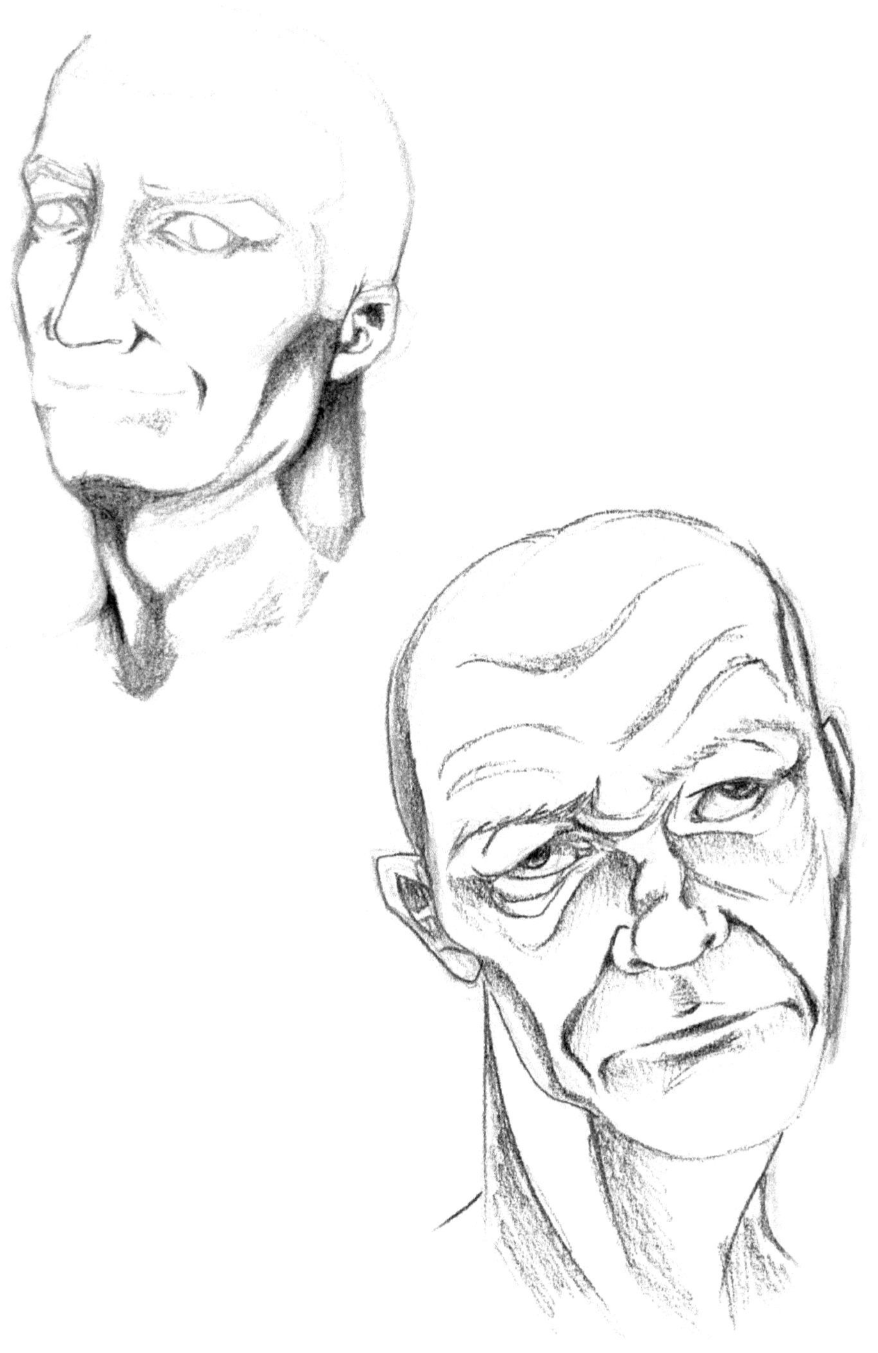

Design: 2024

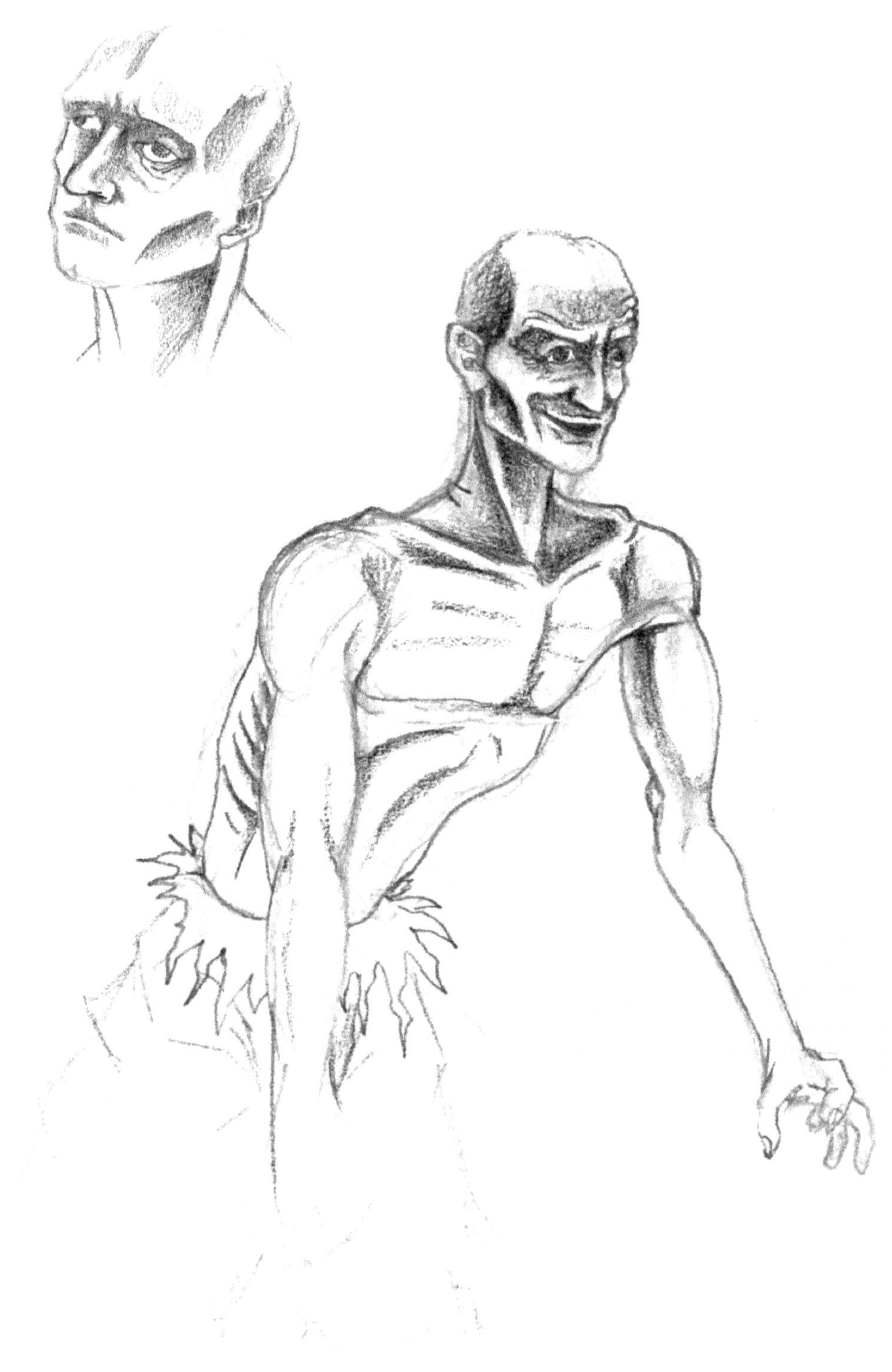

Design: 2024

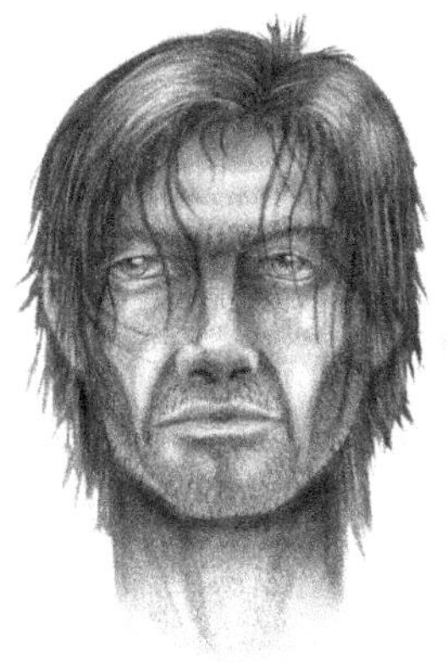

- Marco Doran -

Marco is the second character created from the split of the "Trinity of Man."

The soldier holding a spear in his hand is one of my oldest memories, coming from when I explored forests with walking sticks. The sticks helped whenever I stumbled across hordes of sheep and the guard dogs became aggressive.

From within the Trinity of Man, I feel Dolur took 30 percent and Marco 50 percent.

His initial name was Dorian Marco, inspired by my father's name, but because his daughter was named Mara, and Mara Marco sounded strange, I had to make some modifications.

This character went through some of the most complex design changes.

As one of the first characters I created in the early 2000s, Marco was the spark behind the creation of the rebirth humans.

Initially, James the Gray Wolf had lycan abilities, meaning he would transform into a large, frightening creature with a human face. This possibility remained viable with Marco until late 2020, when the rebirth meant those who possessed it would undergo a transformation that enlarged the body. I removed this detail because I wanted to have the story as grounded in reality as possible and not associated with the concept of lycanthropy.

The rebirth was initially named "DNA implant." Once I realized that term was too modern for a medieval world, I changed it to "beast implant," but that did not solve the issue. And every time I read it, I would read "breast implant," so I changed it to "rebirth" and added the backstory.

The story of Marco's hair can be seen in his very first design of 2004, where I left white strands among his black hair. I opted for a more human shape on the later 2010 design.

This white hair "old man" idea was taken from real life. My father has always had strong white hair. One time, our entire family was on vacation at the Romanian Black Sea, and at a restaurant, a waiter serving me, my sister, my mother, and my father stared at my father and asked my mother, "Visiting the Black Sea with Grandpa?" I remember it infuriated him a lot, while we laughed.

Marco's early designs showed a buffed, strong, capable fighter, but I gradually made him thinner and worn out in order to better fit with the story.

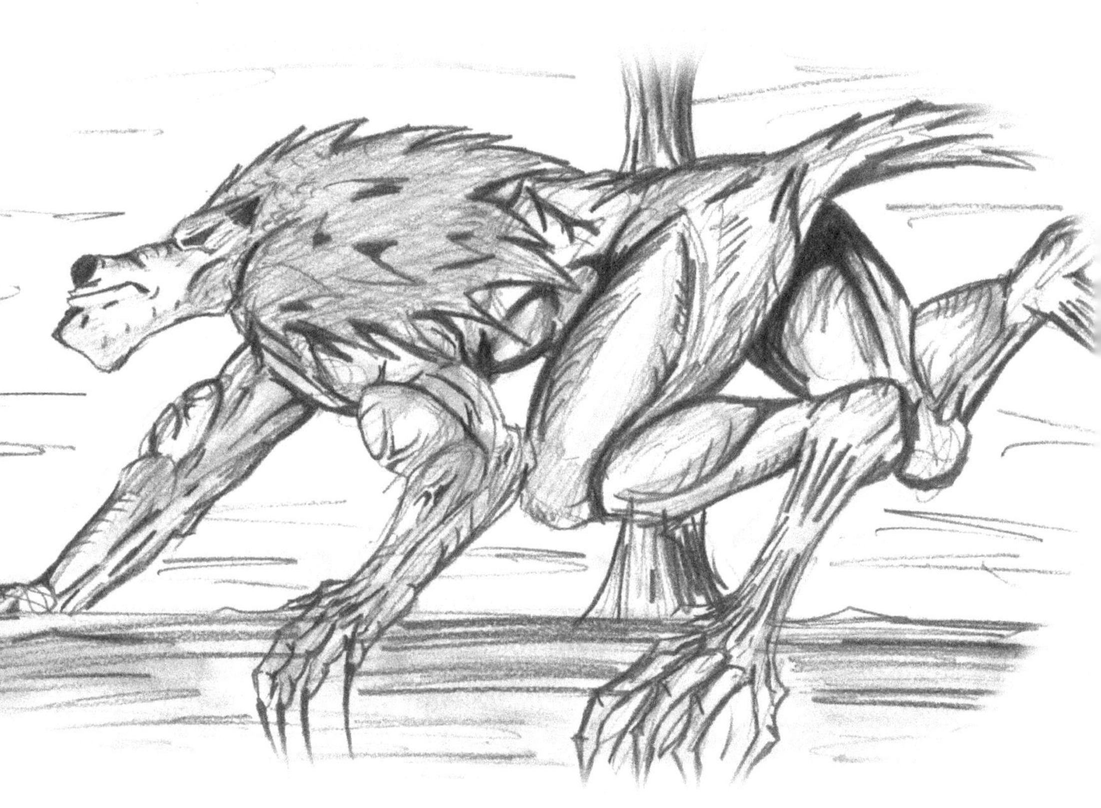

Design: 2003   The first Rebirth design

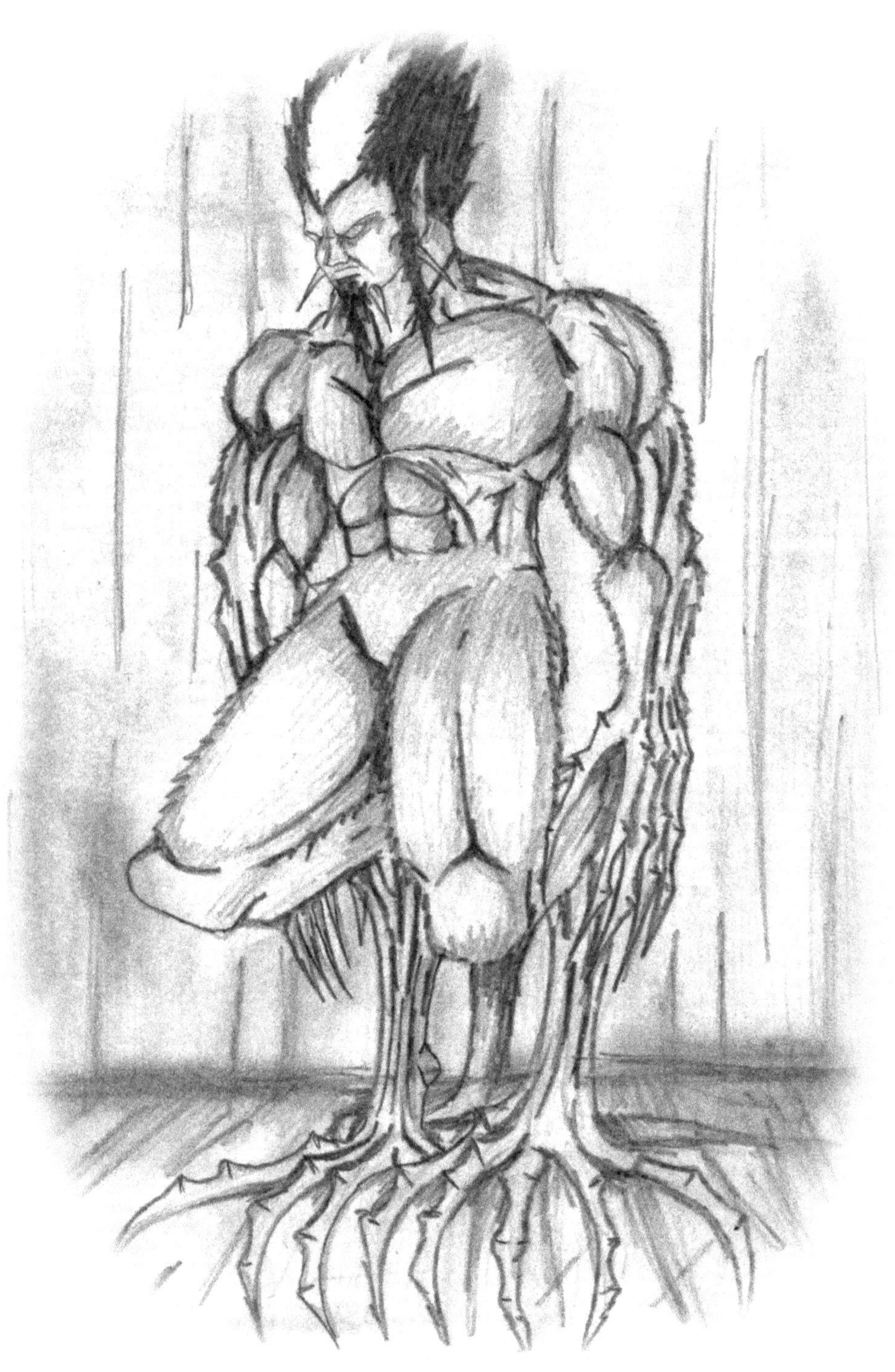

Design: 2004　　　The first Rebirth design of Marco

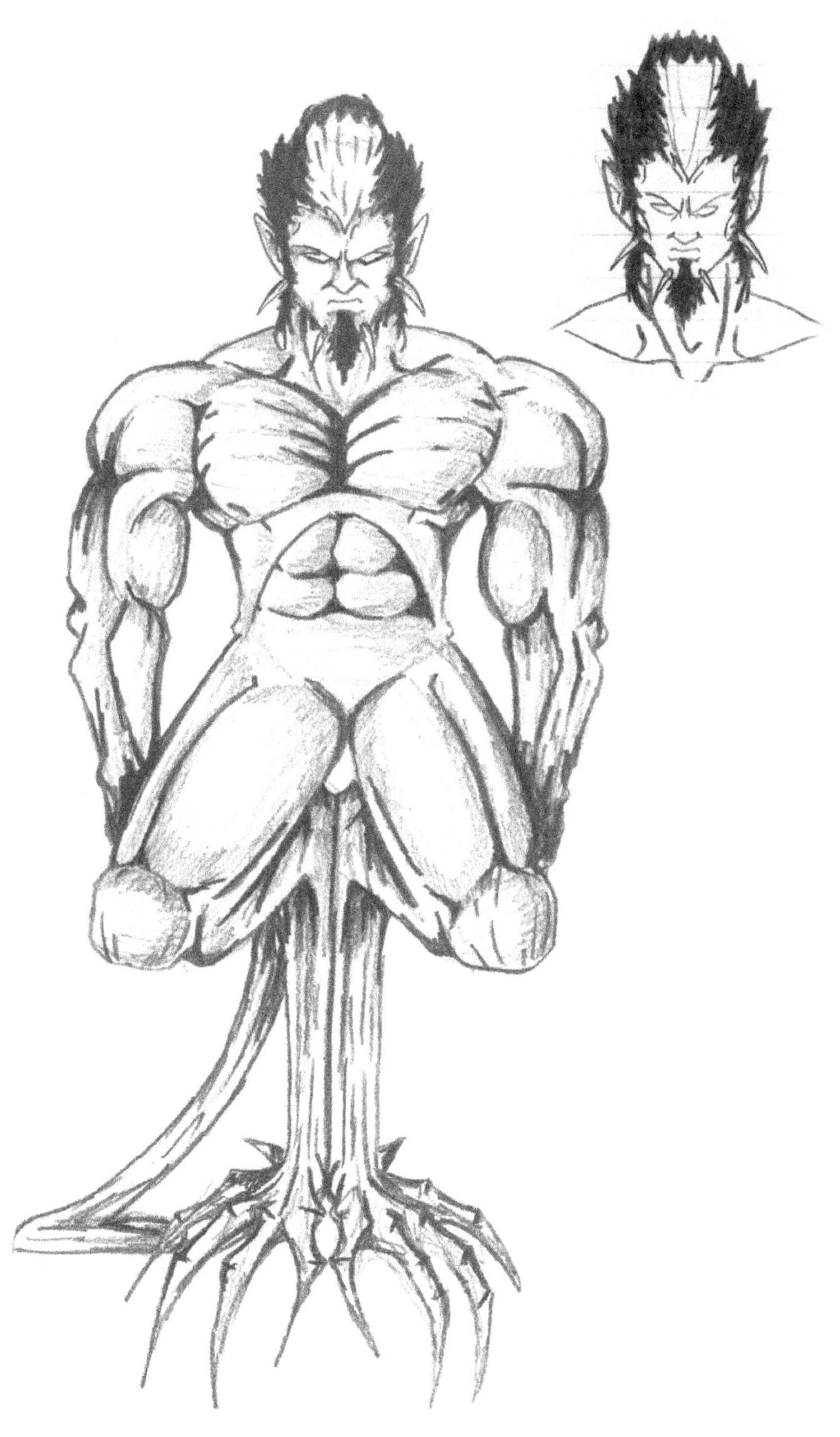

Design: 2004

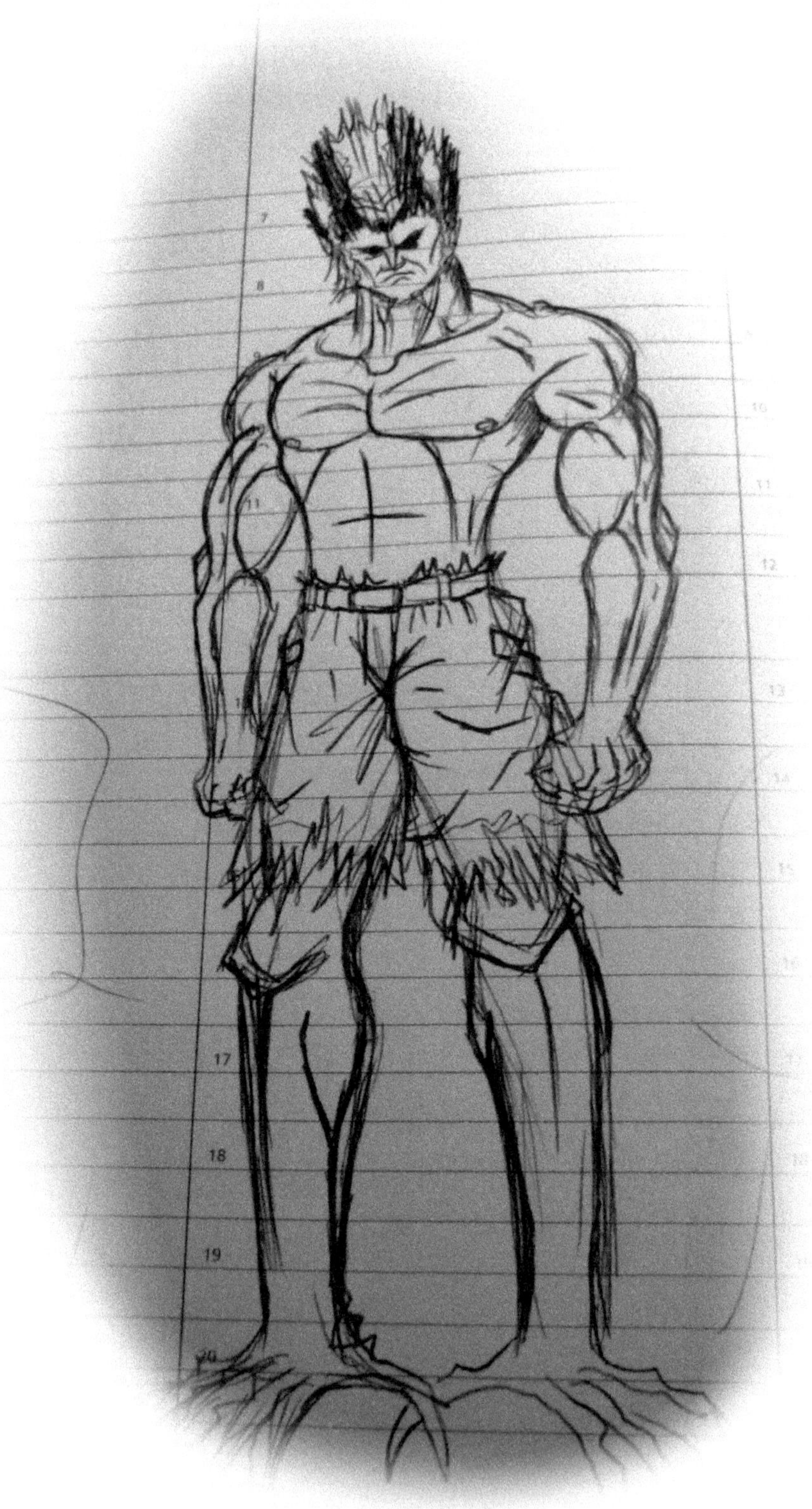

Design: 2010

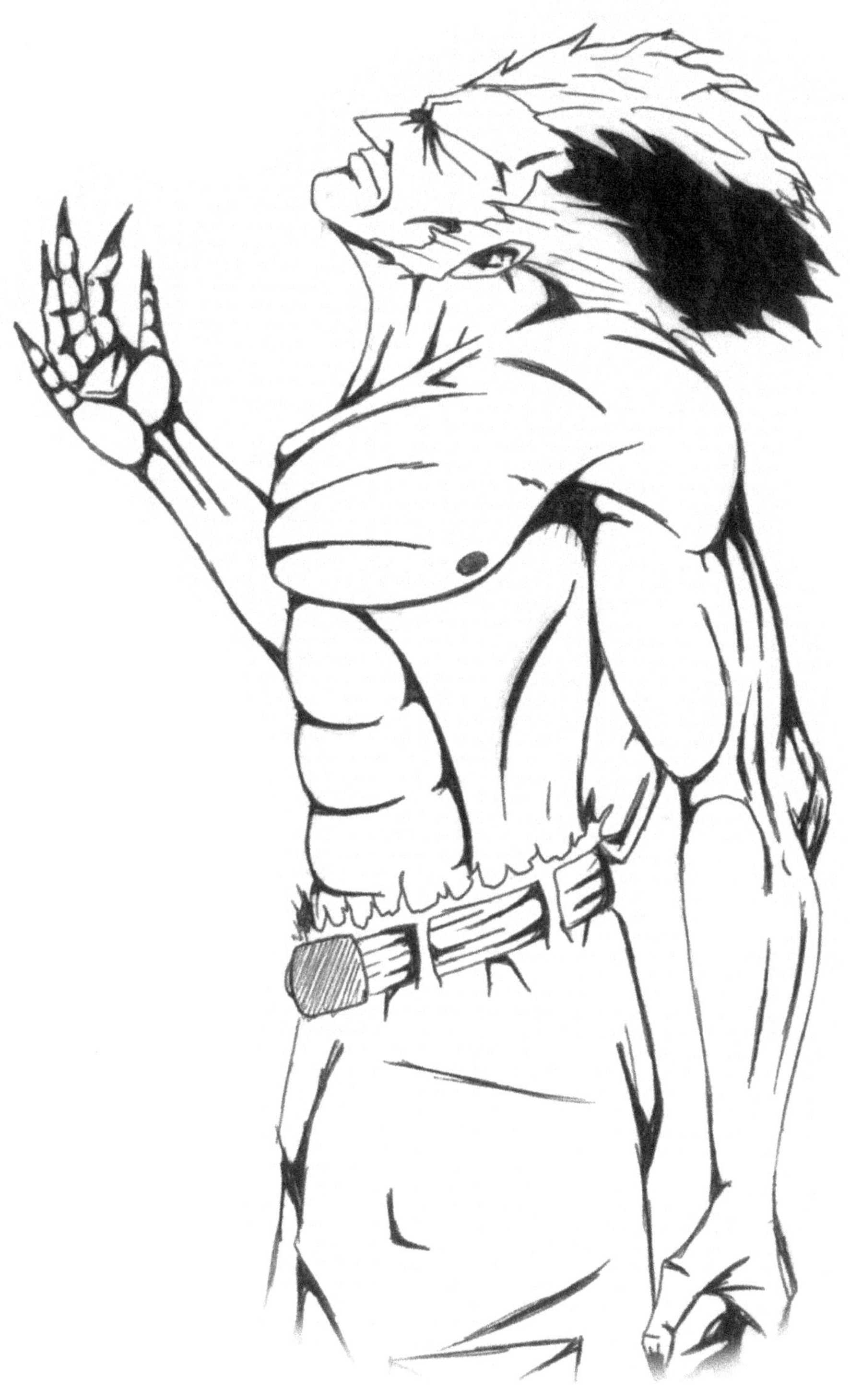

Design: 2010

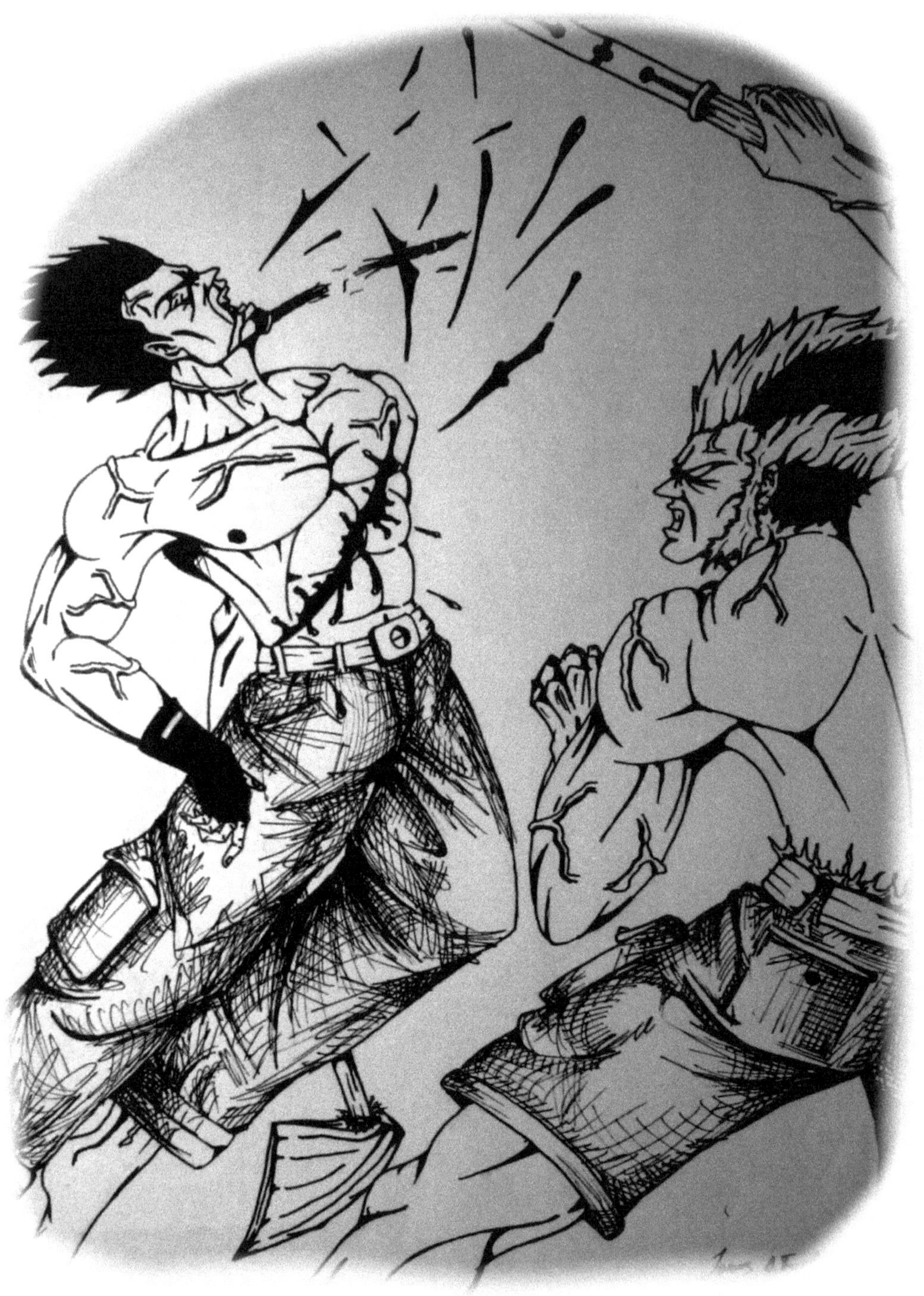

Design: 2010

Marco (right) in battle
Not related to the story

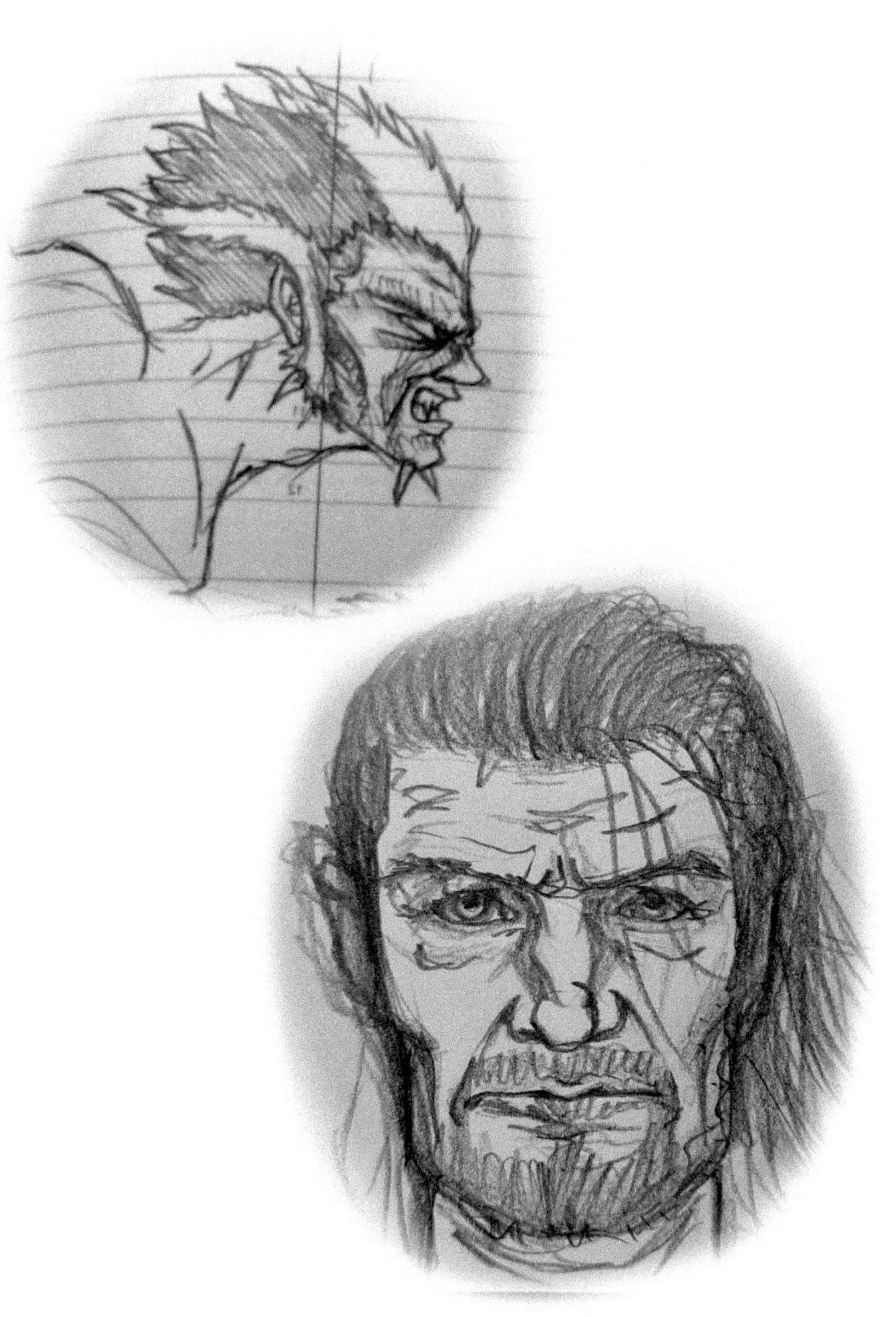

Design: 2010, 2020

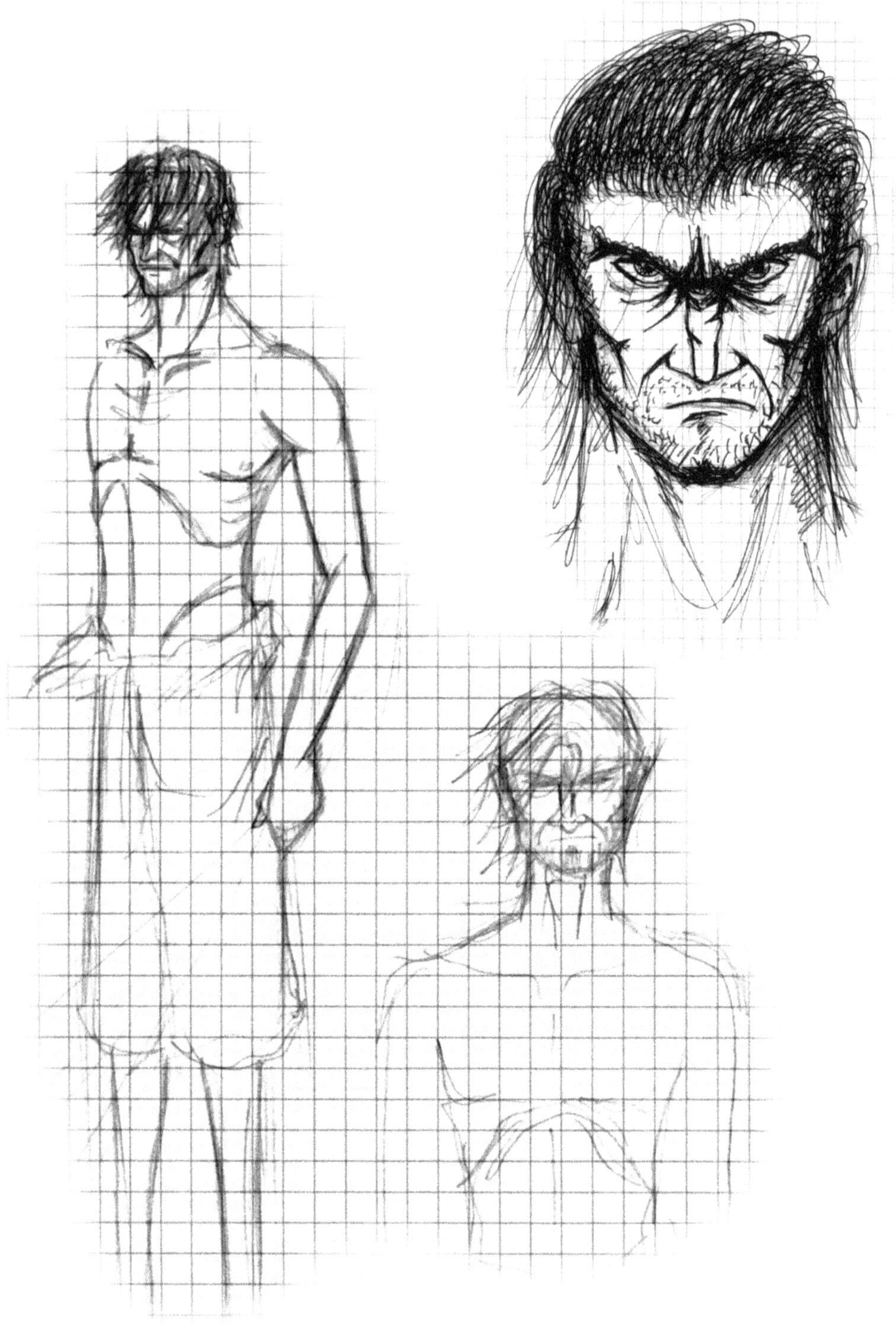

Design: 2017

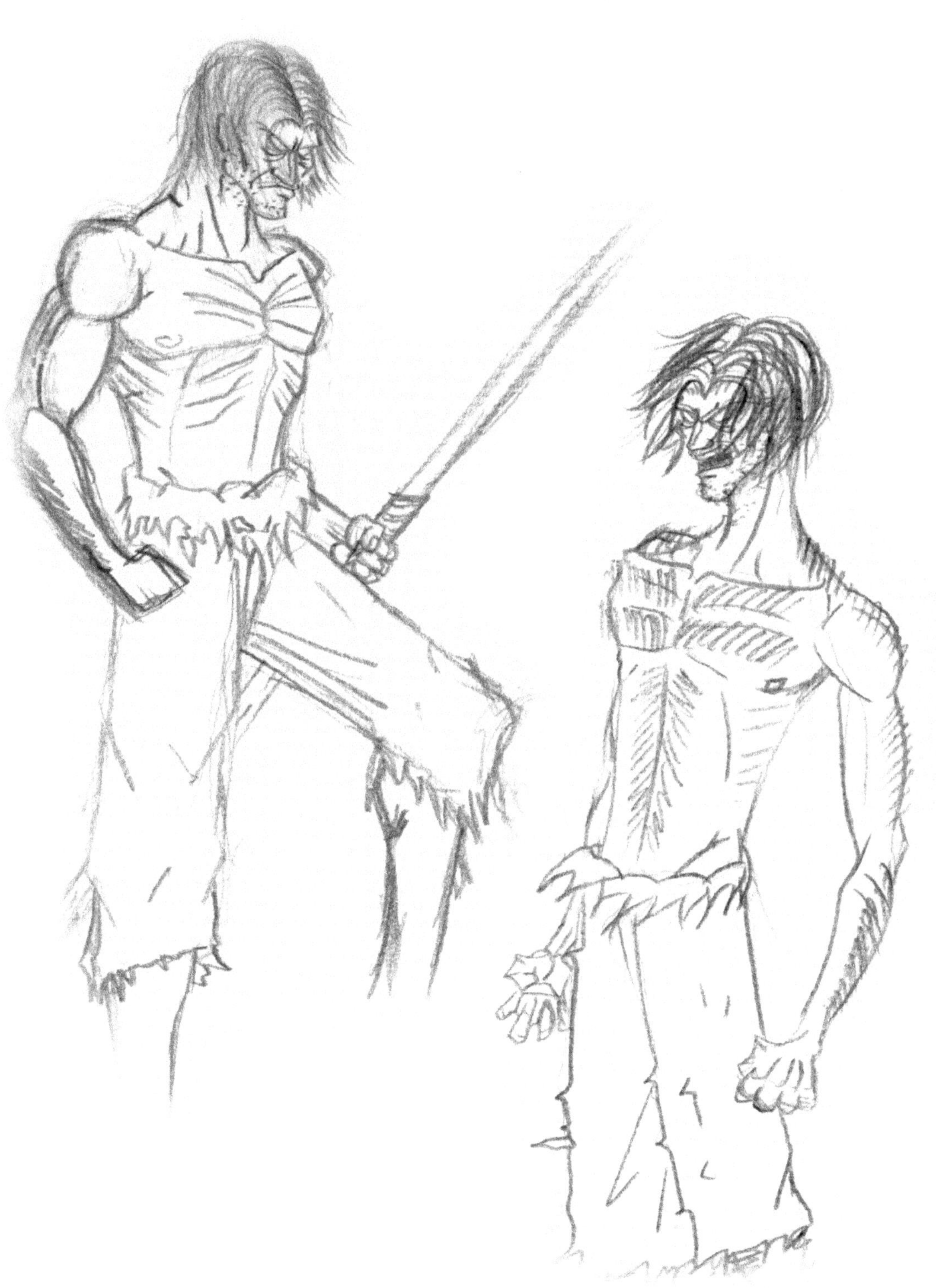

Design: 2019

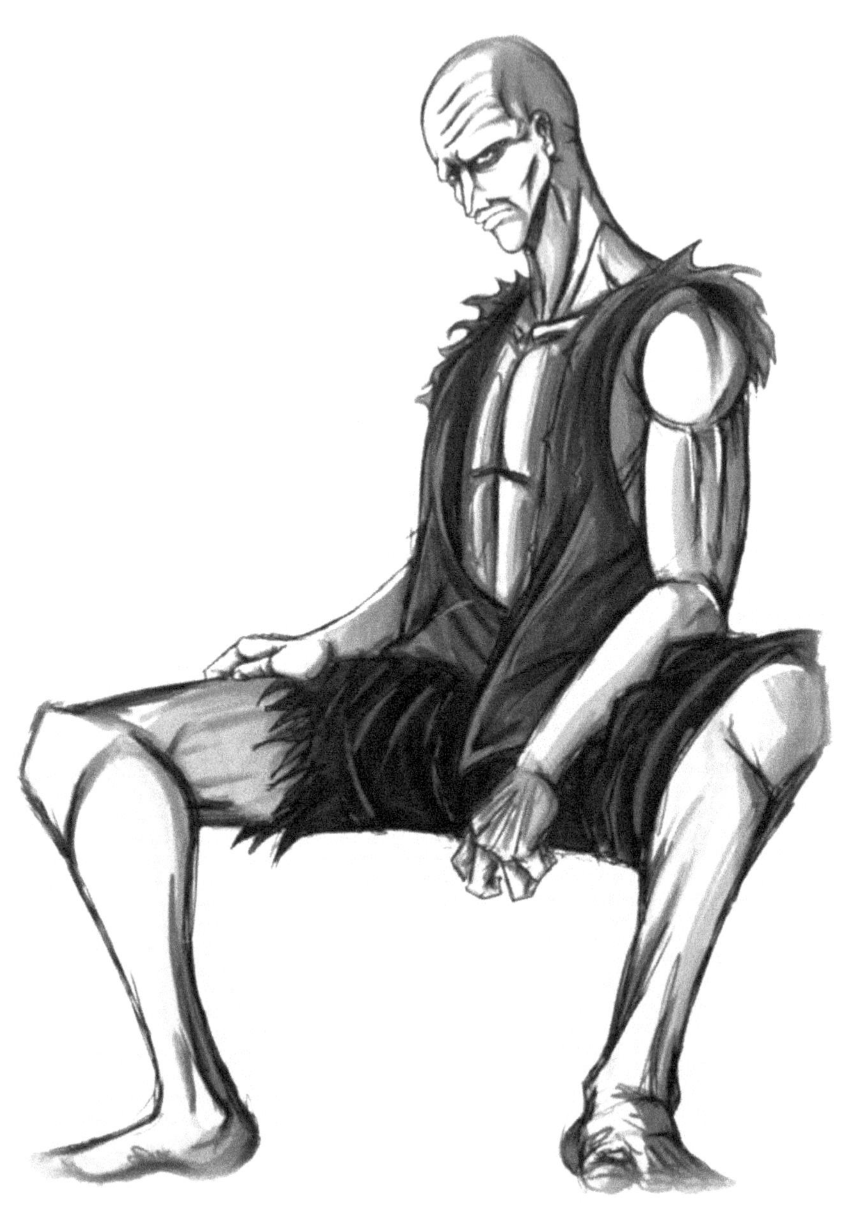

Design of Marco Doran without hair
The concept was quickly abandoned

Digital Design: 2022

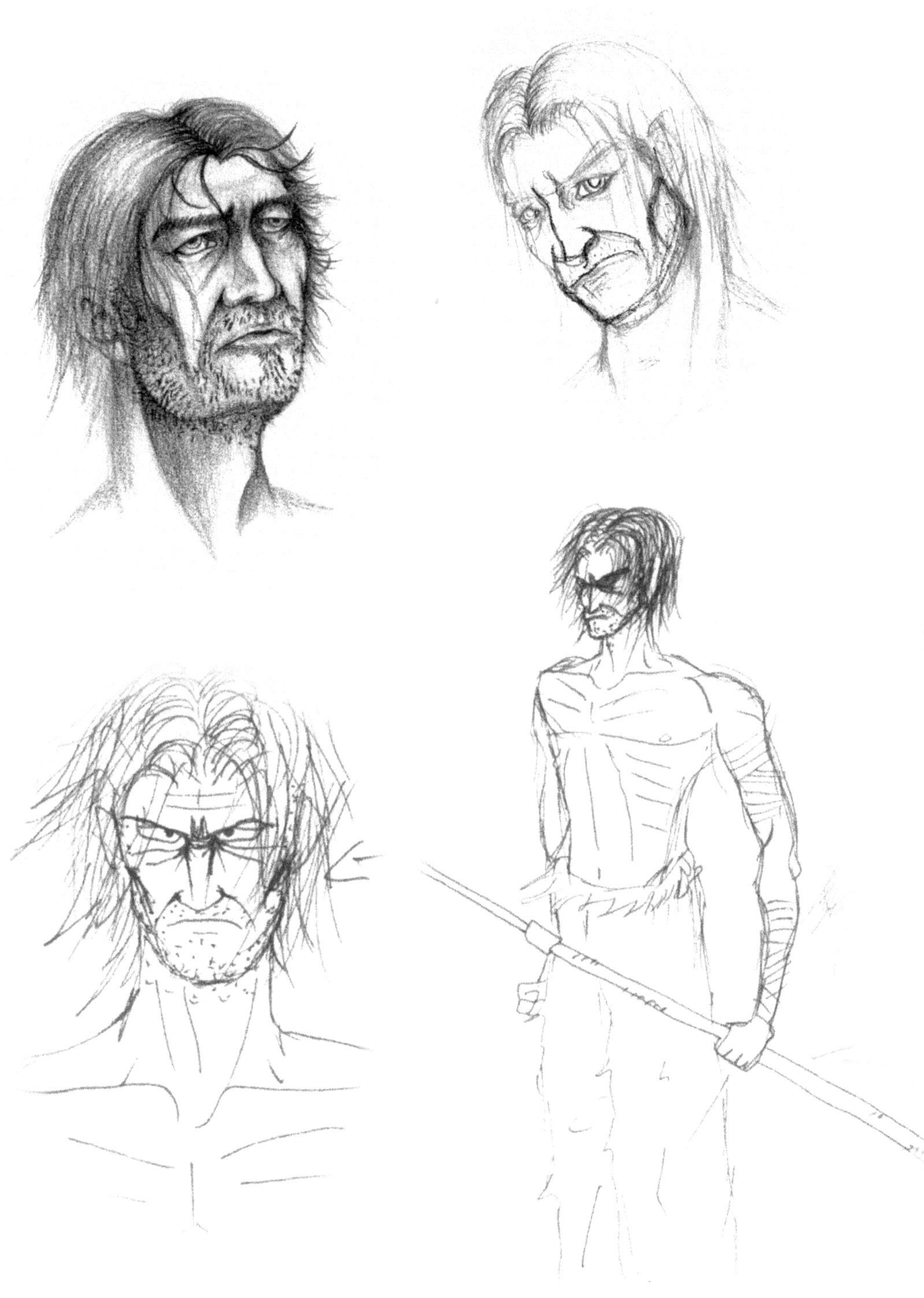

Design: 2023, 2019

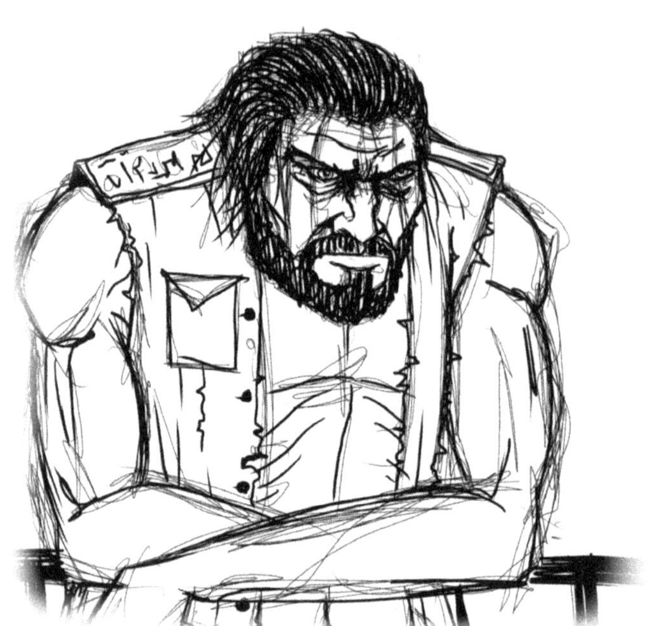

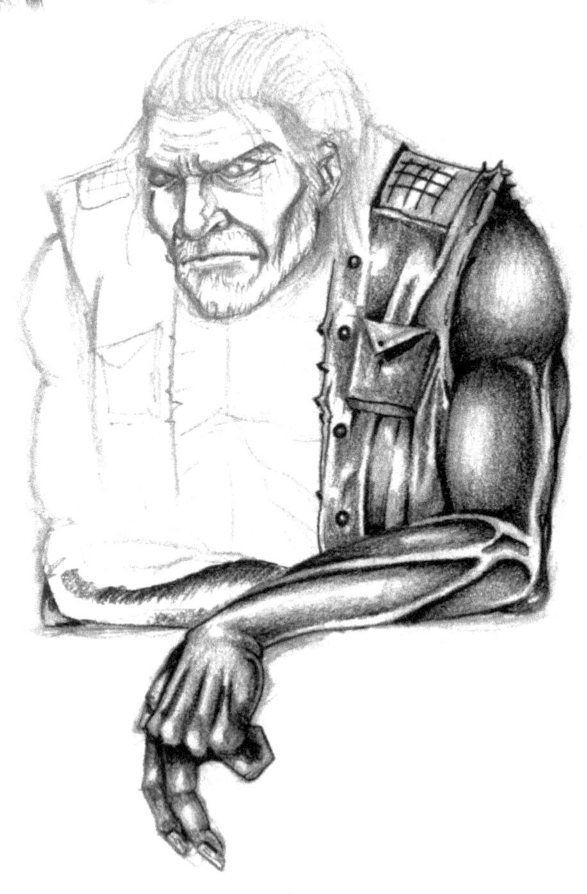

Design: 2024

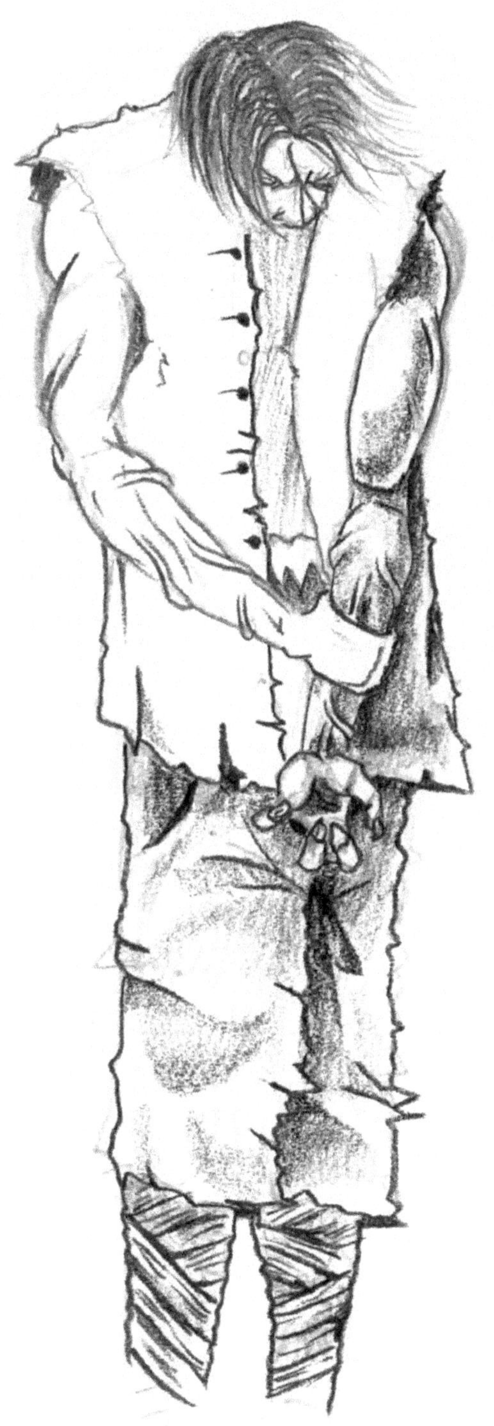

Design: 2024

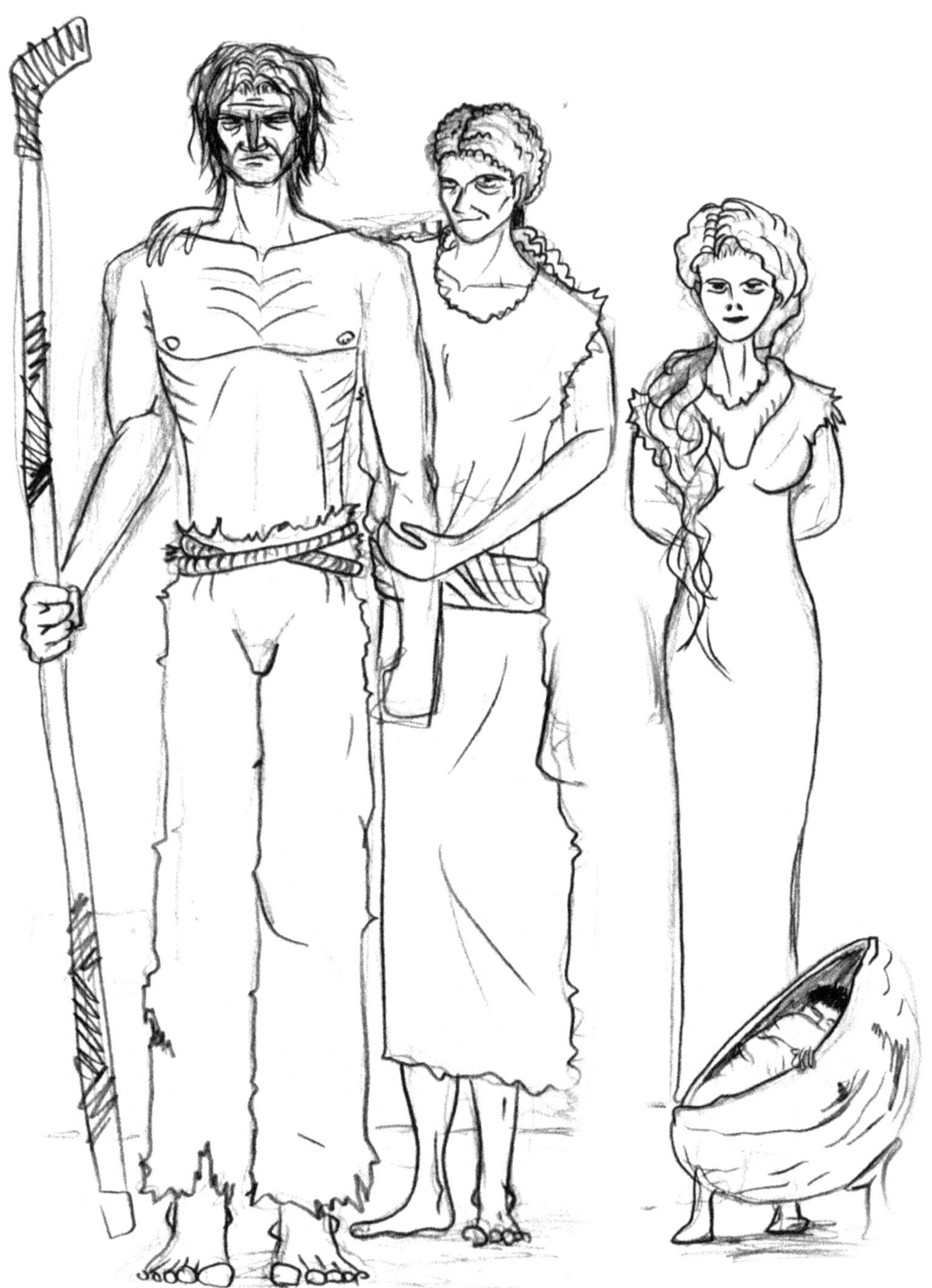

Marco, Cathela, Mara and Molnar Doran

Design: 2021

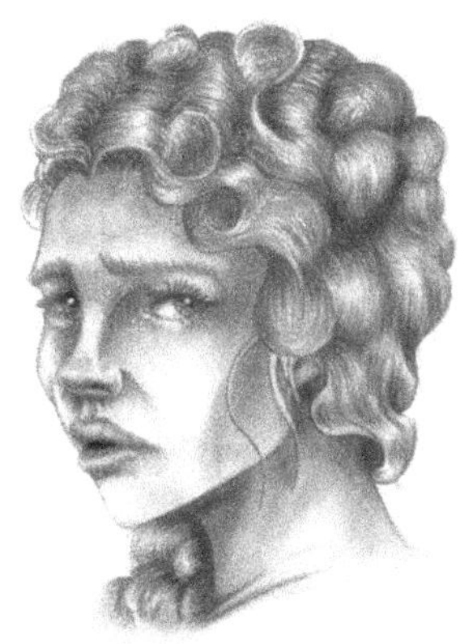

- MARA DORAN -

Mara was created in early 2014. The concept of the green-eyed girl with curly blonde hair was circling in my head even before 2004, but I was unable to materialize a storyline or purpose for her in those early times.

Her first name was Maria, a common Romanian name. I decided to change it to Mara when her last name became Dorian because Maria Dorian sounded strange.

This is one character I had a lot of trouble with drawing. I could never pull off a gentle, cute girl face. My last attempt at her redrawing was in July of 2024, after more beta readers told me the former 2023 design didn't quite fit her description. And they were right!

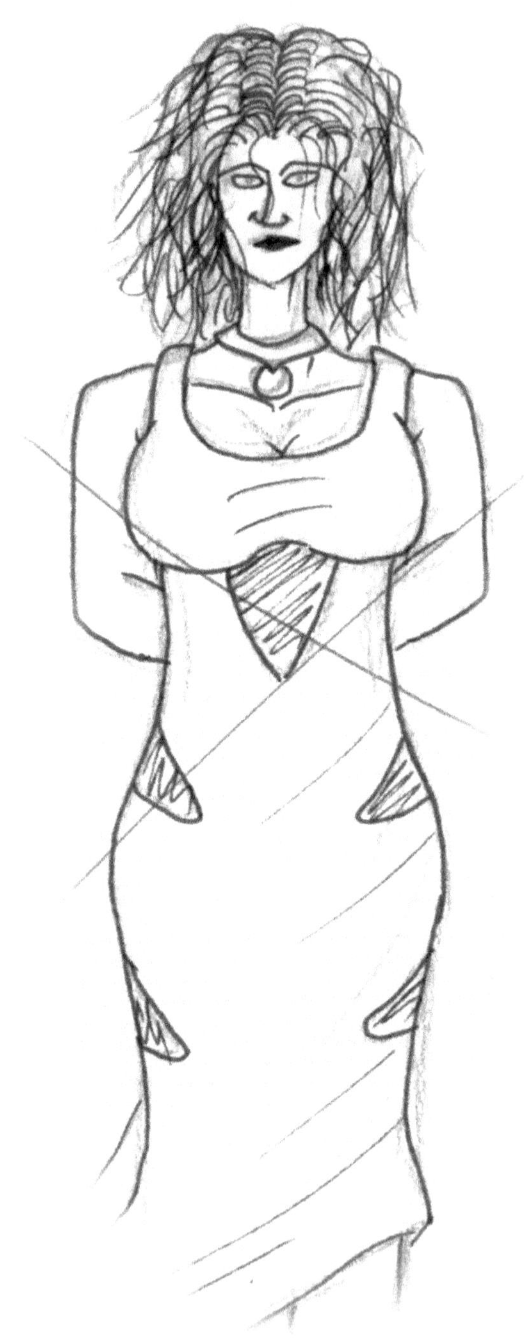

Design: 2018

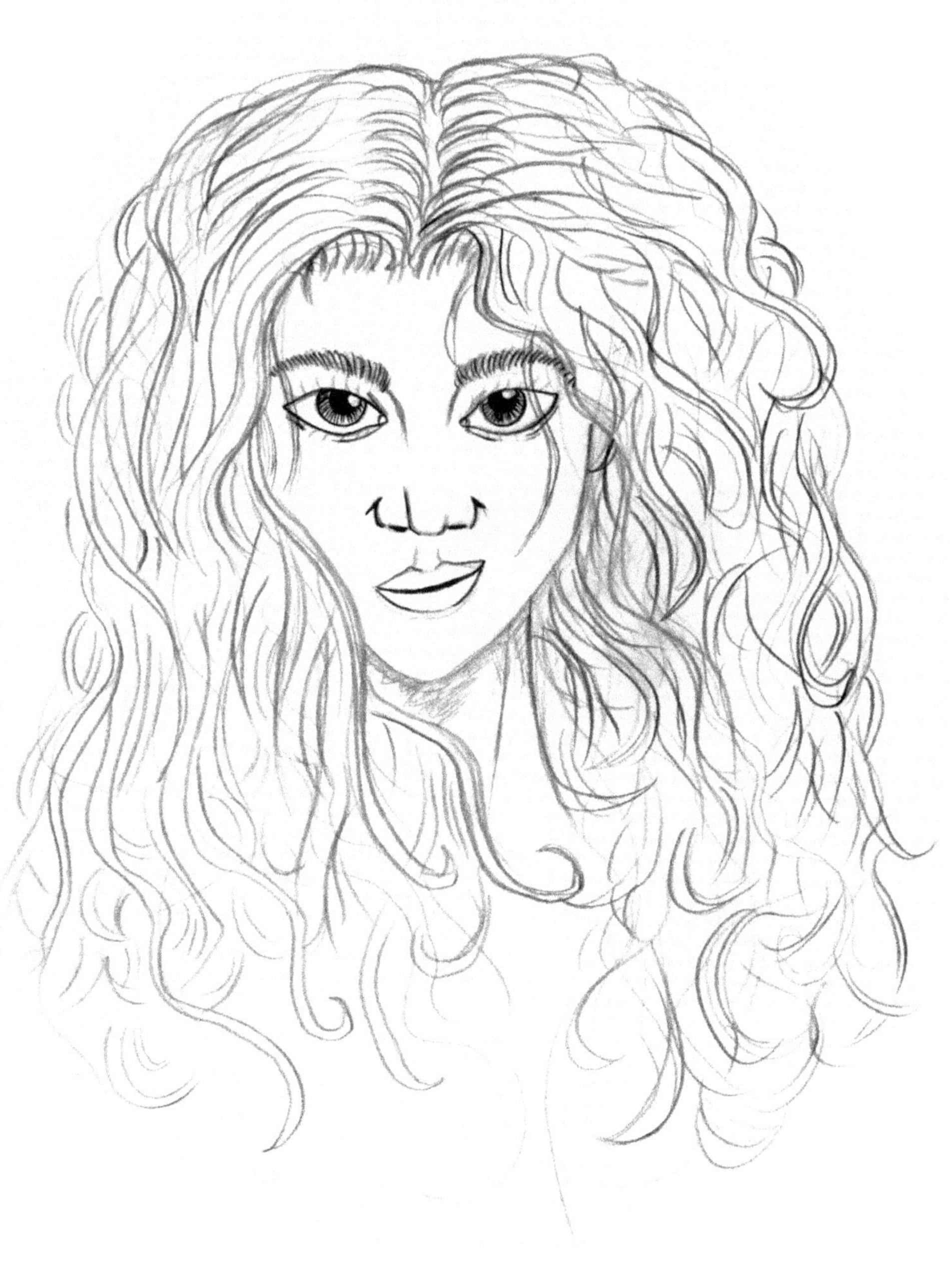

Design: 2020

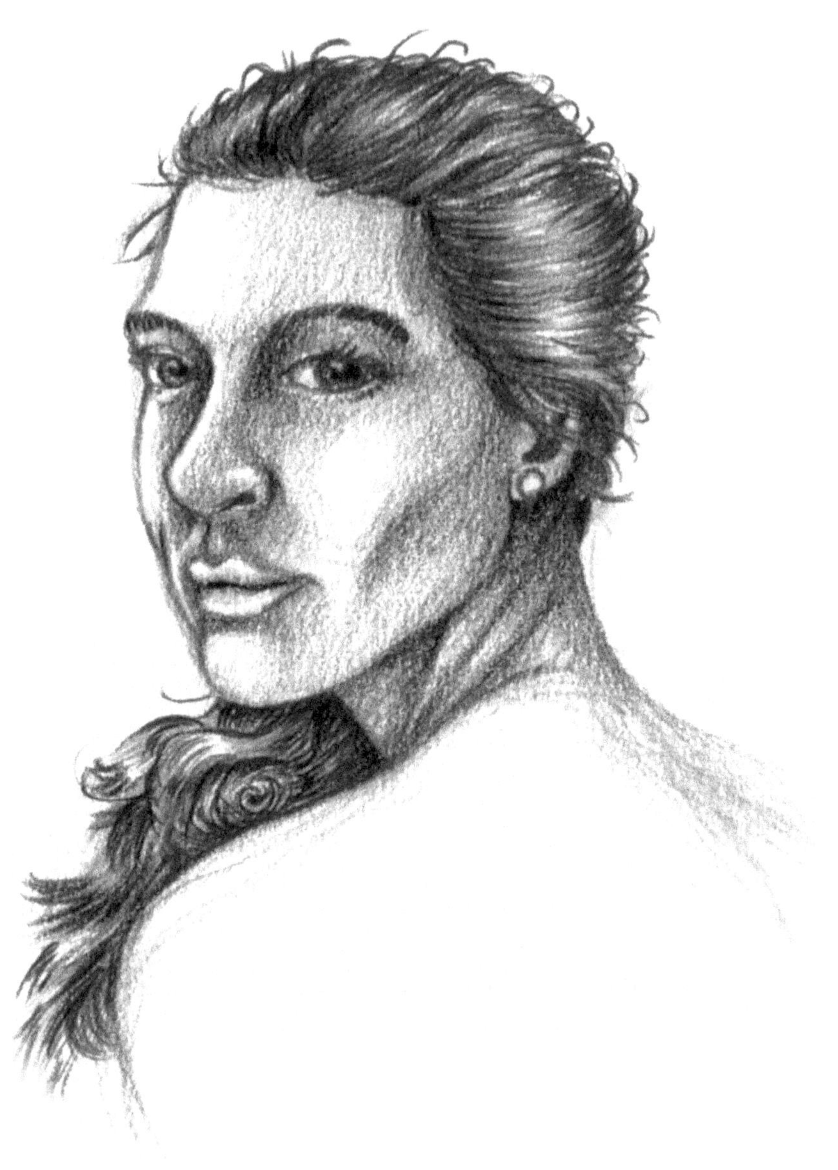

Design: 2023

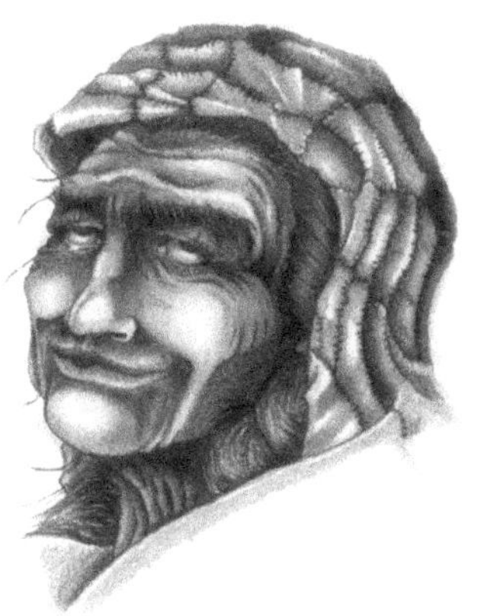

- THE RAT MOTHER -

The Rat Mother went through three name changes.

The Gifted Mother: It was too common, found in so many other franchises. Her first design had long, unkempt hair that flowed over her shoulders and outside of her hood. I removed that concept in order to have her more grounded and real, hiding most of her hair inside her hood.

The Gifted Sister: In 2019, I had the Gifted Mother and the Gifted Sister. Both of them had the same role, so in order to reduce the ever-growing number of characters, I remained with only the mother, but I gave her the name of the Gifted Sister. This name also didn't convince me, as it removed the protective and caring part of what a mother would resemble in the Rat Huts.

The Rat Mother: I decided to offer her this name in July of 2024. I felt this name fit her perfectly.

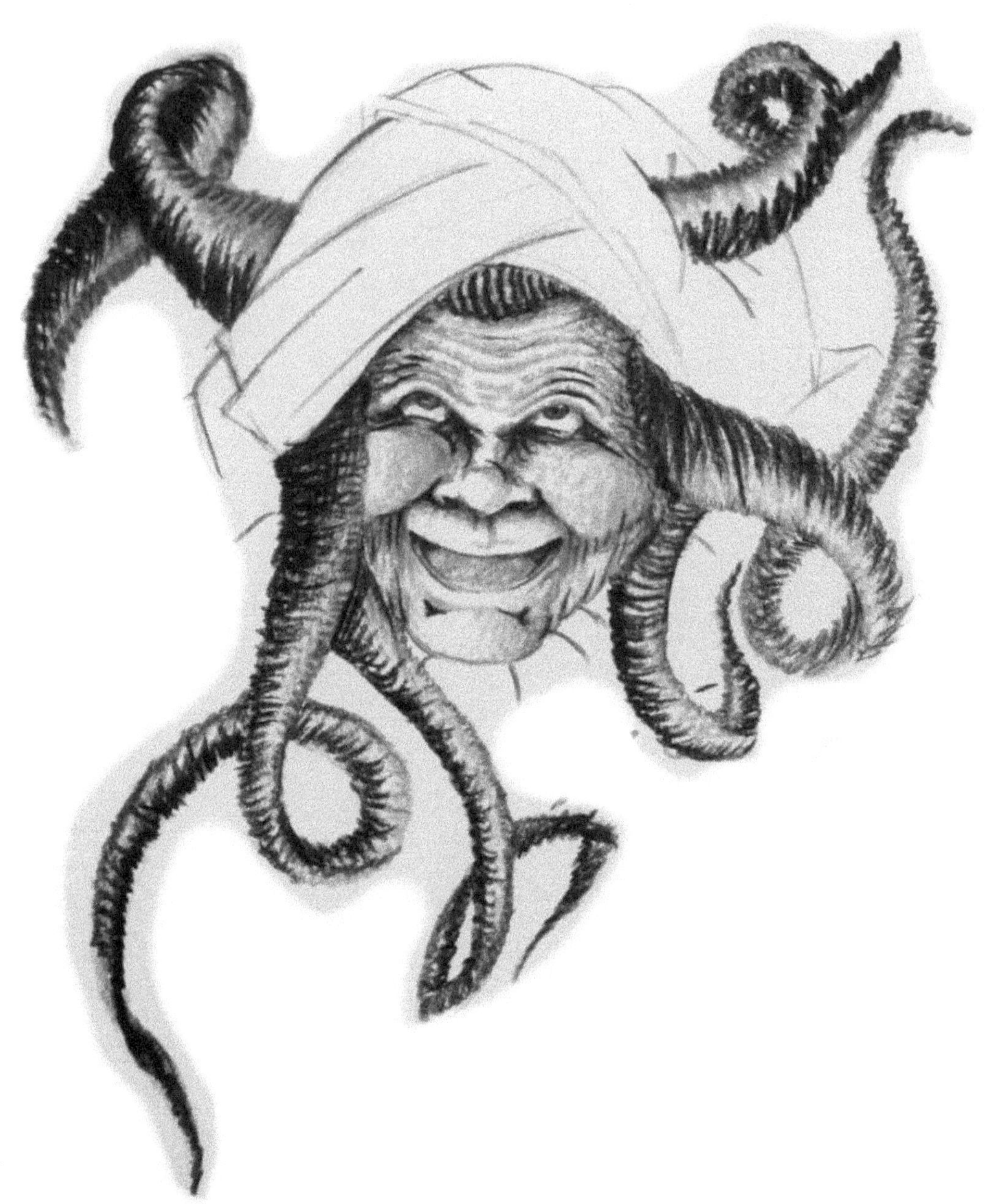

Design: 2021

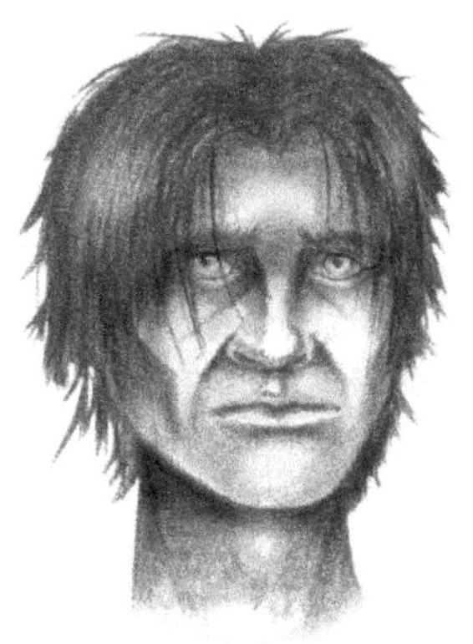

- Matu Ensur -

Matu was the first new character when I decided to write the story of *Favors Within Ashes* in August of 2014.

He had a common Romanian name—"Matei." I decided the names of the characters inside this world would be similar to the kingdoms they came from, so his name needed one of the following letters: o, u, m, n, t.

It was difficult to draw him with features that did not resemble strong, giant, evil men.

I chose to draw and add Matu's portrait to the book in June of 2024. He was one of the last drawn characters. I did not intend to draw him but began sketching in my free time. The decision not to use strong shading on his eyes brought out the fear in his gaze, and I knew that had to be Matu.

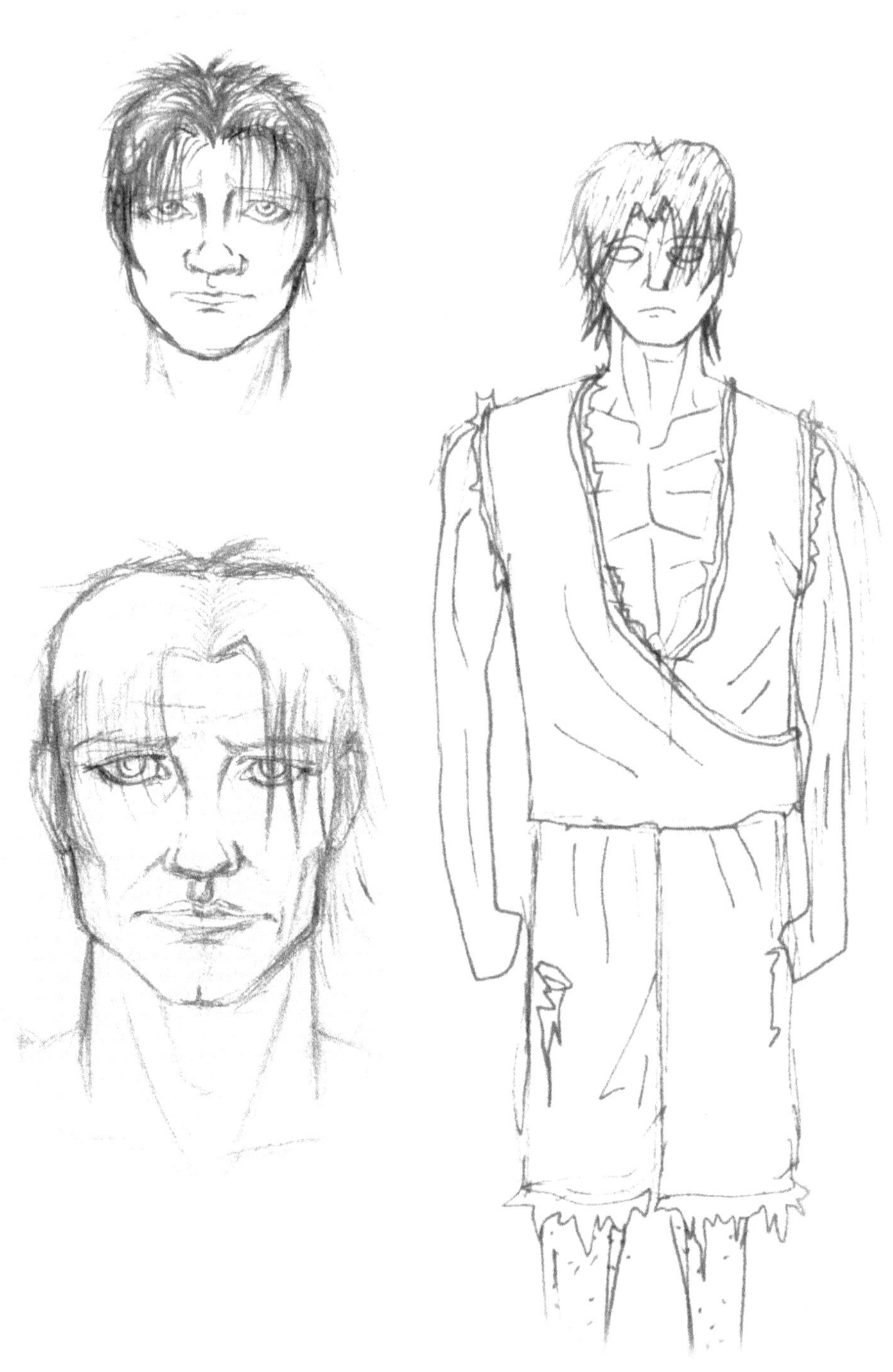

Design: 2018, 2024

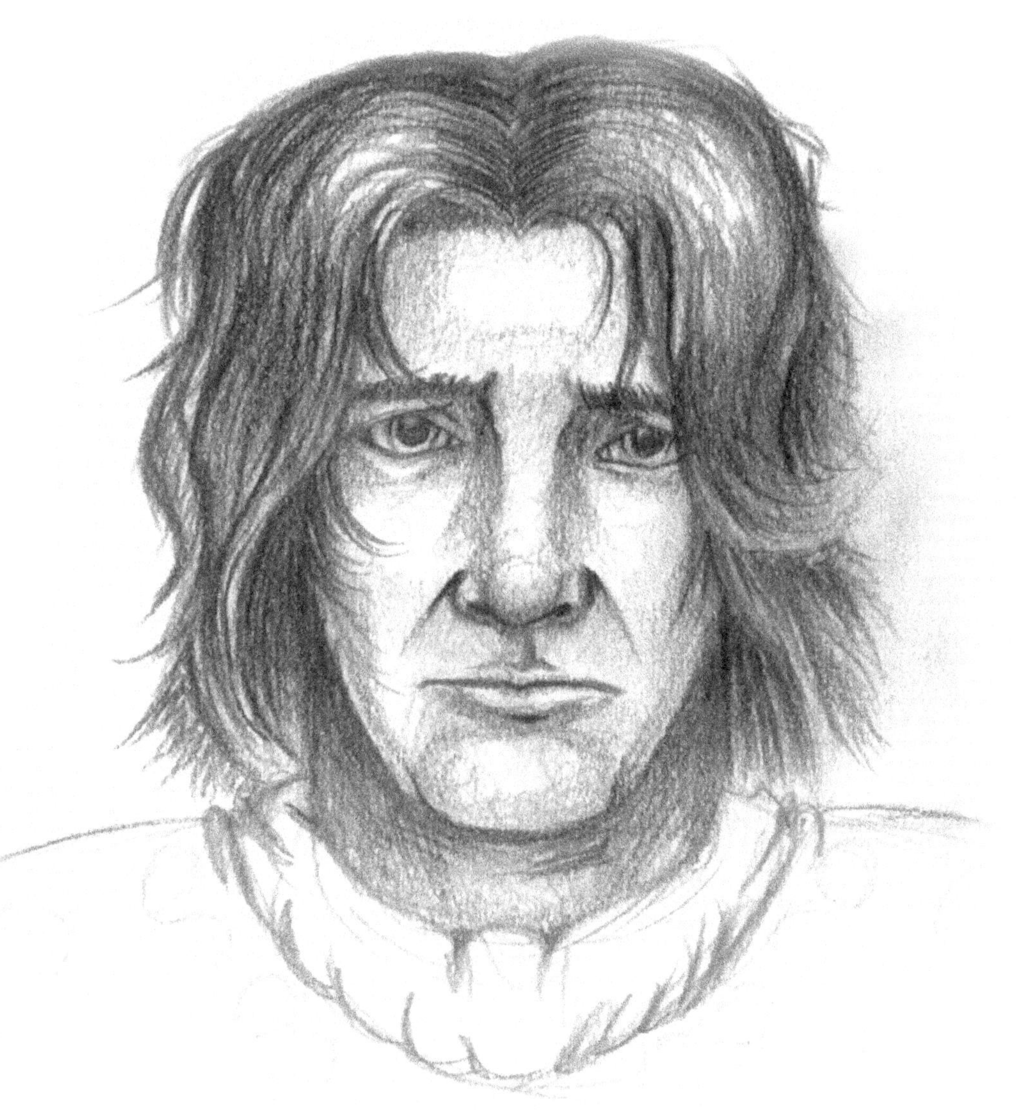

Design: 2021

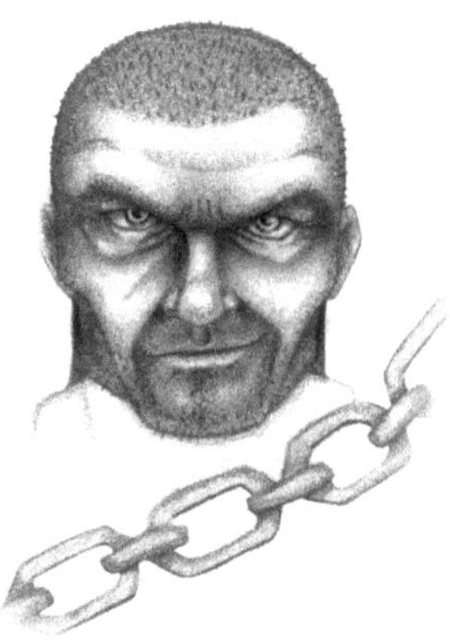

- Sir Breko Isedon -

Breko Isedon is one of the first antagonists I created and sketched between 2000 and 2003. His initial name was Chris because a lot of the common names in the nu metal–style media I consumed were Chris, John, Jack, James, etc. At that time, I had not created the concept of the legionnaires, but I knew he needed to be one of the "bad guys."

His second name was "Woodon Brad." I've always had a hard time coming up with names. I created this name in 2014 when I was working in a hotel in Austria and was staring at the forest one summer evening after a hard day. I used the term "woodon" to create his first name, and Brad, which in Romanian means pine tree, for his last name.

His final version, Breko Isedon, is the name I took from a legionnaire whom I deleted from the story, as I merged his character with another existing one. At that time, this was the only instance I merged two characters into one.

I changed his hairstyle, cutting it shorter with each redesign. The 2000s-era long, braided beard seemed impractical, and after adding chains to his arsenal, I knew it would be a major problem, so I eliminated it. The hair he sported in the 2018–2020 era seemed too modern for a medieval world, so I decided he would just go with a short shaved-scalp style.

What I always knew was that I wanted Breko to use an axe for a weapon.

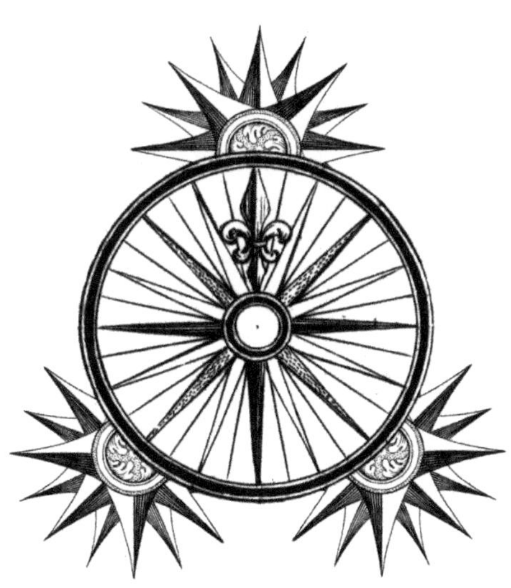

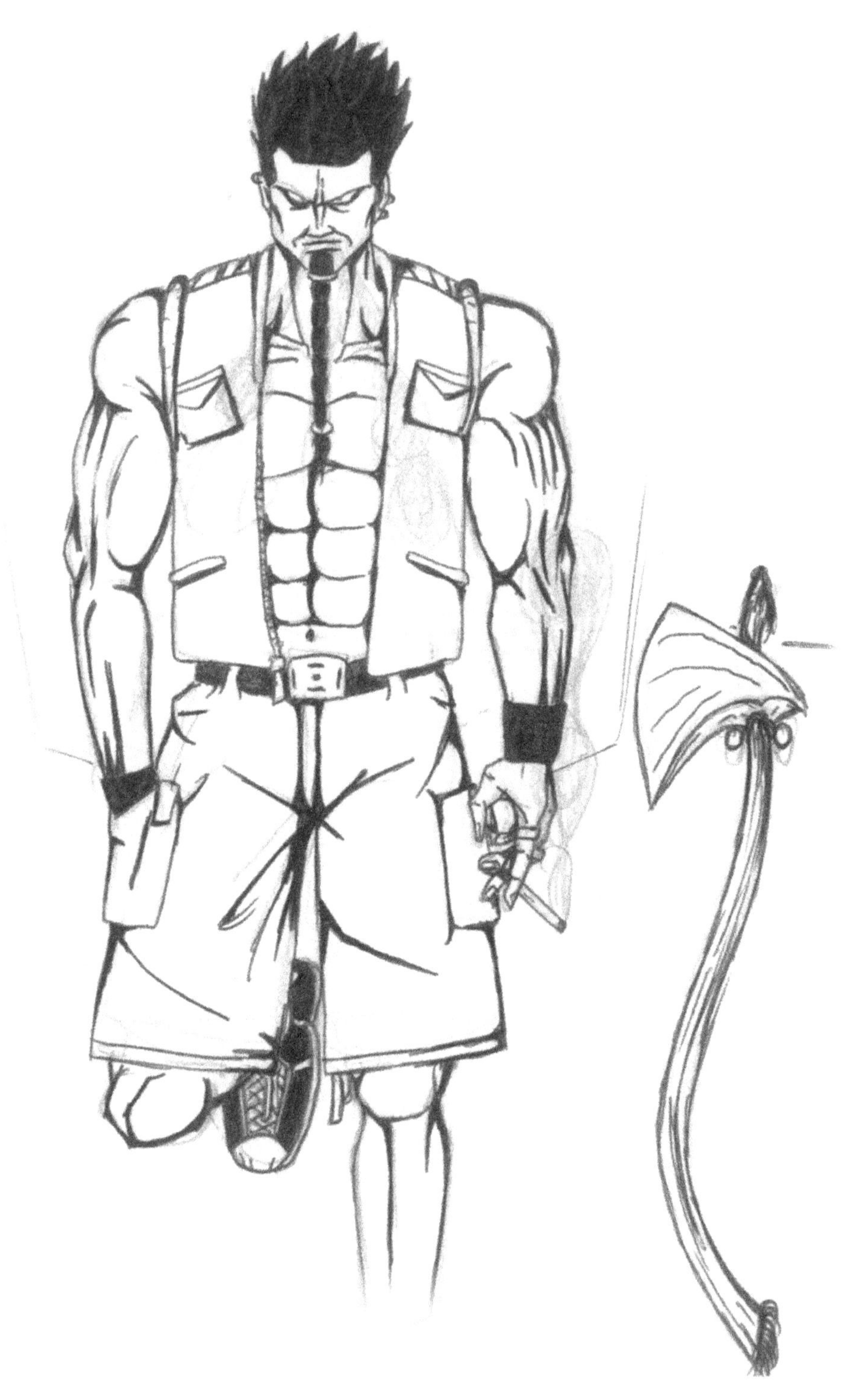

Design: 2010

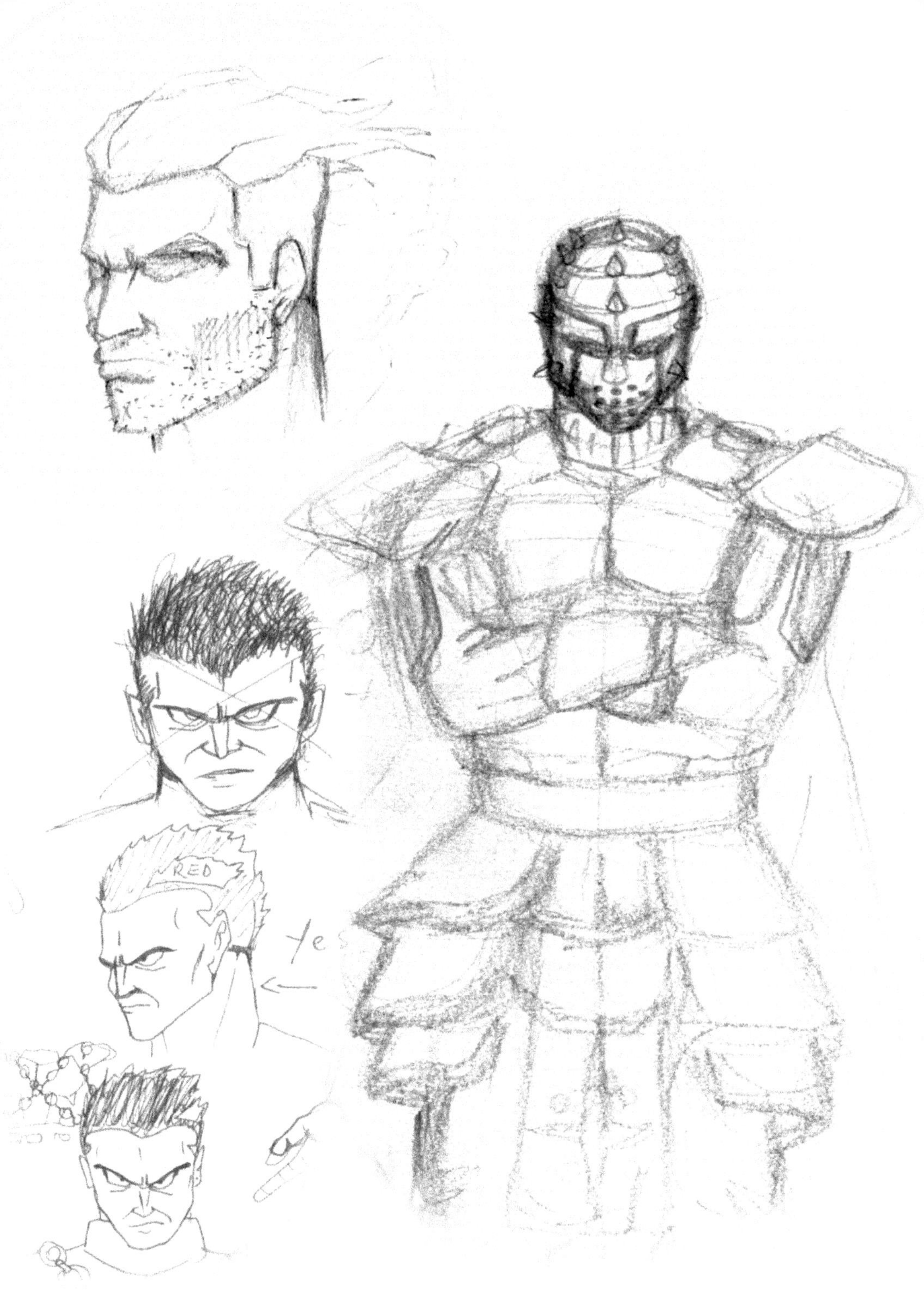

Design: 2019, 2020, 2021

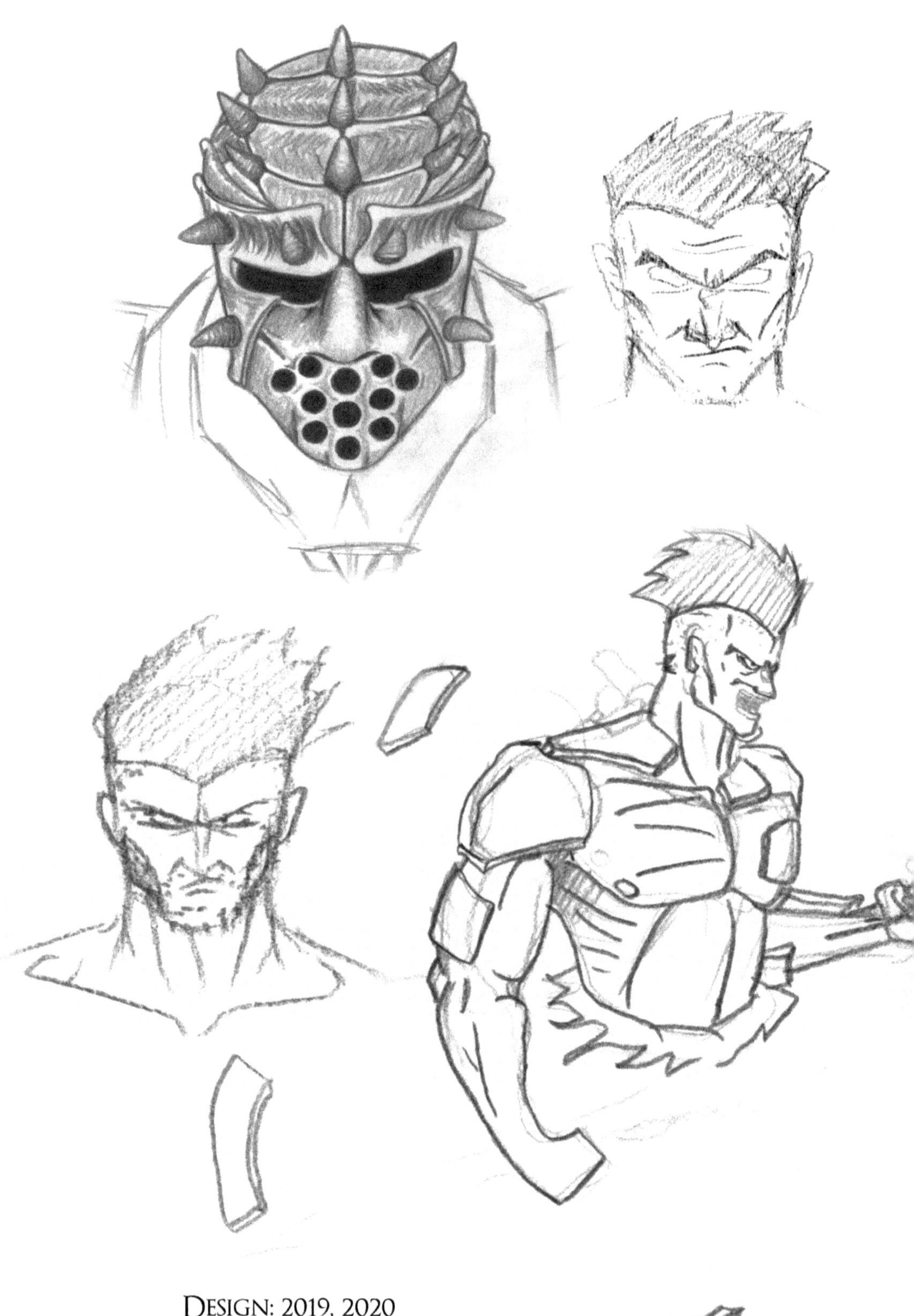

Design: 2019, 2020

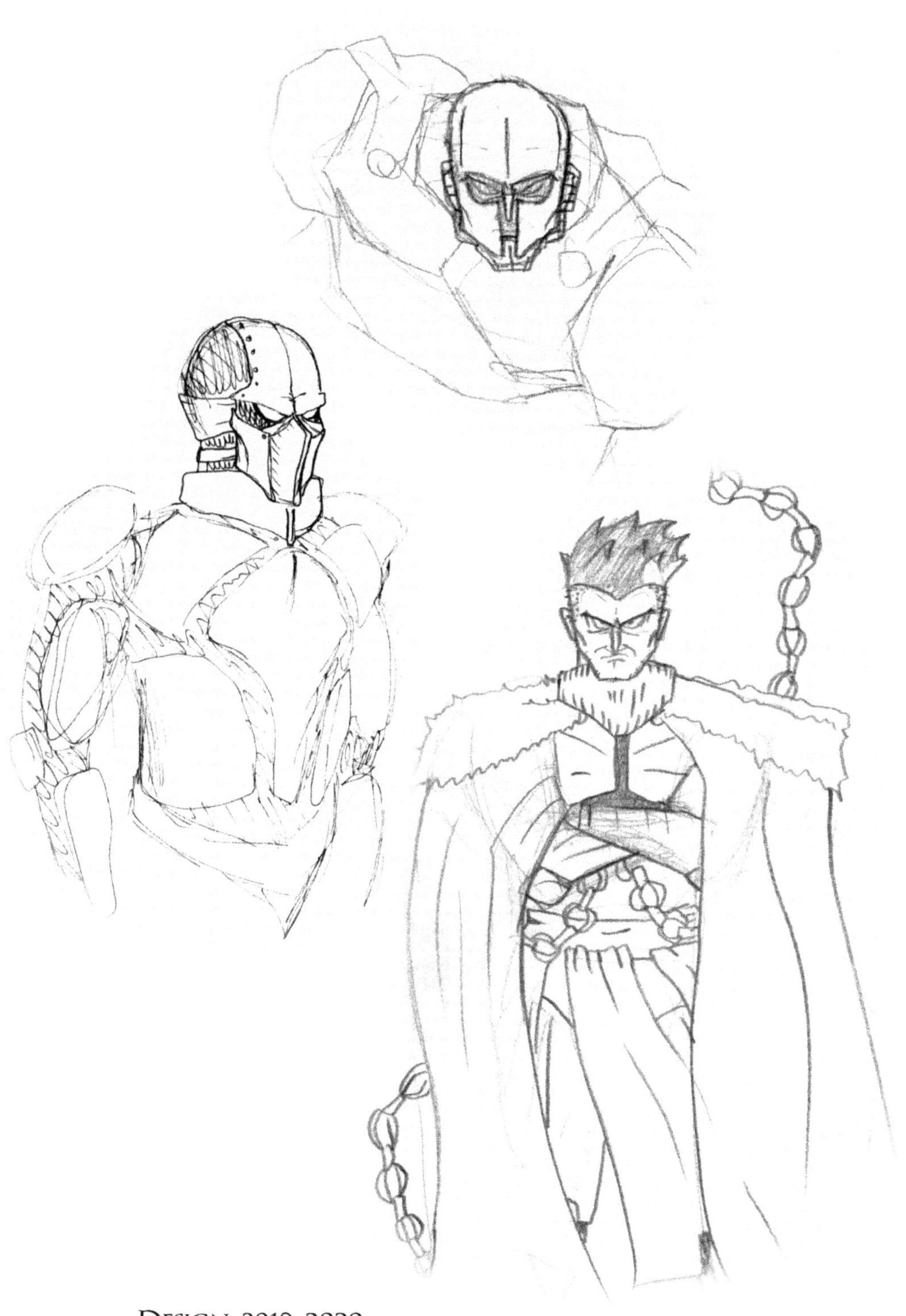

Design: 2019, 2020

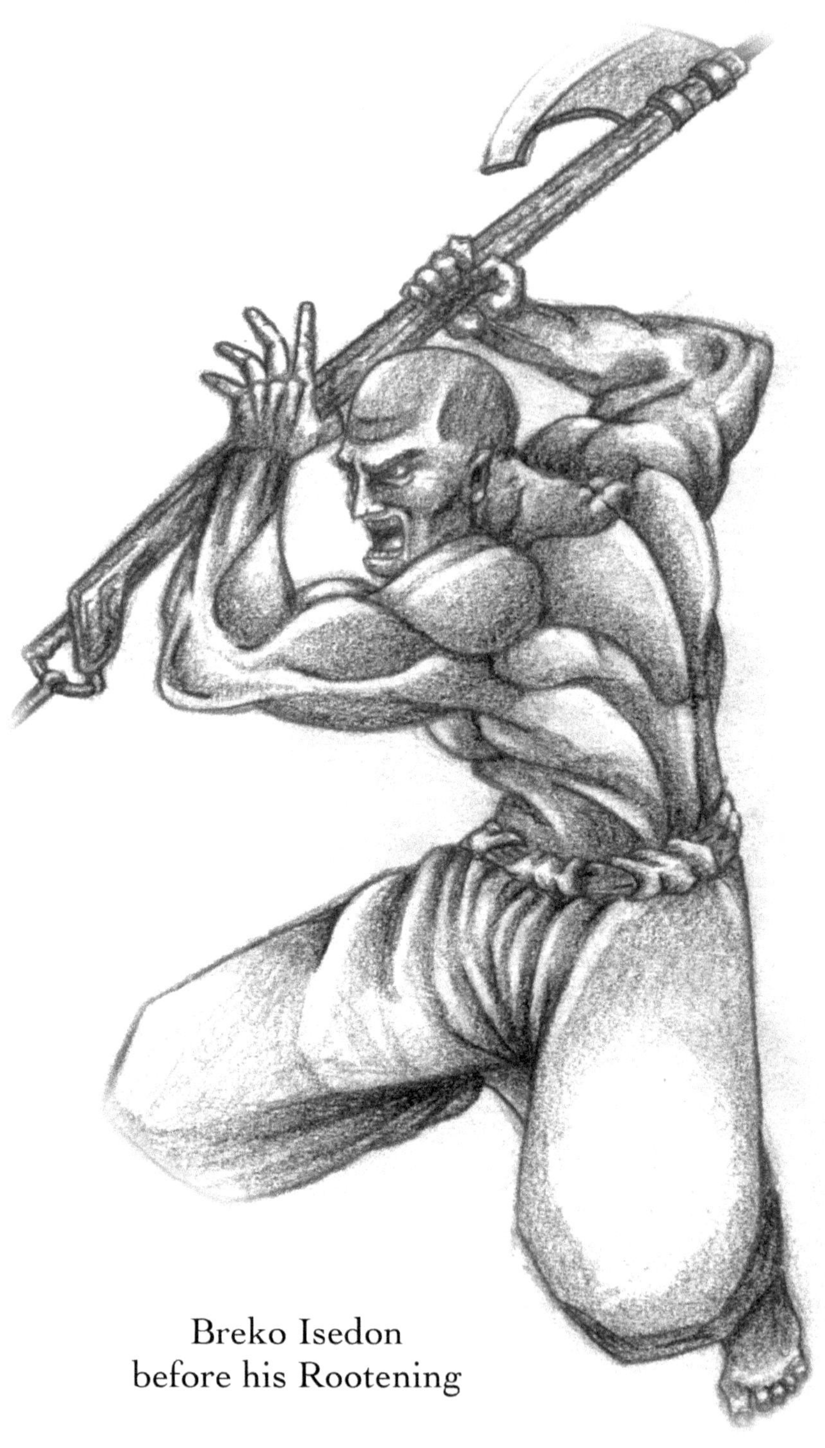

Breko Isedon
before his Rootening

Design: 2021

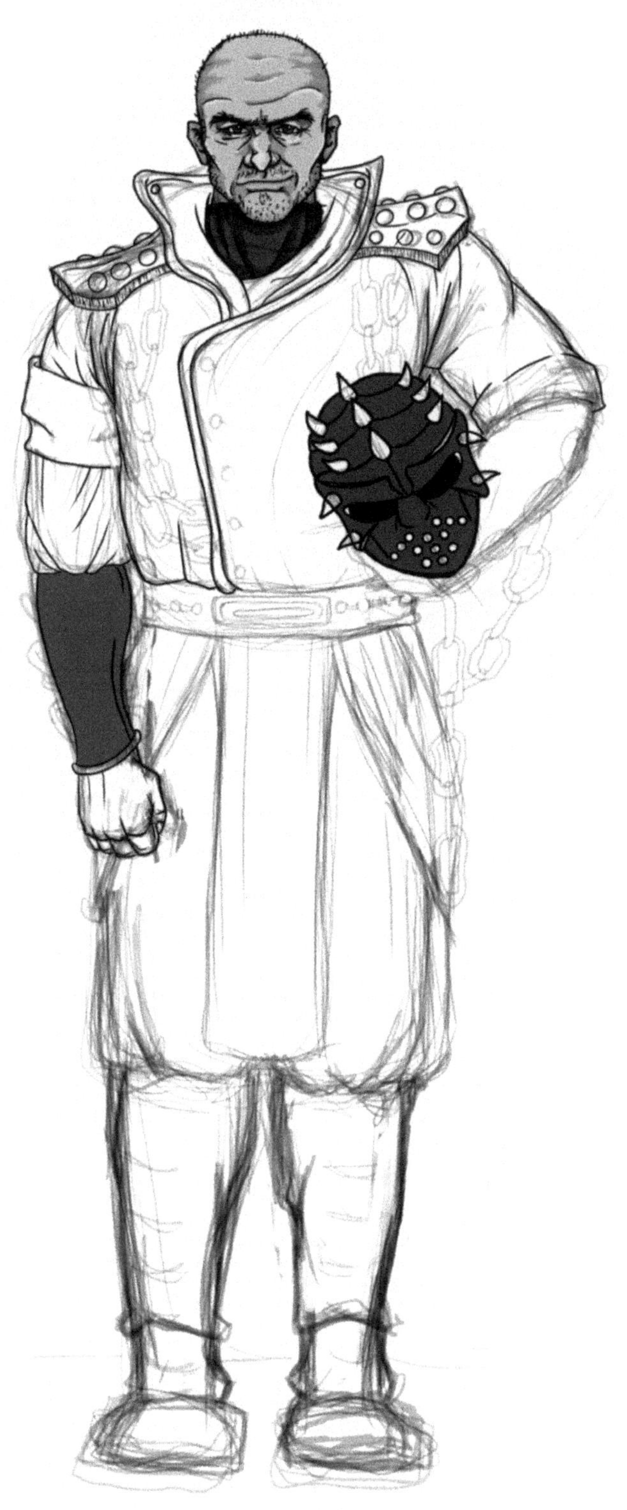

DIGITAL DESIGN: 2022

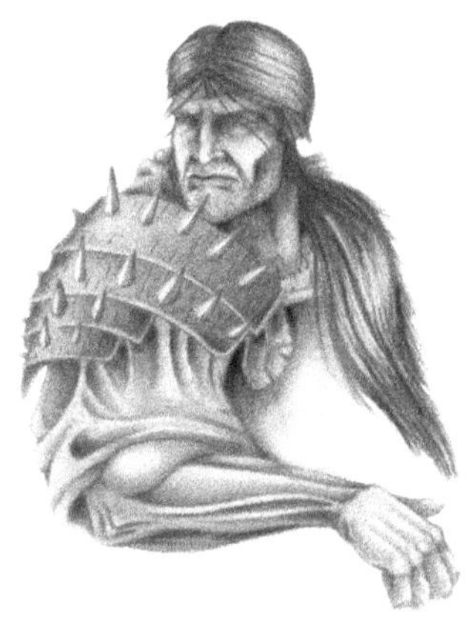

- Niklas "The Dead" Khed -

Niklas Khed is one of the characters I enjoy writing about very much. His name was one of the first ones that wasn't American, Romanian, or a strange imagined name. I heard "Niklas" a lot in Austria, and initially he was simply Niklas "the Dead." But starting in 2012, I wanted all my characters to have first and last names, and I knew I had to find a last name for him. I came up with one that rhymed with "dead" in order for his names to sound good together. So that was how Khed was created.

This character needed to represent unpredictability. Massive, loud, rude. I wanted him to be imposing. I took more interest in his appearance after 2022, settling on a strange armor set, a chaotic mixture, showcasing his careless character.

Something I love about him is that he is the first (of what I hope many) characters I have tattooed. My client saw his drawn design on the wall in the shop where I tattooed and liked him a lot. He told me he wanted to have him, and we brainstormed the design. Because the customer wanted to have a tree branch and a dark-themed tattoo, we selected Niklas to be hanged in order to incorporate the rest of the design. Niklas's position in the tattoo has nothing to do with his evolution within the story.

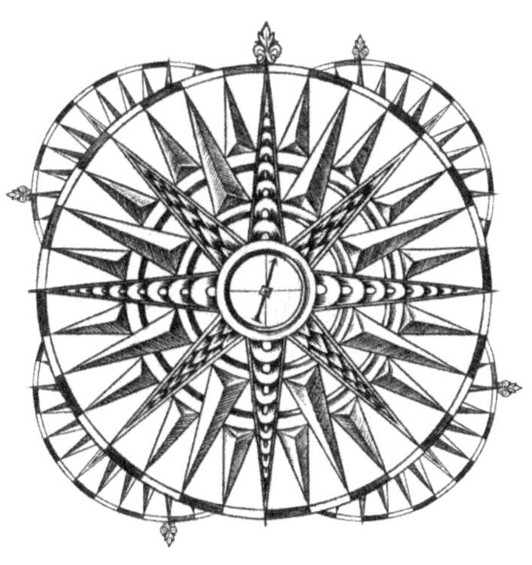

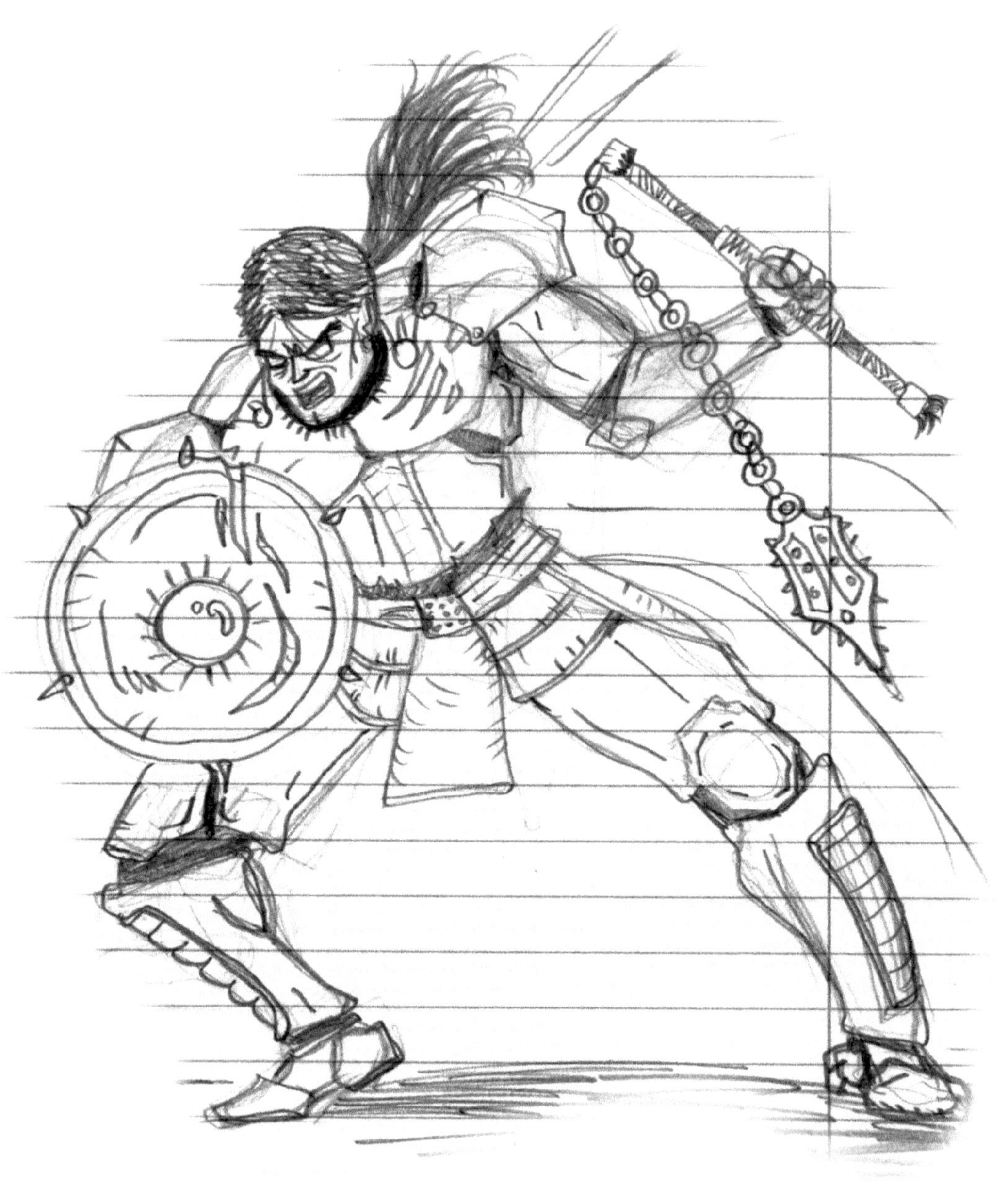

Design: 2018

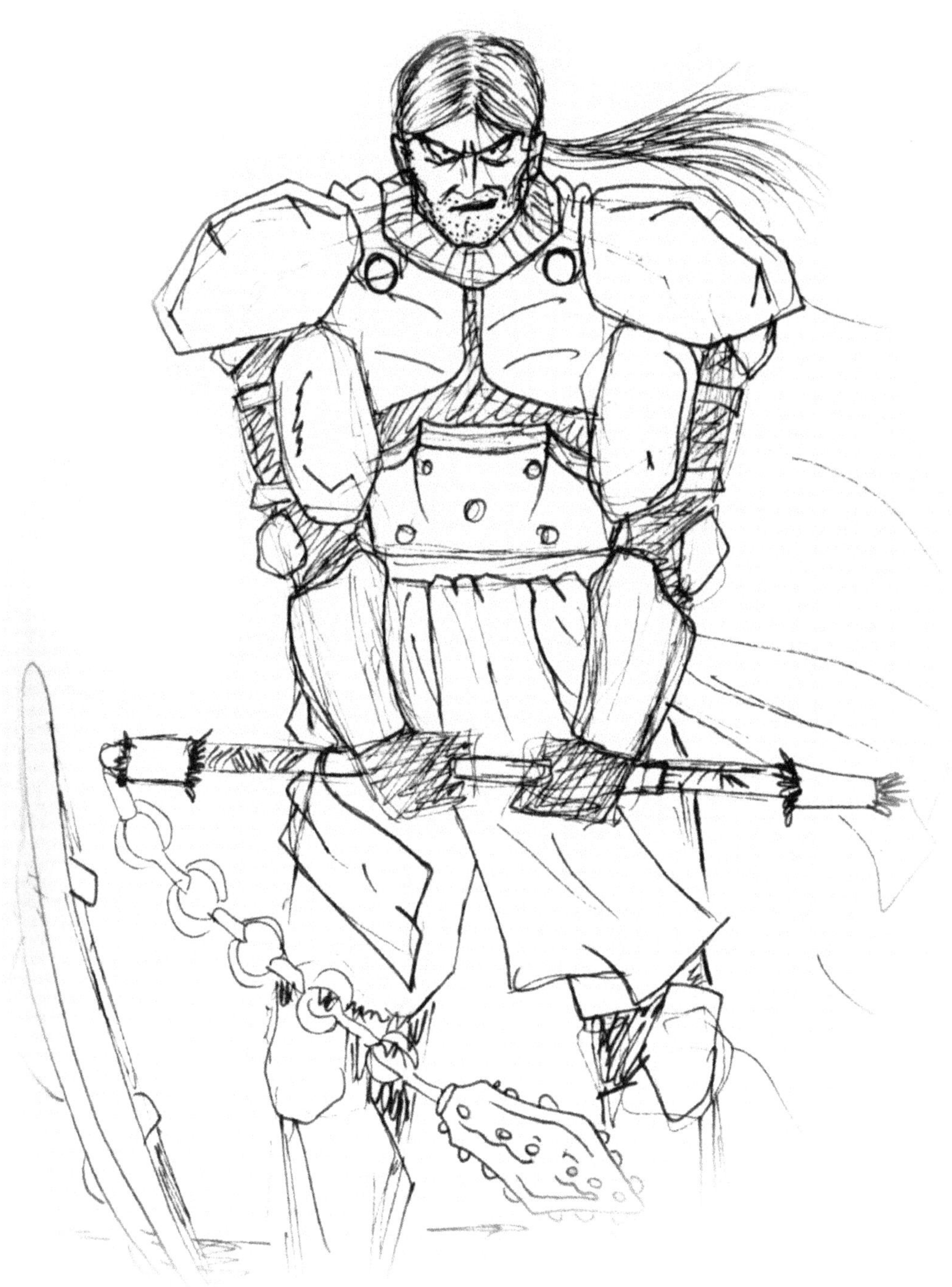

Design: 2019

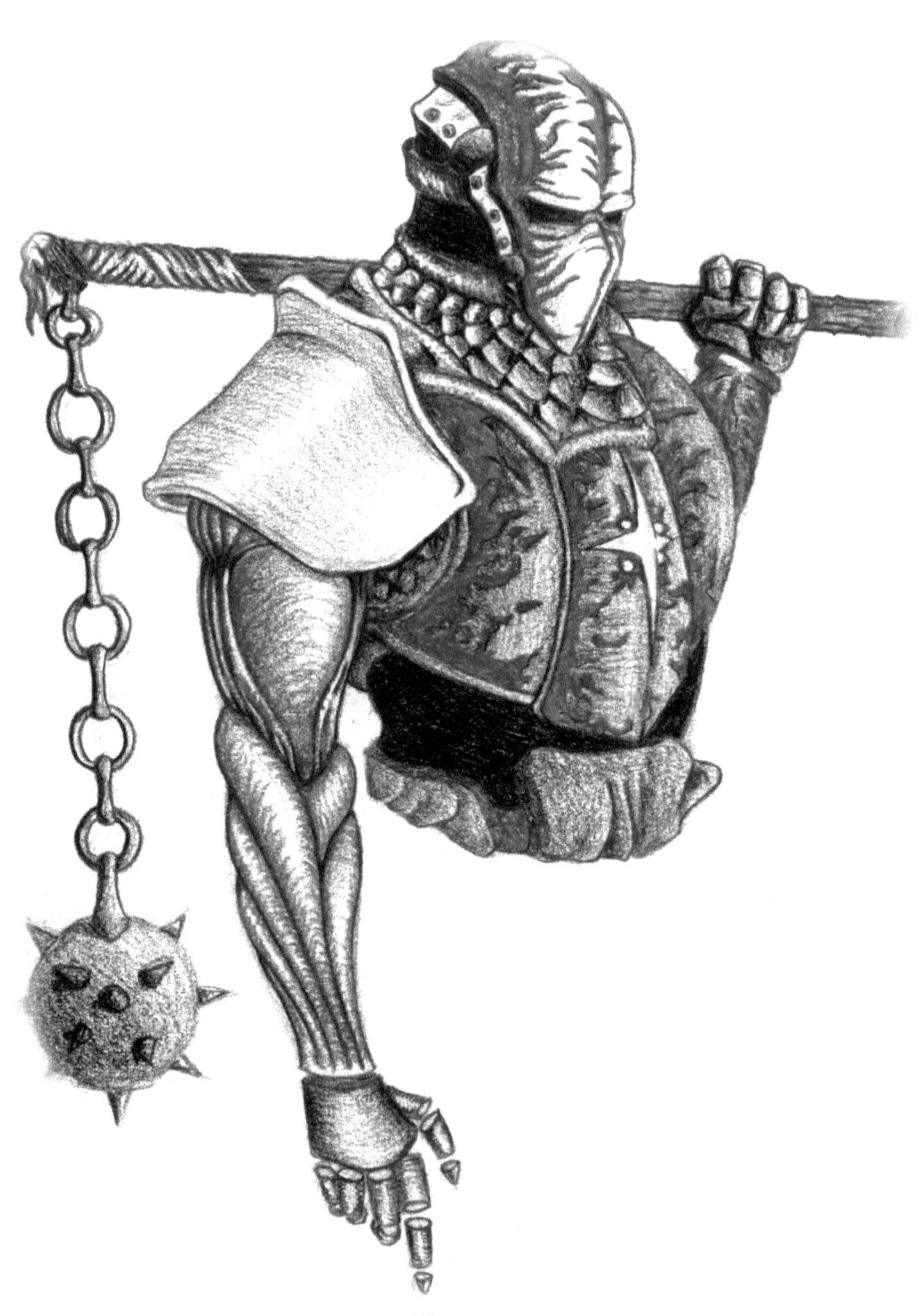

Design: 2021

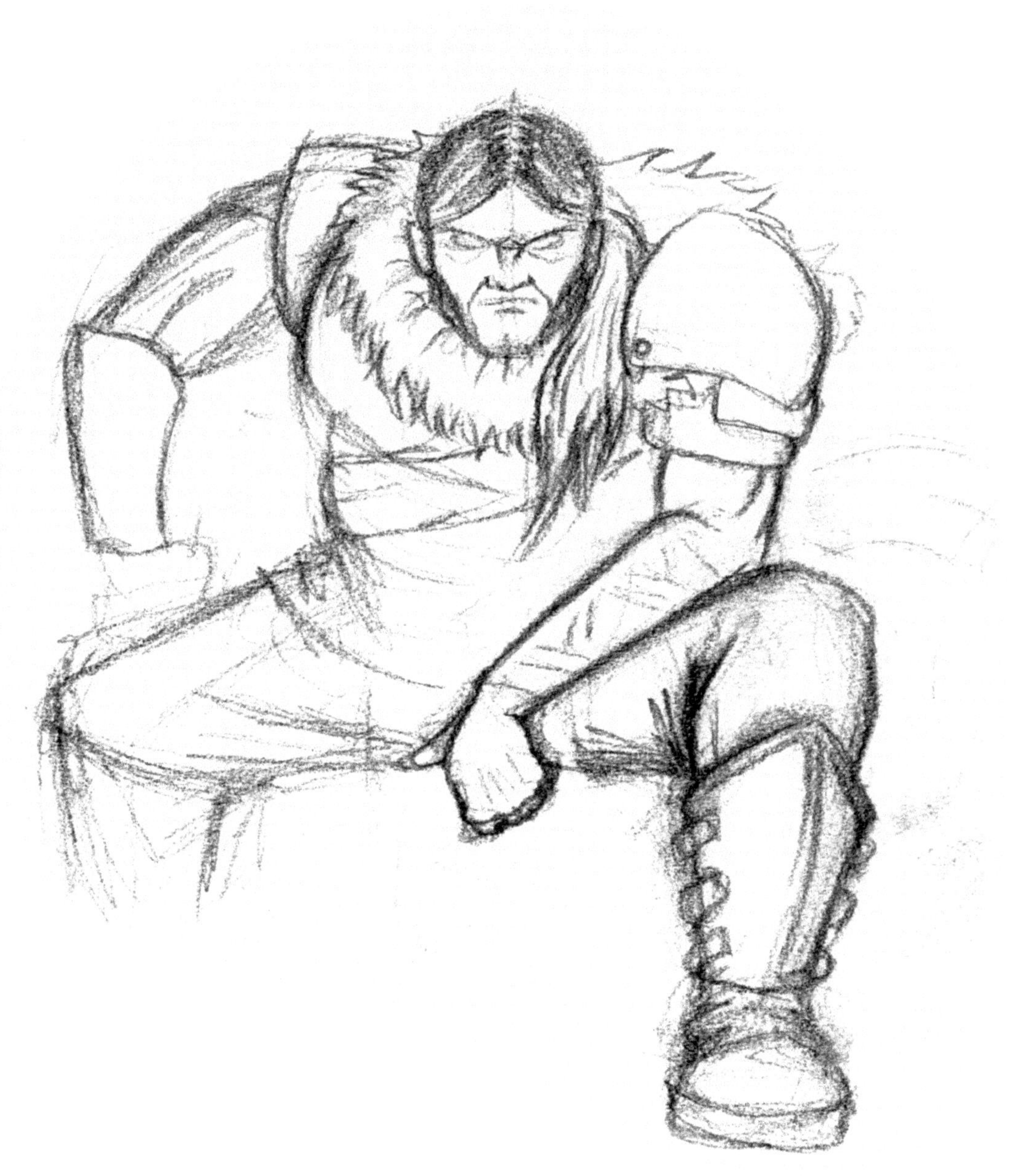

Design: 2022

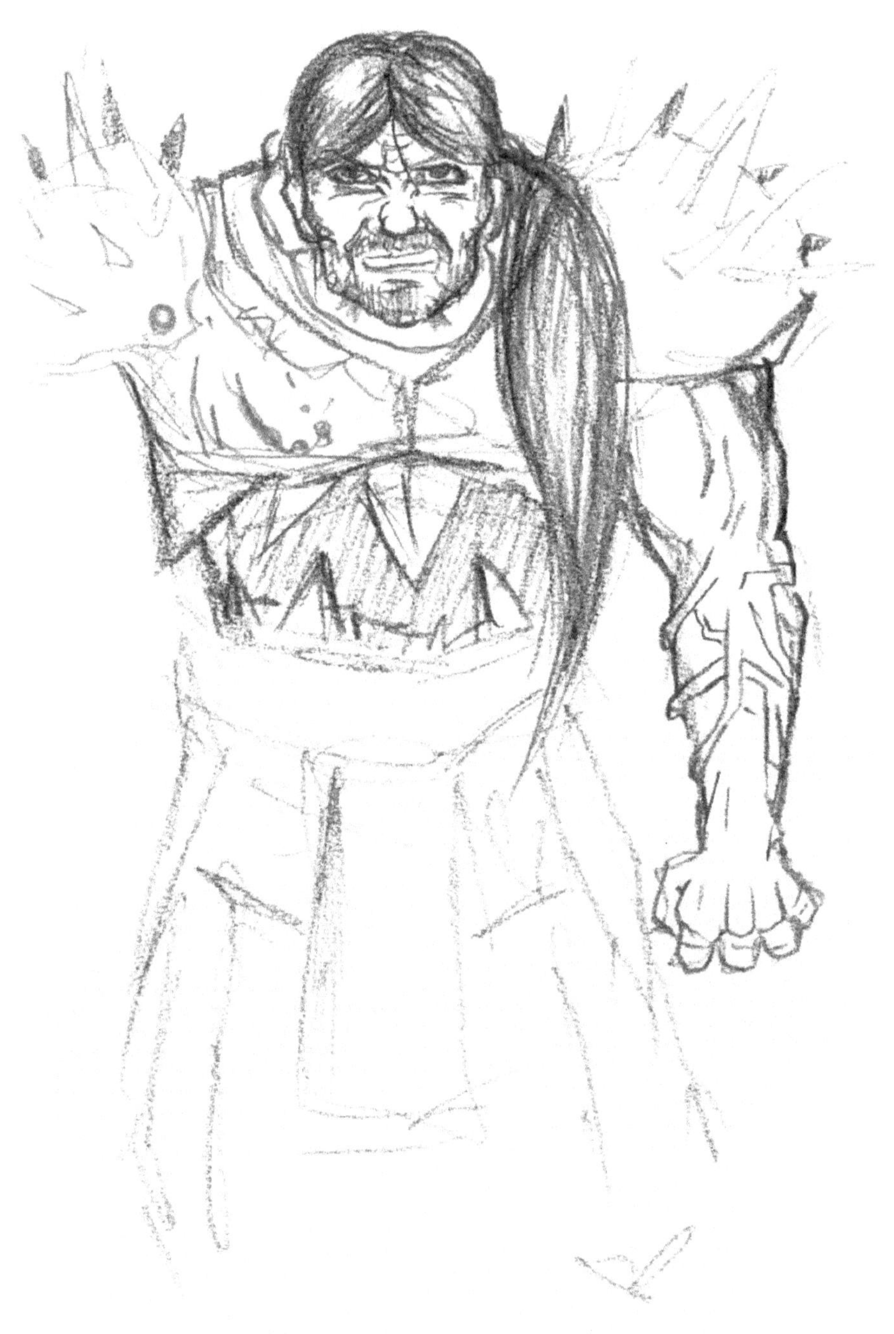

Design: 2022

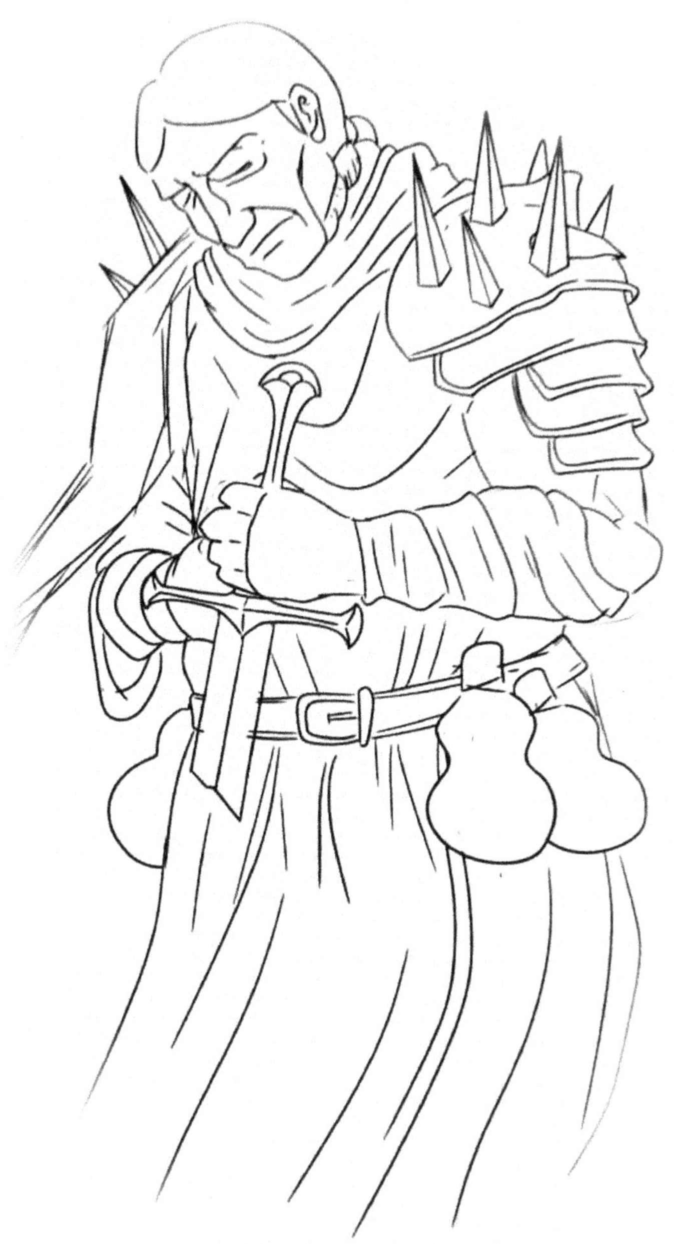

The sketch of Niklas, drawn at the request of my client

Design: 2024

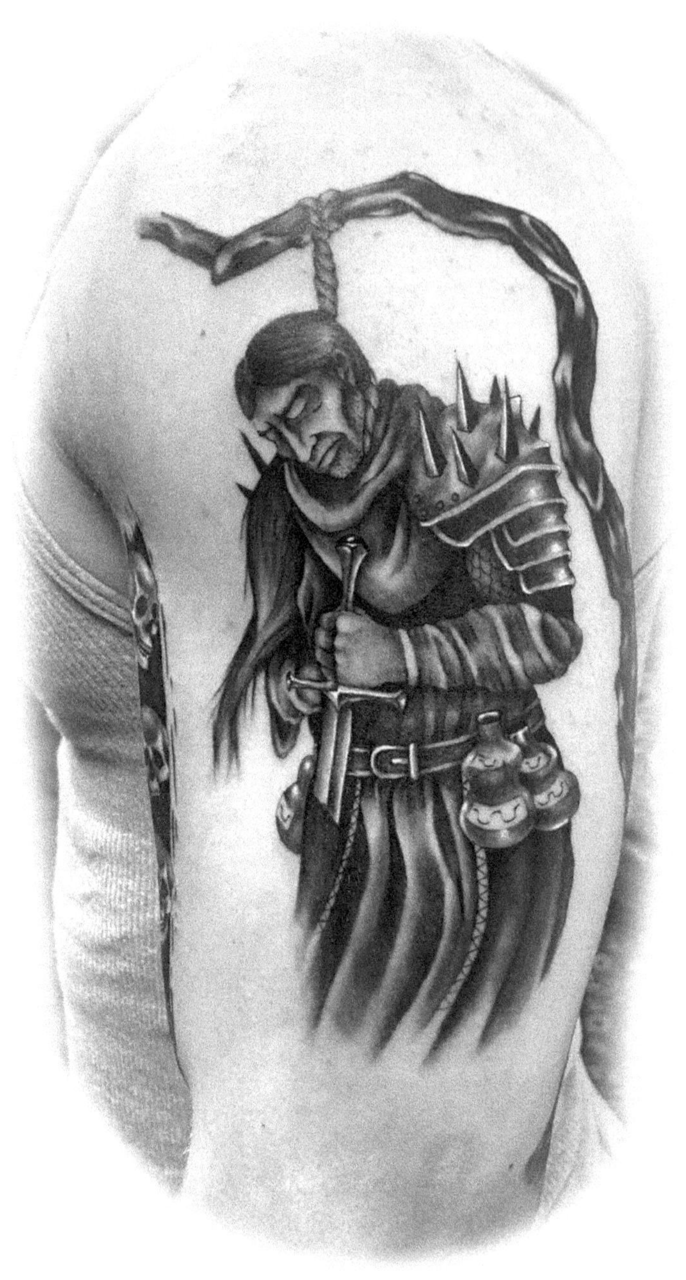

Finished tattoo of Niklas Khed
Does not represent events in the storyline

Tattoo: 2024

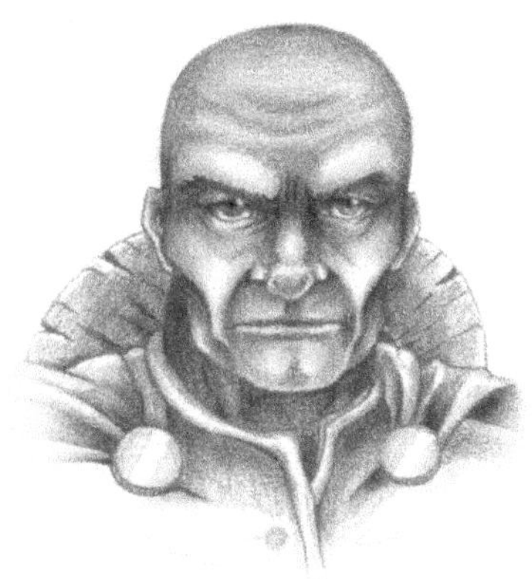

- ROSTEN LATVON -

Moving further from the Victorian era of the story, I created Rosten Latvon as a military man. Silent, strong, and rugged.

His weapon of choice was the whip because I wanted to express his command over the oraks and animals he controlled. His concept began as Marco's reliable and loyal sidekick when the story followed a more generic anime storyline in which a gang of misfits came together for a greater purpose.

In early 2014, I decided to erase Rosten from the story, and later on in 2017, I brought him back as the commander of the Royal Blade. I believed his demeanor and personality would fit well in the position of a leader.

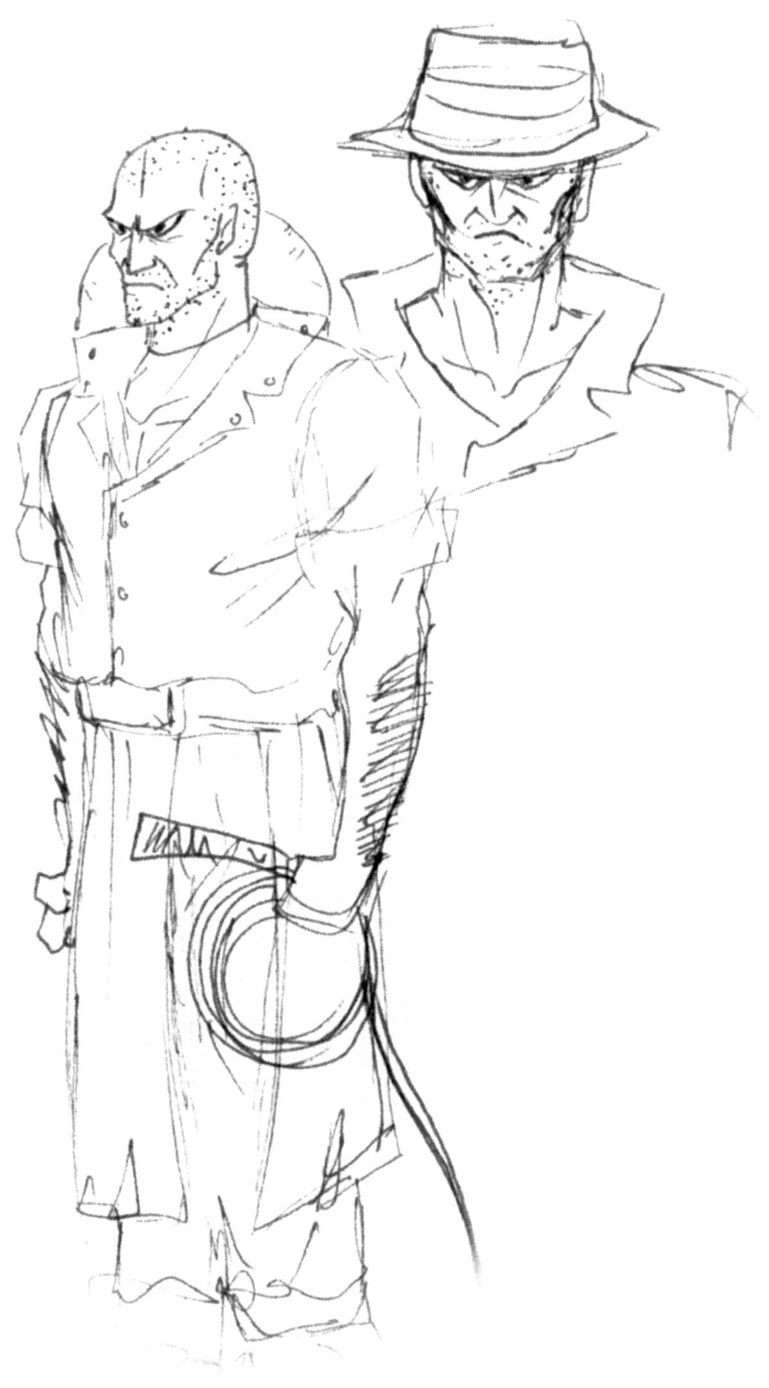

Design: 2018

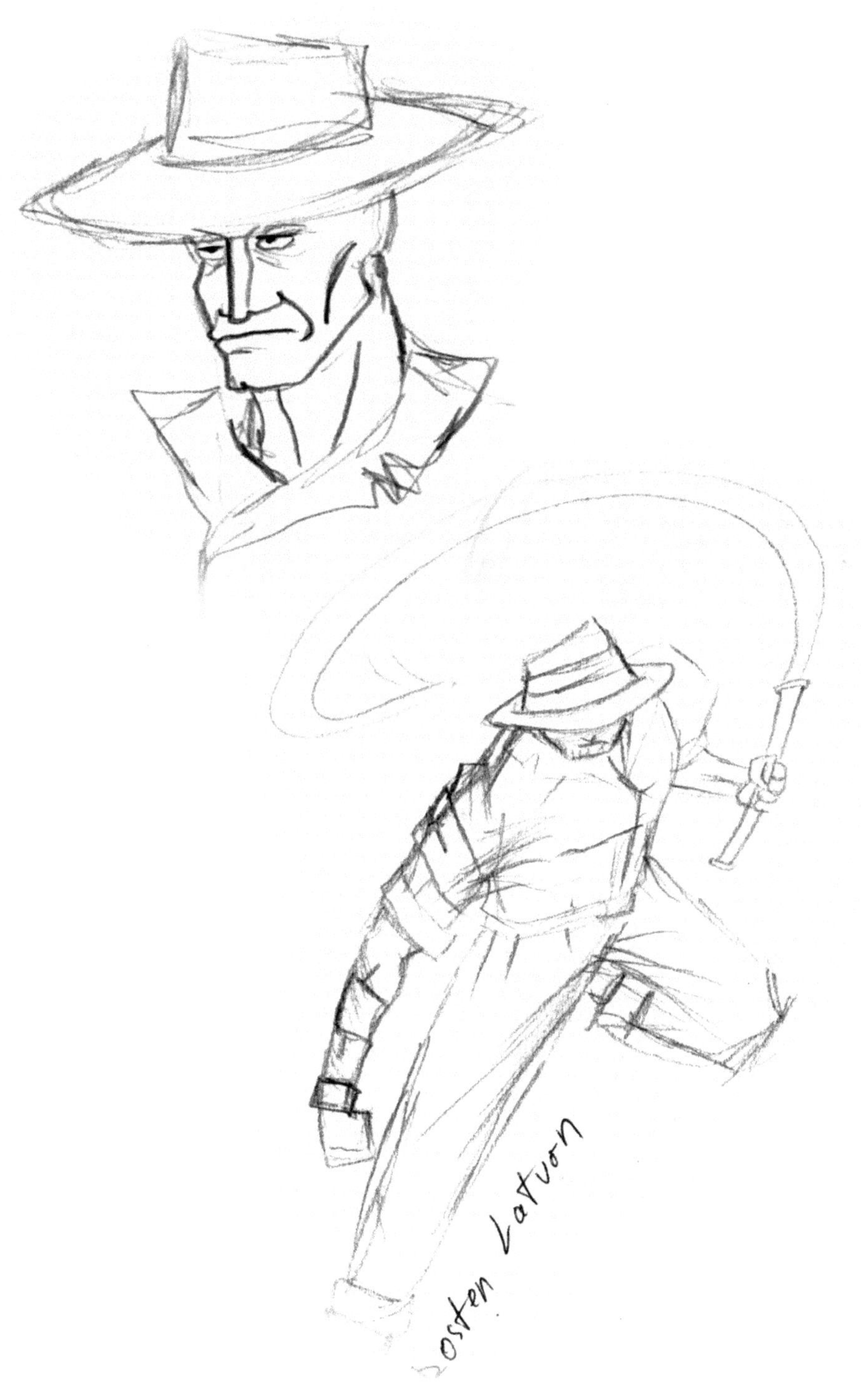

Design: 2018

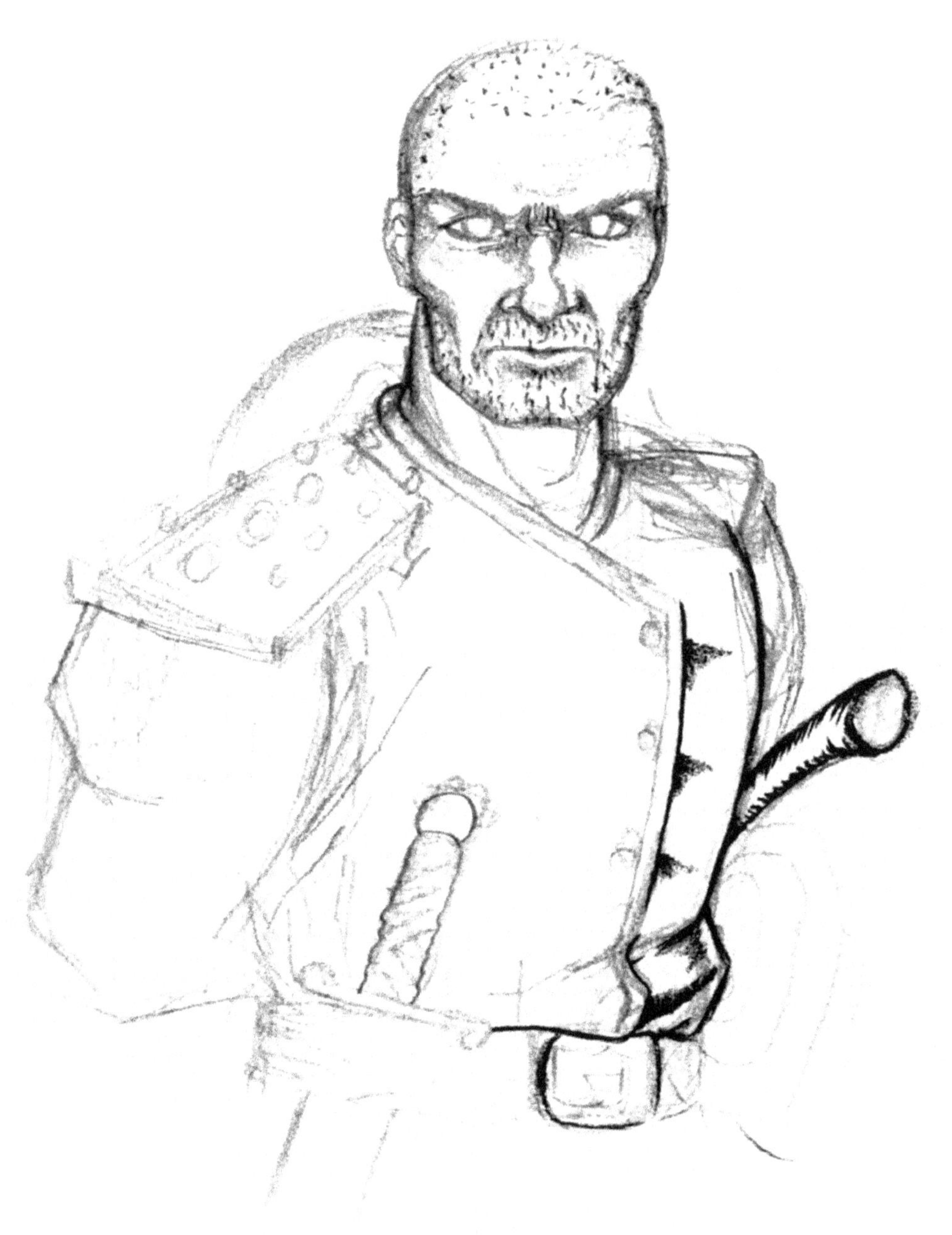

Design: 2024

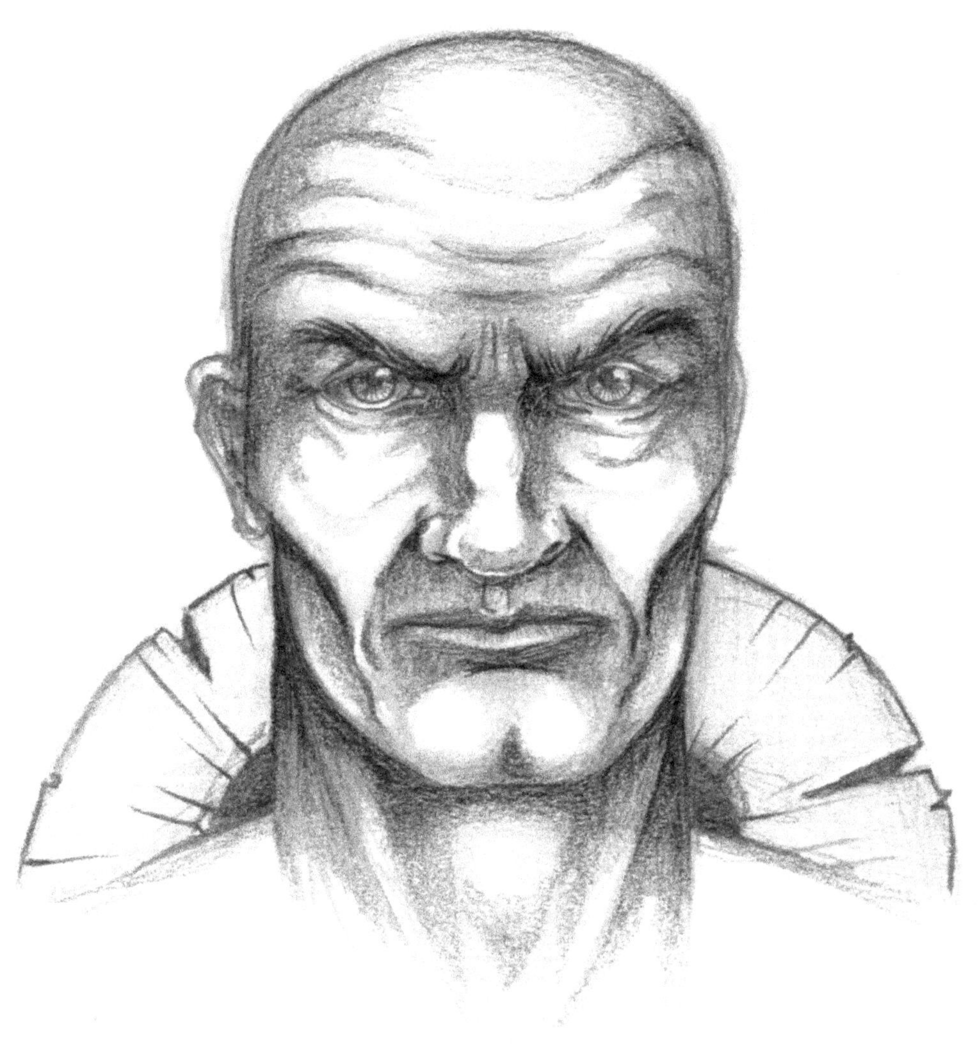

Design: 2024

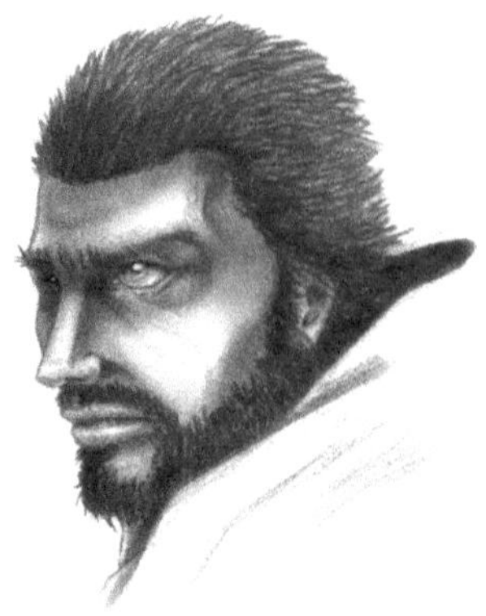

- Baron of Trade - Amah Tetran -

Another instance where one character was split into more is with the counselor.

In 2014, King Kristoff had one counselor, Amaho Tetran, who would oversee all within the lands of Canoria. I presented him as a wise old man.

Later on, while developing him, I realized that just one man could not handle all the tasks of the Crown, so I started creating more of them. Thus the many tasks of the original "counselor" were split into Amaho and Stephano.

This character creation will forever be a strange one for me because for the only time in the story, I needed to switch characters. I noticed somehow Amaho's and Stephano's stories intertwined, and I needed to go back to the start and swap the two. But after a little bit of thinking, I decided to switch their names so that it would all better fit.

So in 2019, the character of Amaho Tetran received the name, title, and story of Stephano Siktah, and vice versa, in order to better fit with the path they were on.

In 2022, I changed their title to barons, as counselor seemed too modern.

In 2023, I removed the "o" from Amaho in order to avoid the similarity in their first names.

Sometimes when I write about them, I still confuse their names and need to double-check.

His last design, from 2024, brought a younger version out to fit his character better.

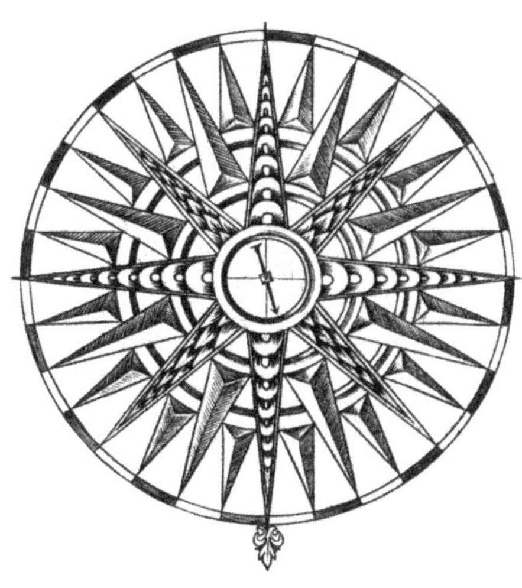

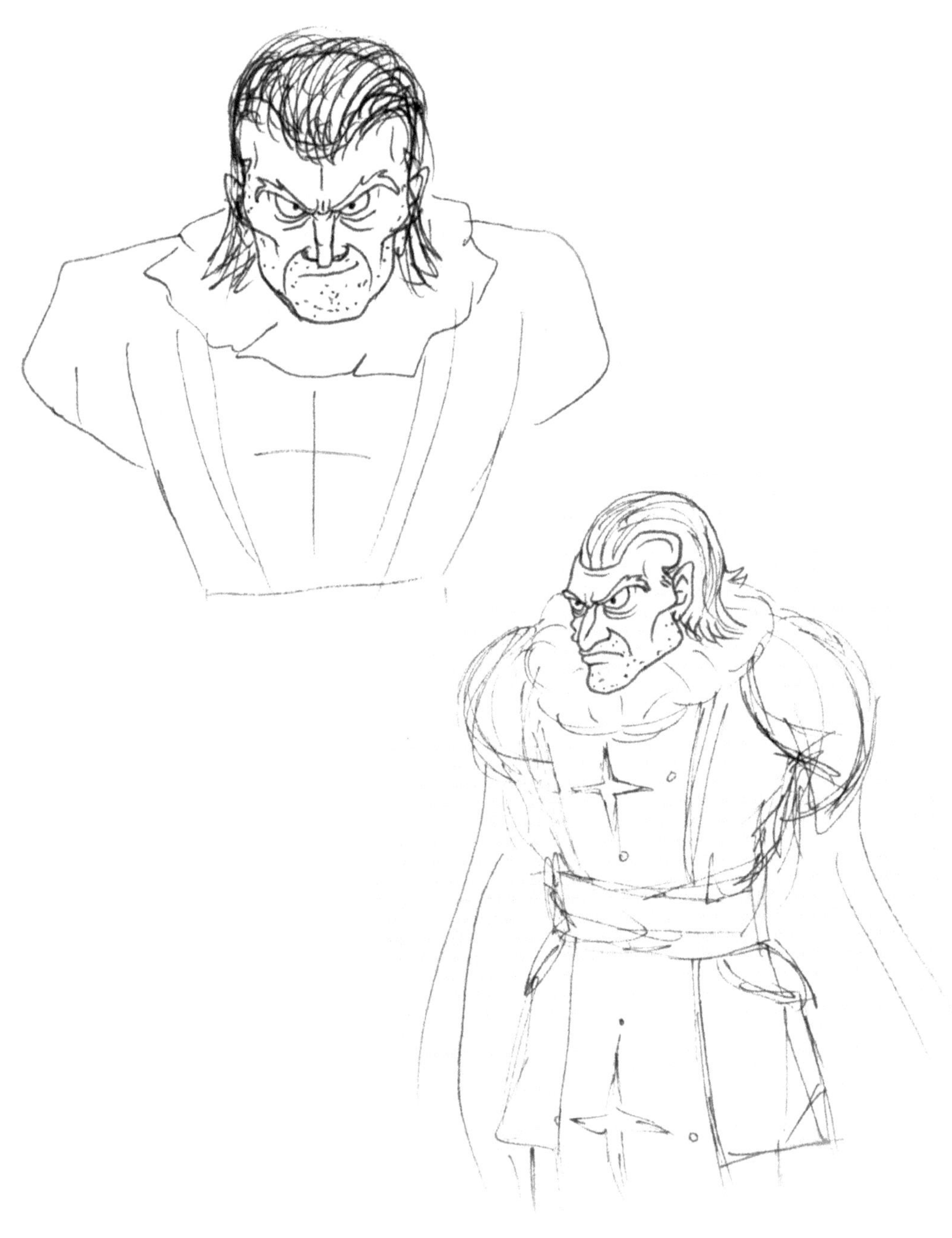

Design: 2018

The original Baron

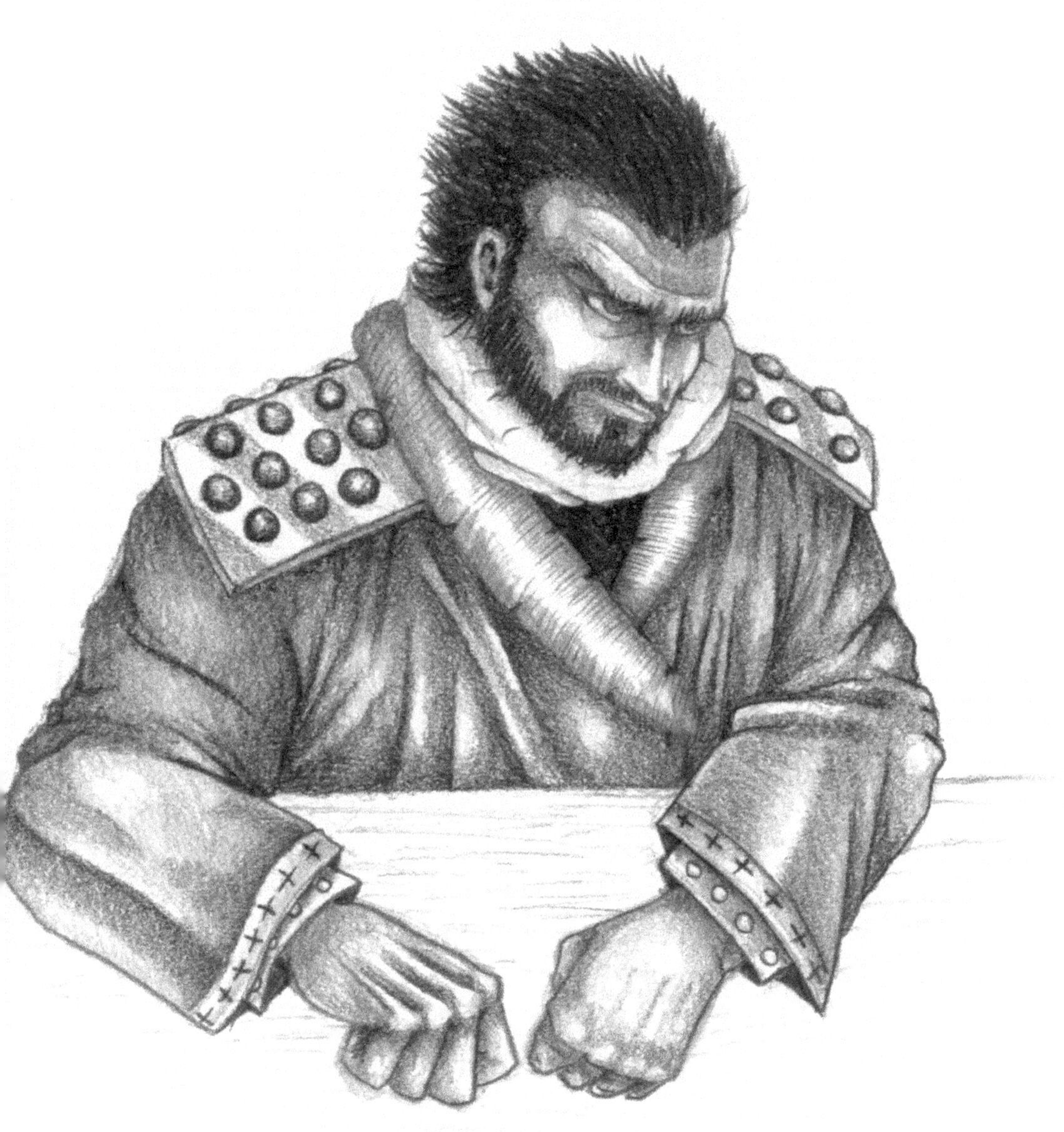

Design: 2024

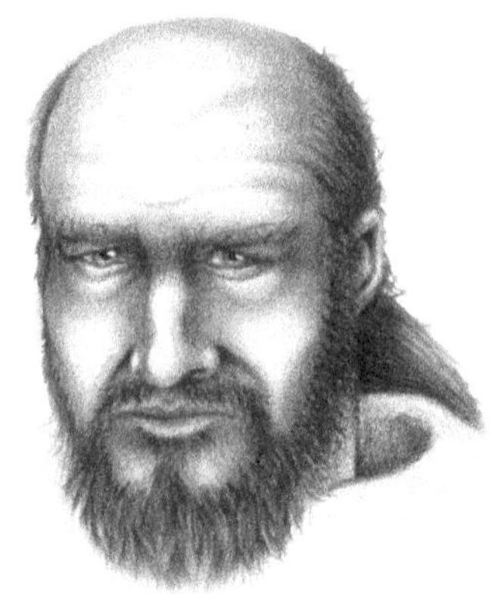

- Baron of Mortar - Stephano Siktah -

Created out of necessity and the need for more barons, Stephano's early designs were of a cocky, arrogant, outspoken man, which did not fit with his personality. Amah's designs, of a more obedient man, fit him better, and then came the confusion, where the way they looked did not fit their personalities. Thus the change was necessary.

Stephano received a younger look in 2023, and I felt this was one of the best characters I managed to draw in comparison to what I imagined him to look like.

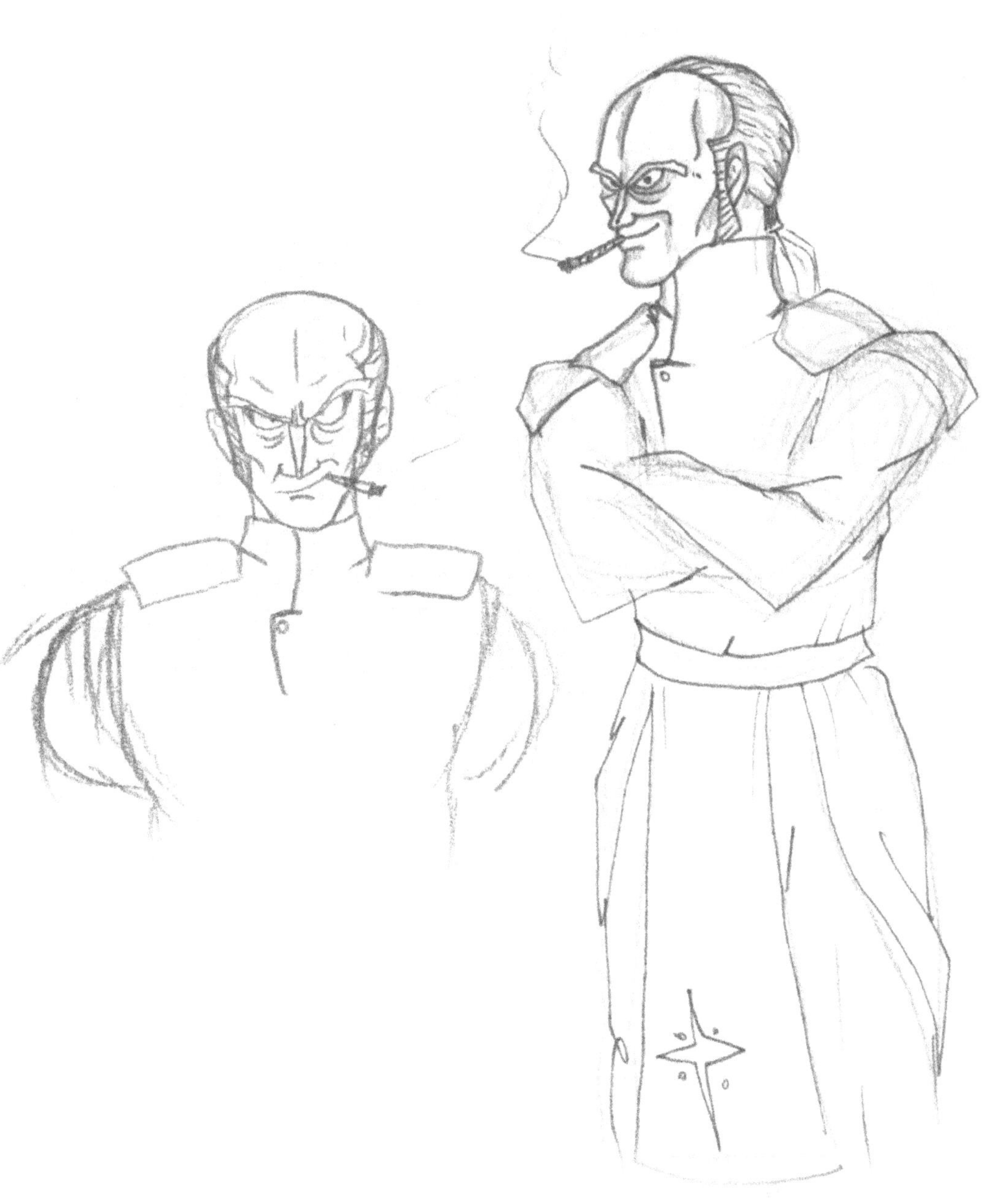

Design: 2018

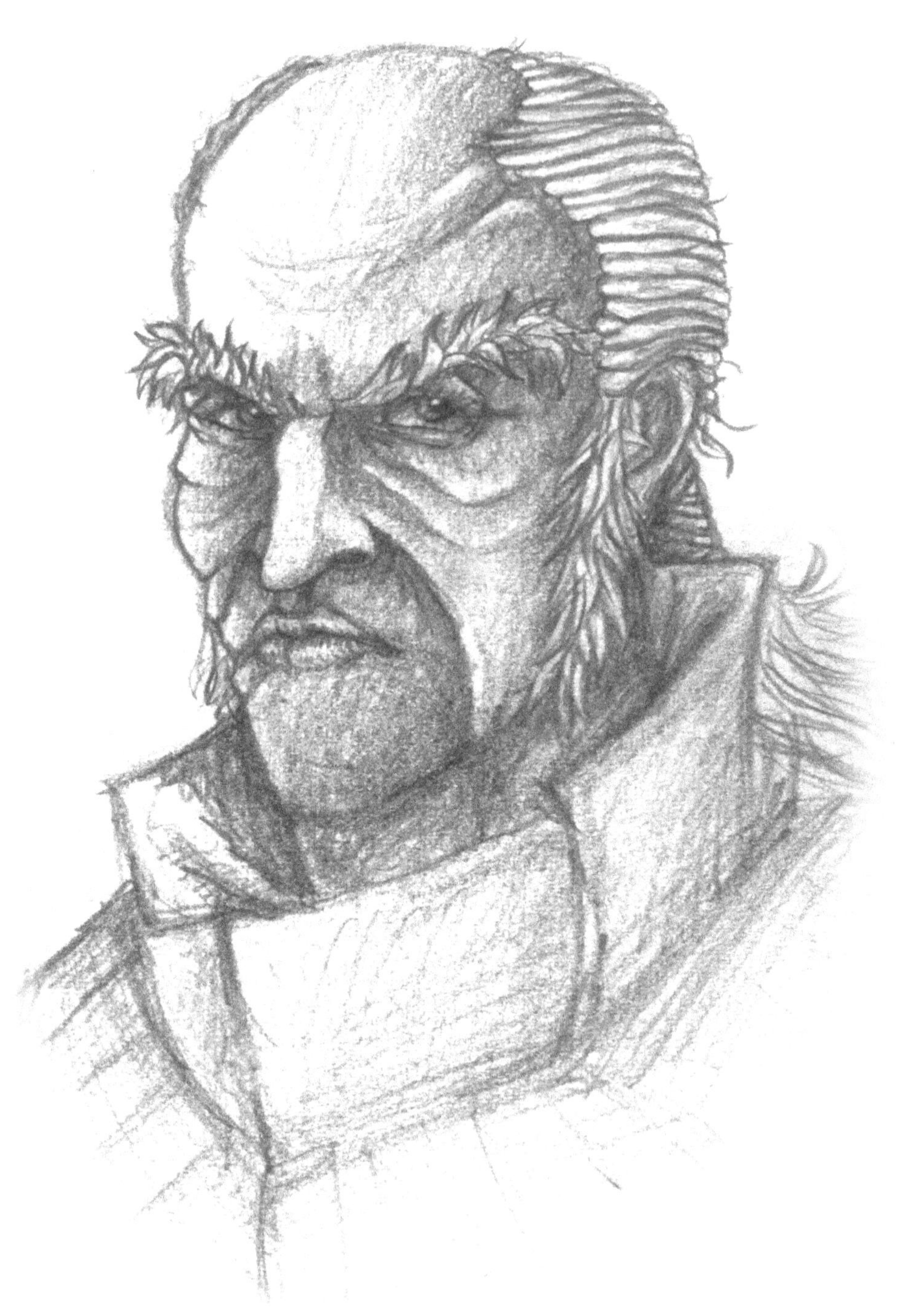

Design: 2021

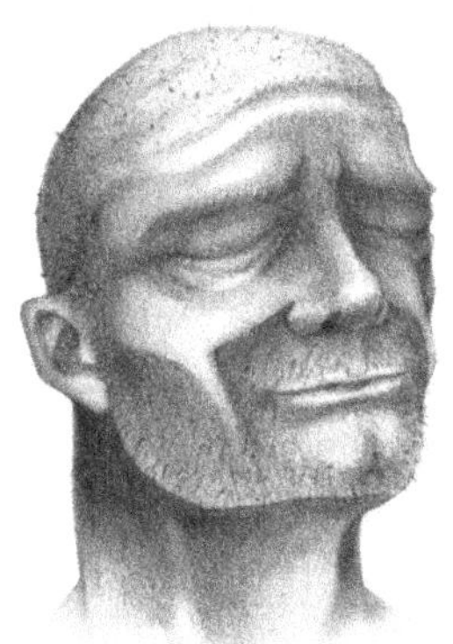

- Baron of Wisdom - Ediron Rutal -

The concept of the only counselor and his king still lingered with me, and I knew I had to create such a companion for Kilean.

In 2017, after falling asleep on a bus coming home from a music festival in Romania, I dreamed of an empty library. No one cared for it and it began to deteriorate. I then knew I needed a librarian to gather, protect, and share information.

His concept first came to life through a song I wrote for the band I founded in Romania, called "Cenușa Soarelui."

I drew him in 2019, and he was the librarian. His name quickly changed to the Bookkeeper and remained as such until the spring of 2024 when I felt that the English term for the Bookkeeper would not fit. Translated to Romanian, the Bookkeeper would mean "the keeper of books," but in English, the title has a strong association with accounting. In order to avoid confusion, he became the Storyteller in the middle of the copyediting process.

Ediron is the only character who was first created through the form of a song.

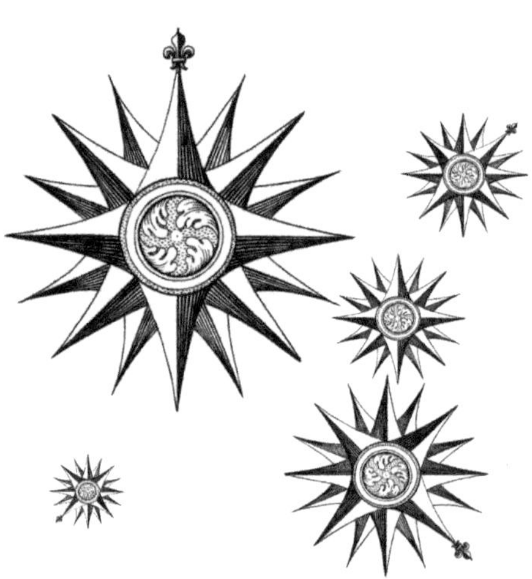

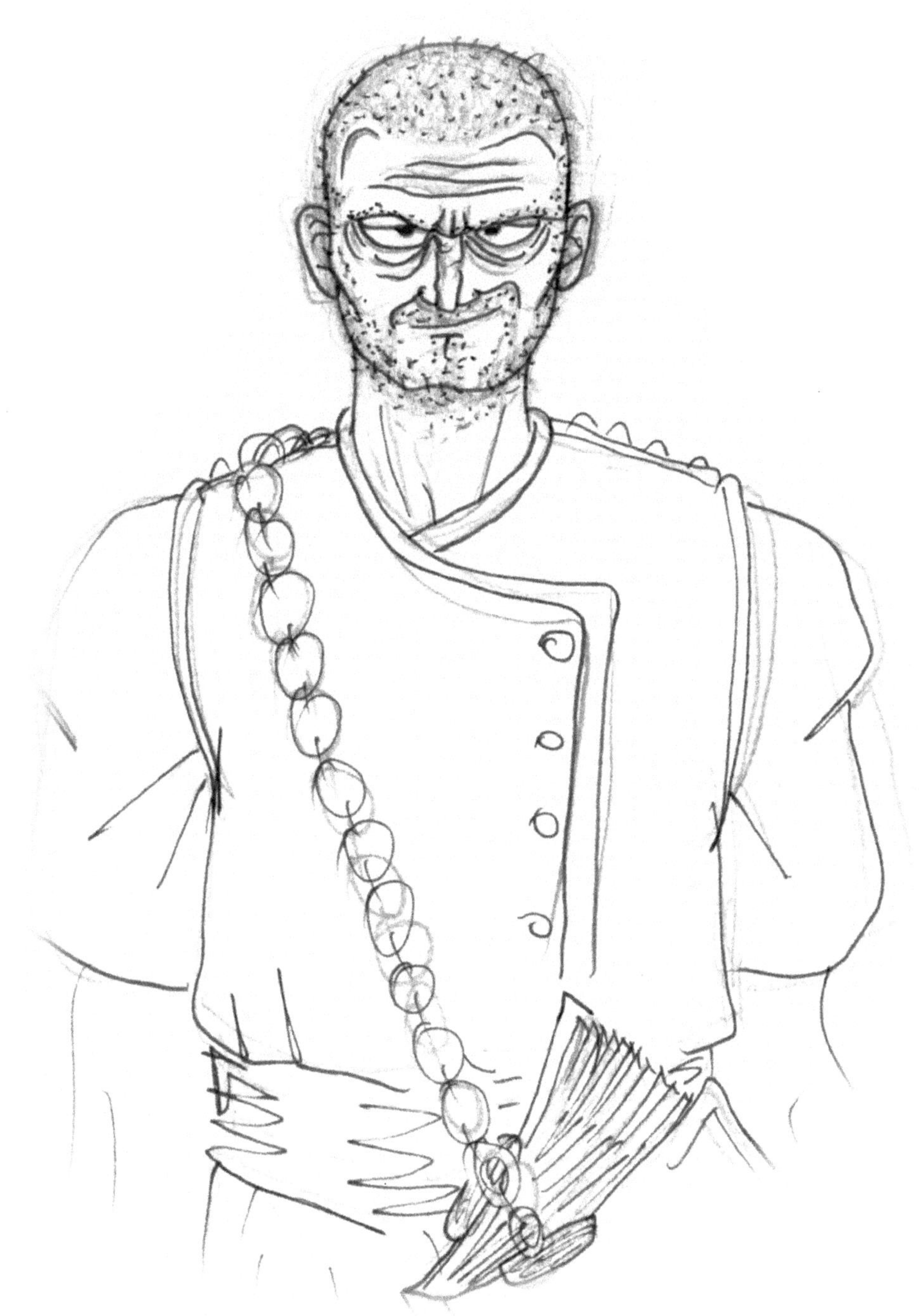

Design: 2018

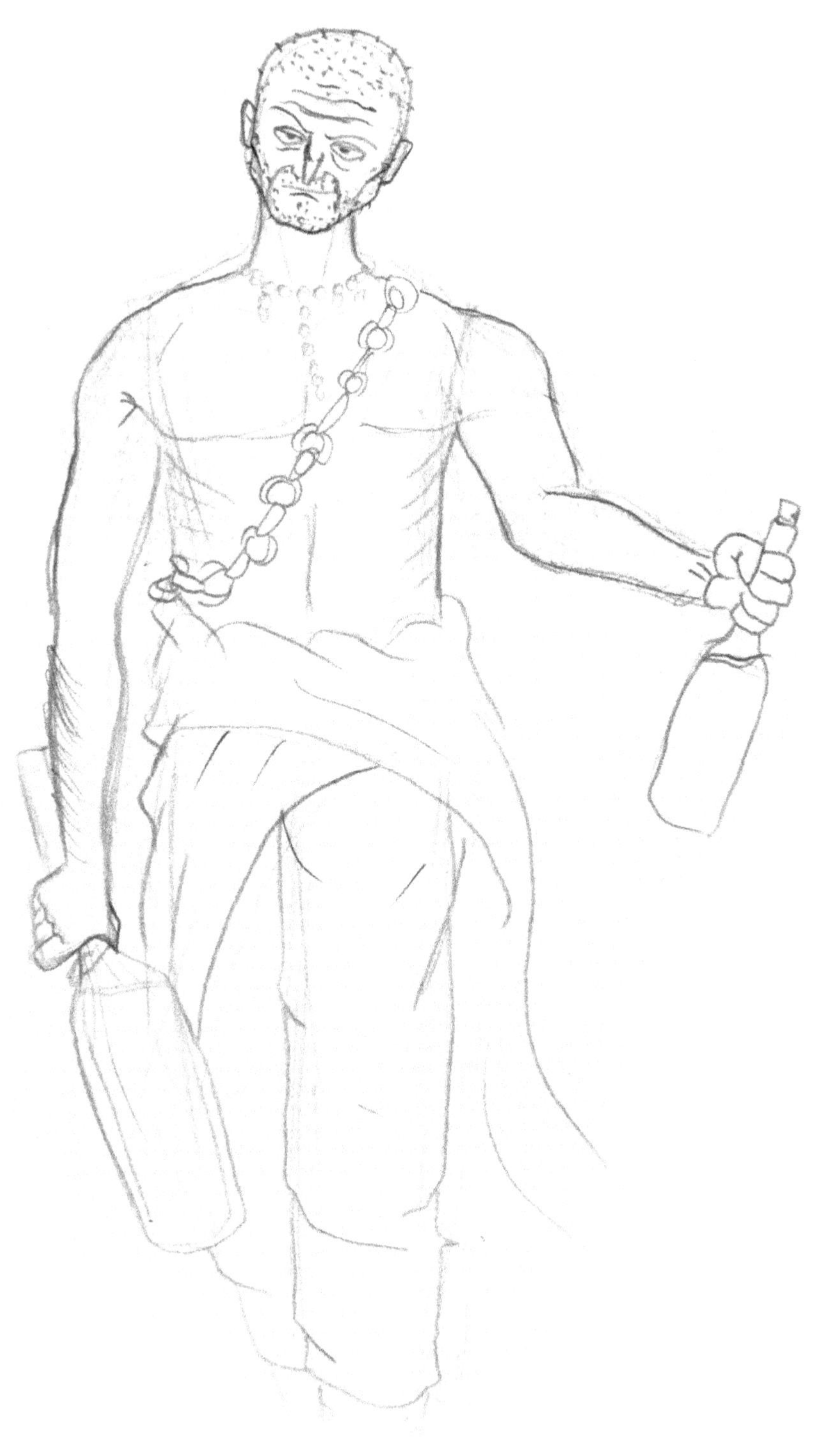

Design: 2021

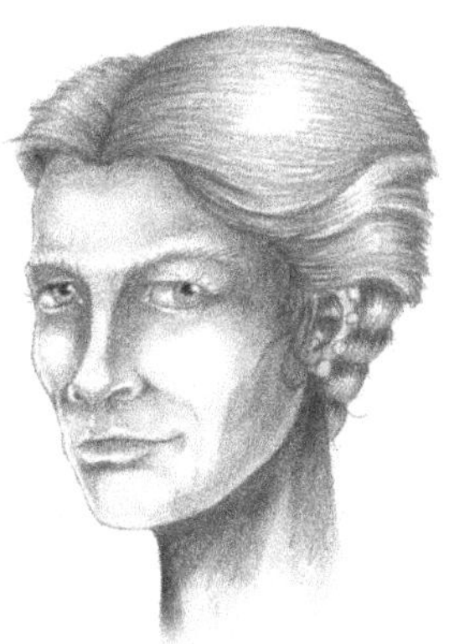

- Princess Tamara Steol -

I knew the world of Dautrinias was not a mirror to the kingdom of Canoria. I needed to present princesses of beauty and fairness, like in the fairy tales my mother would tell me of, along with lands delving in peace and prosperity.

Her design had many issues in 2019 because of my inability to create softer, nonaggressive faces.

Her final design was created in 2024, after I decided to include the portraits inside *Favors Within Ashes*.

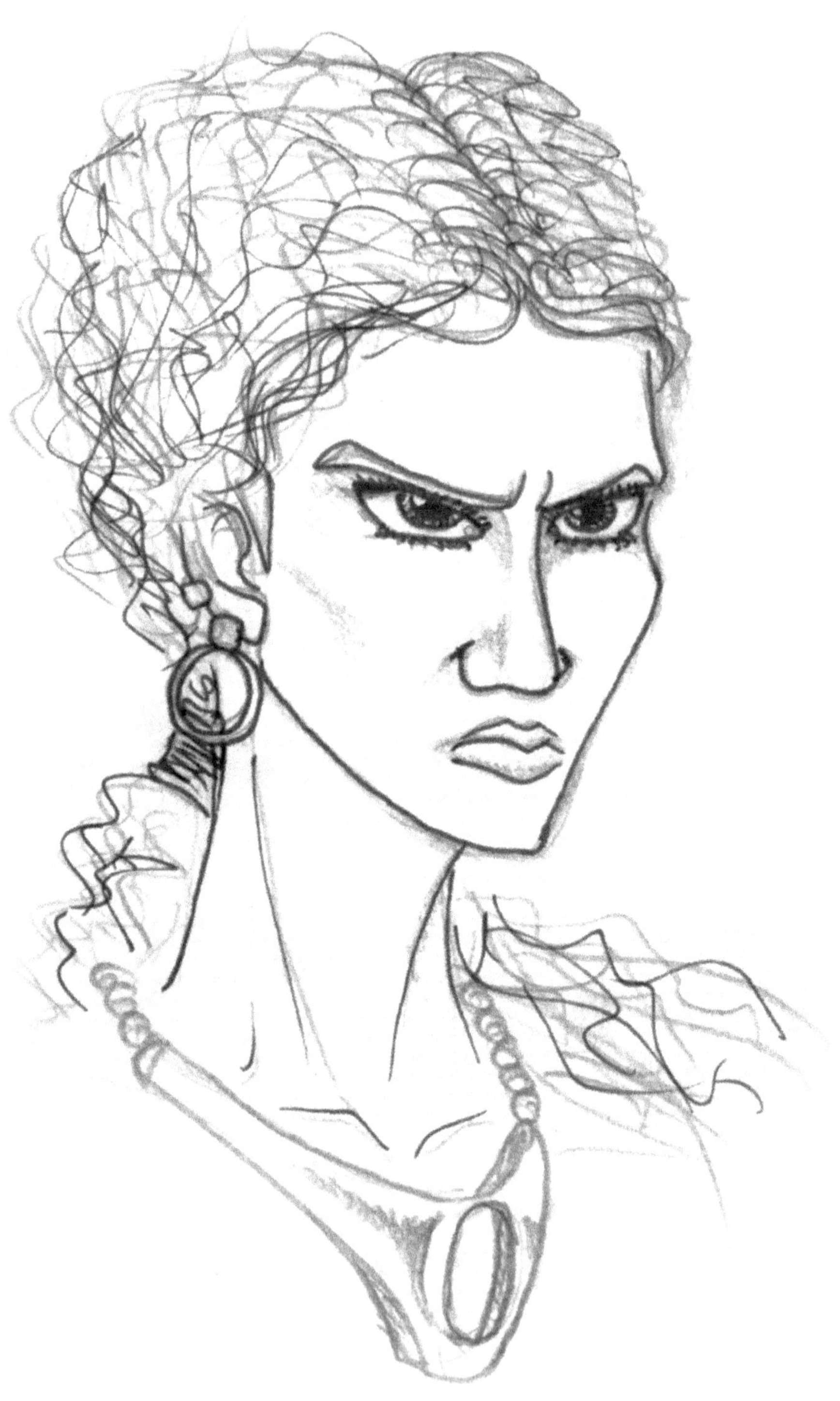

Design: 2018

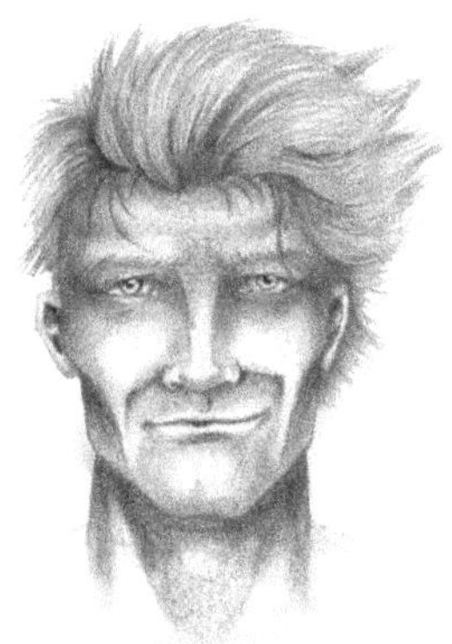

- Prince Alexander Steol -

After first establishing the main storyline of the series, I knew this story would belong to the grimdark or dark fantasy genre. But I knew I didn't want the entire world to be so harsh. Not everyone had the conditions found within Canoria, so I began sketching and creating the first versions of my very own prince charming through Alexander. A gallant man, brave, honest, and fair. As opposed to any of those found in Canoria, he needed to have a calm and attractive face untouched by signs of battle, thirst, or hunger. When working on his redesign in 2019, I struggled to create characters who did not look evil or angry, so I decided to leave his design for a later time, revisiting him in 2024.

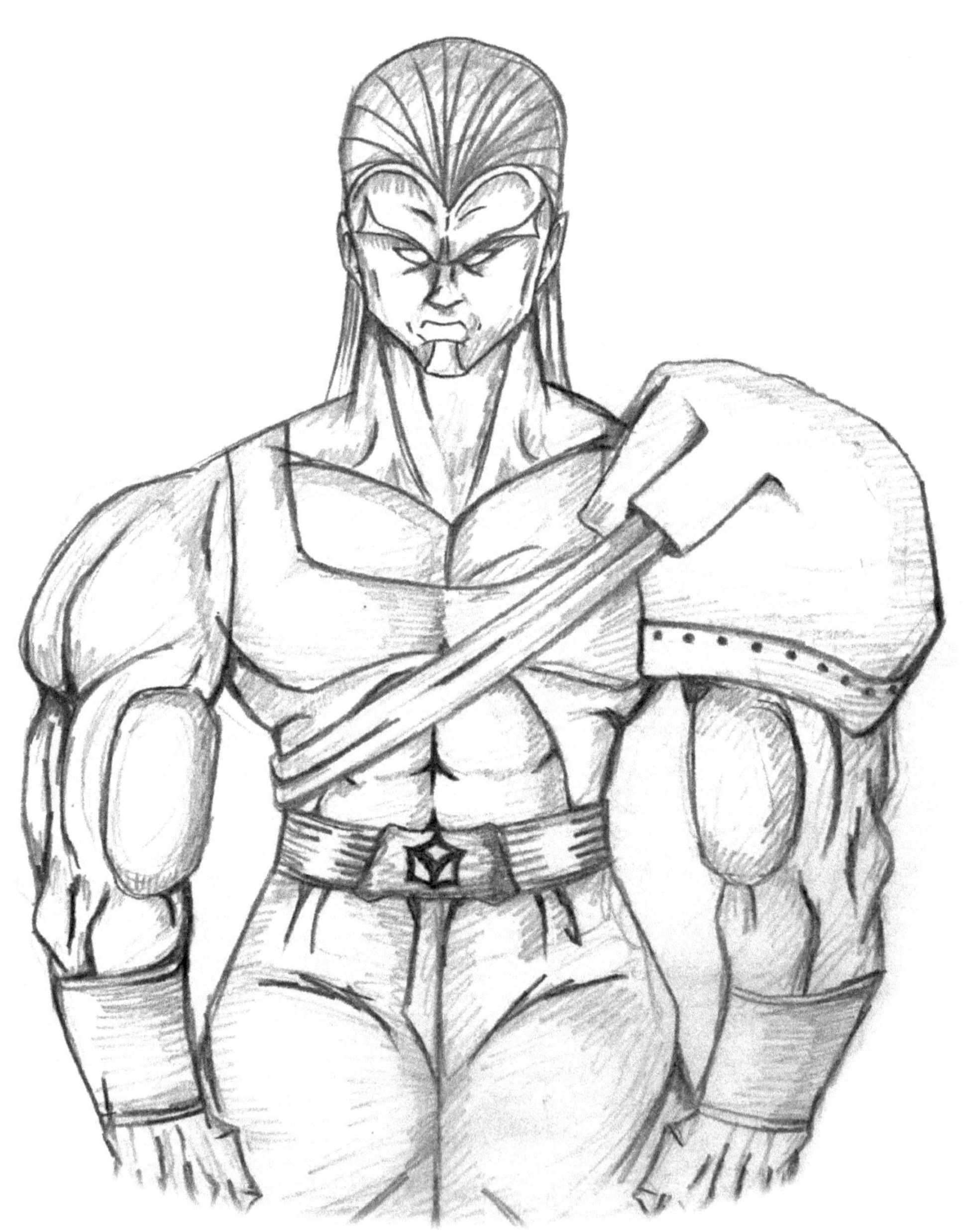

Design: 2003

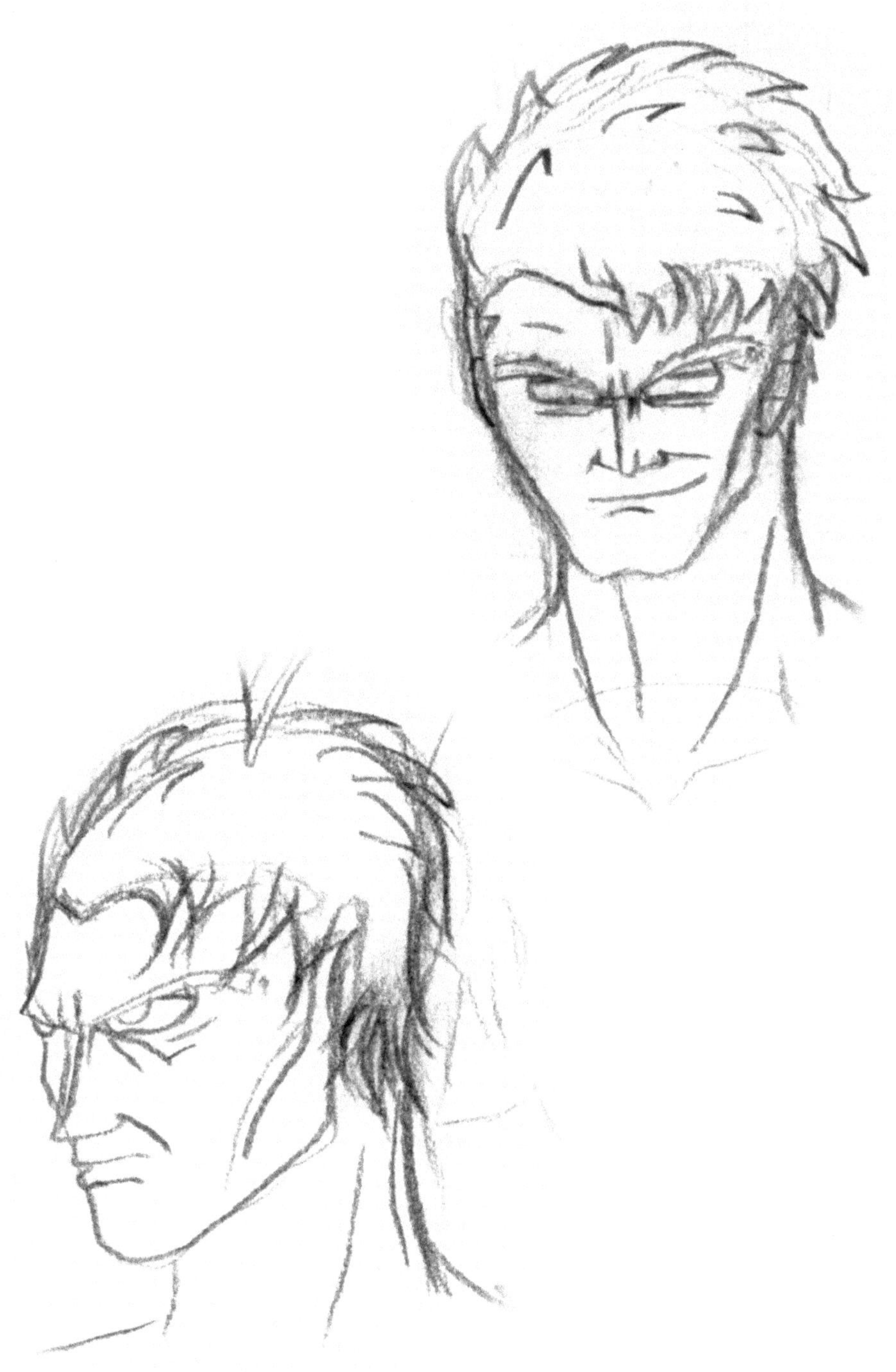

Design: 2018

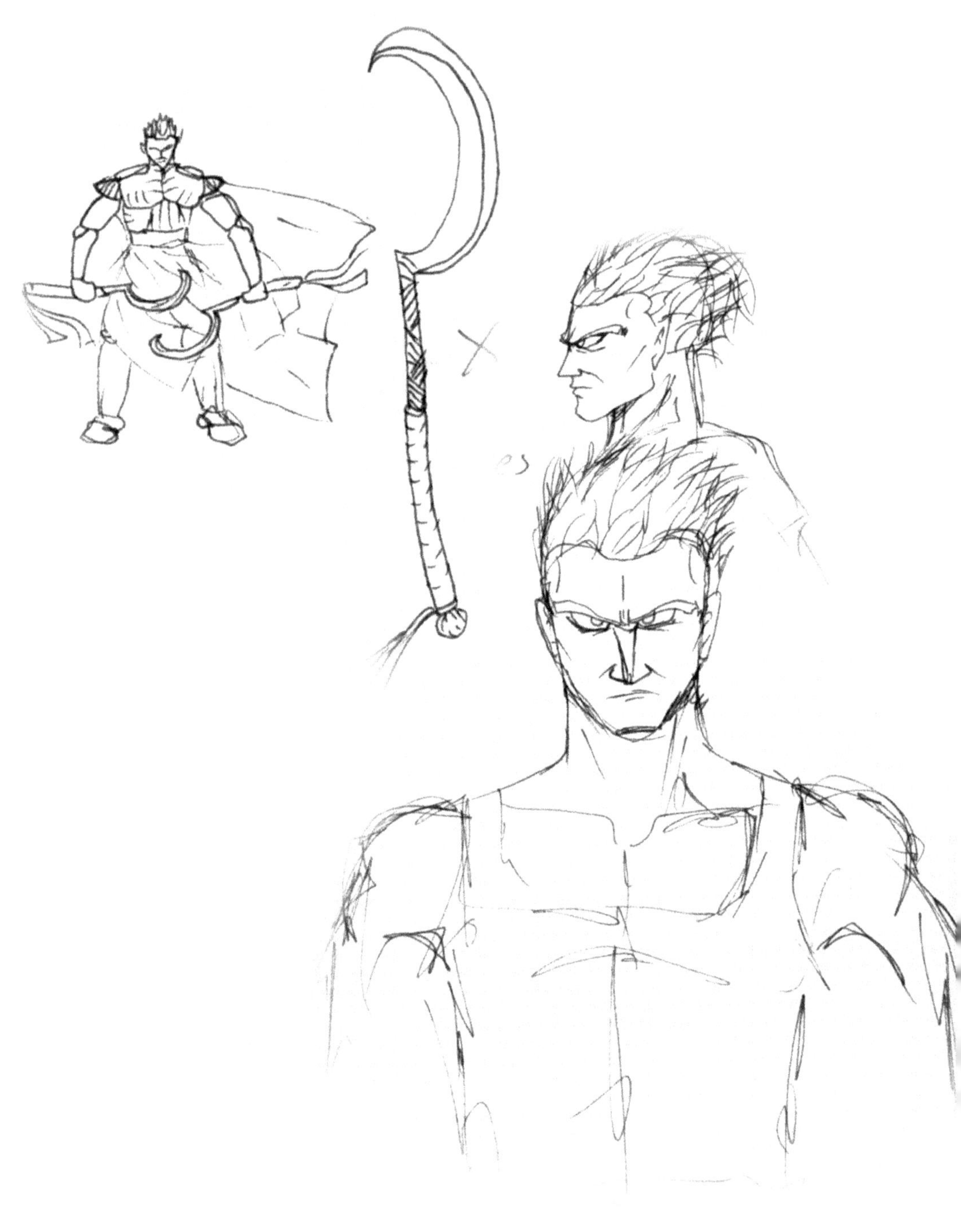

Design: 2018

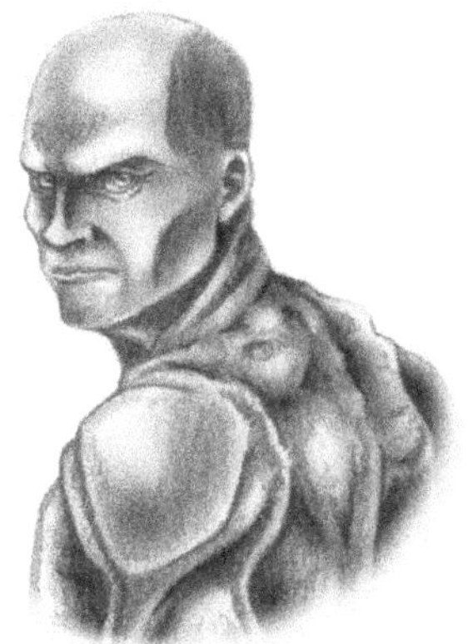

- Prince Seran Steol -

I initially drew Seran as an older man. When imagining him, I kept forgetting he was younger than Alexander. He had more facial hair, and I even thought of adding a braided beard like his father's, but he was too young to have such a dense beard, and that would have been against his beliefs, considering the path he takes on in the story.

I decided to draw more of his body, and not focus just on his face, in order to showcase his stature and efficient physique.

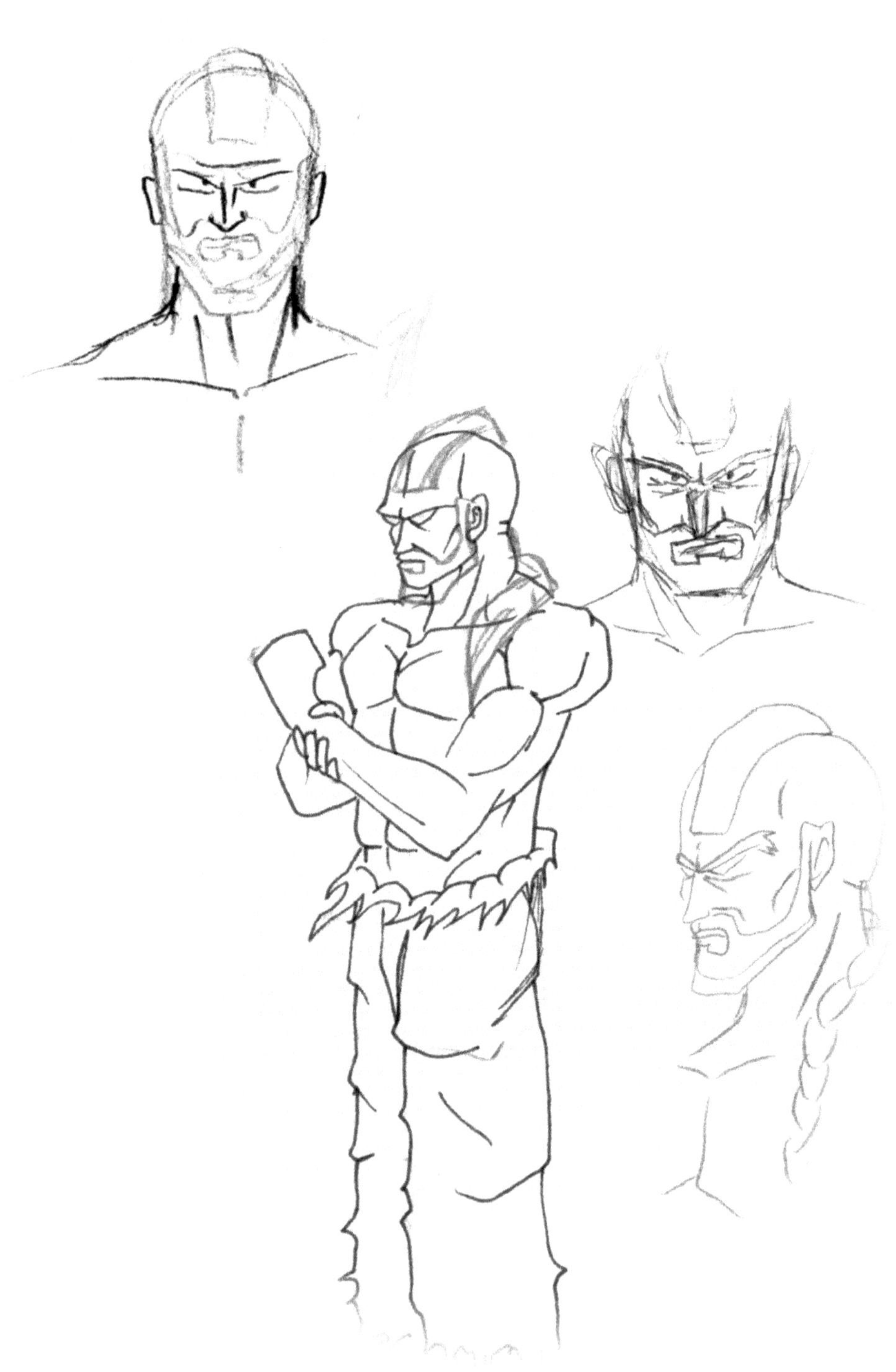

Design: 2019

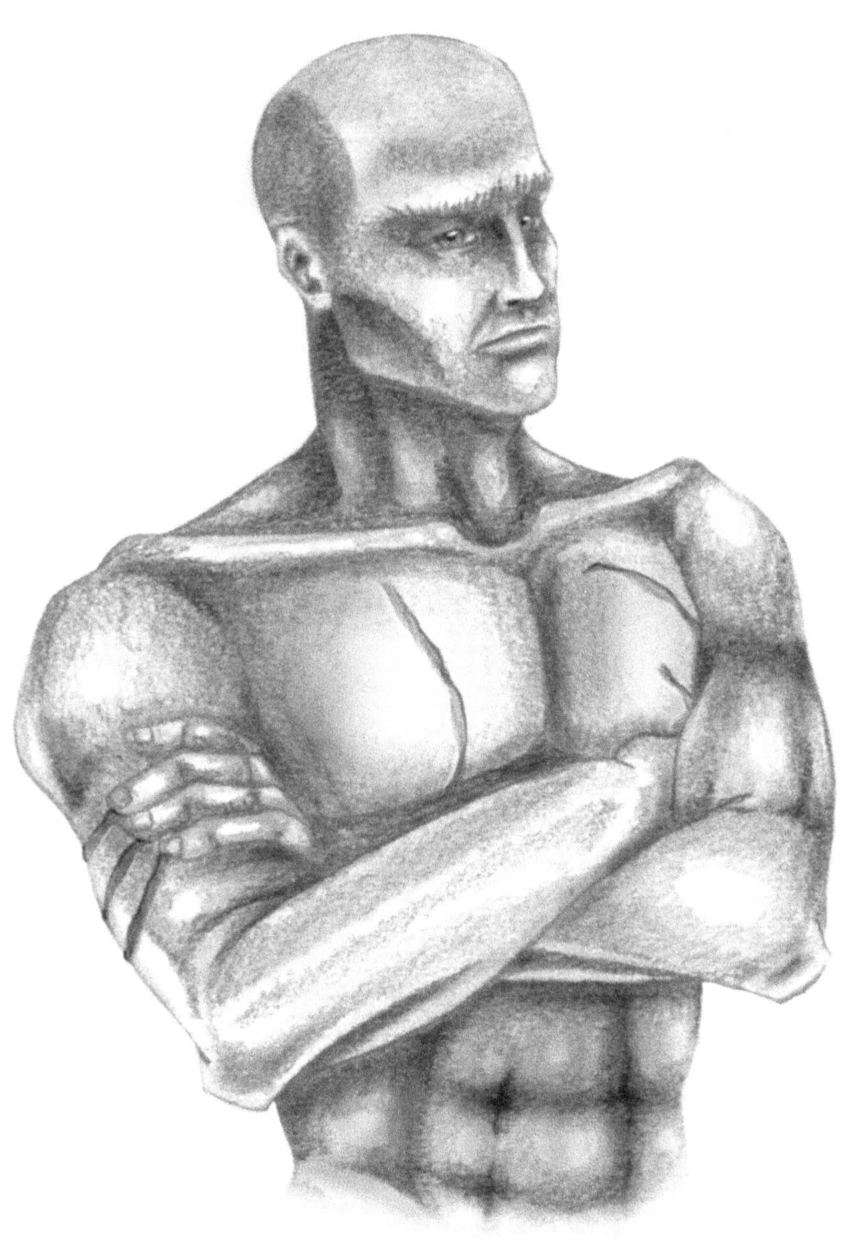

Design: 2024

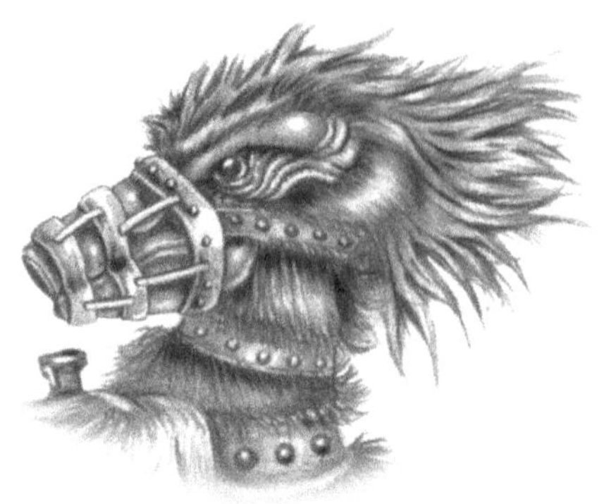

- THE RULEK -

From the very beginning, I decided I wanted to have fantastical creatures in this world.

For the transport of wares, supplies, or humans, air seemed to be the fastest method and most cost-effective, considering these animals could be tamed and proved to be loyal.

I knew I did not want to have a creature with reptilian features. Dragons and wyverns are prevalent in all mediums of fantasy, from books to movies/series to gaming, so I wanted to go in a more falcon/eagle direction.

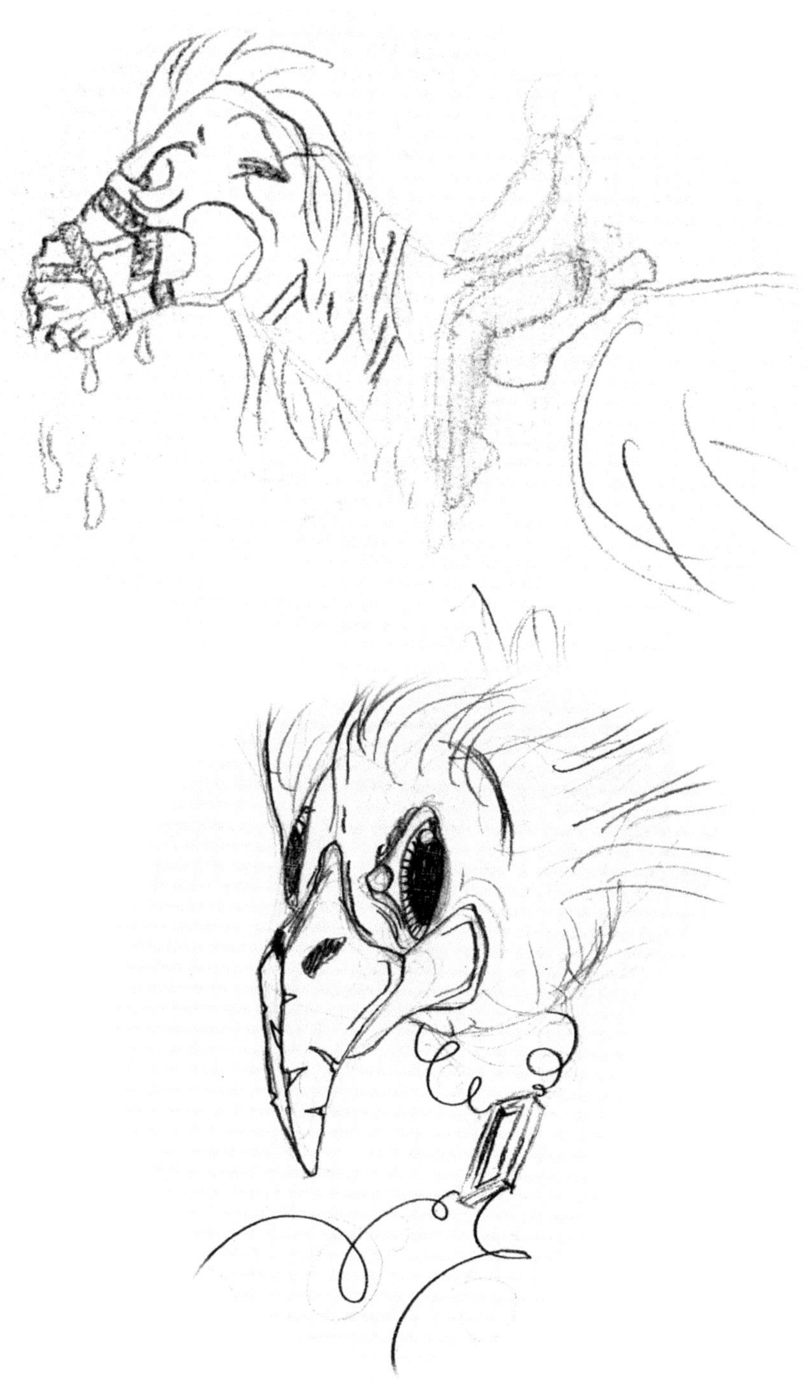

Design: 2016, 2018

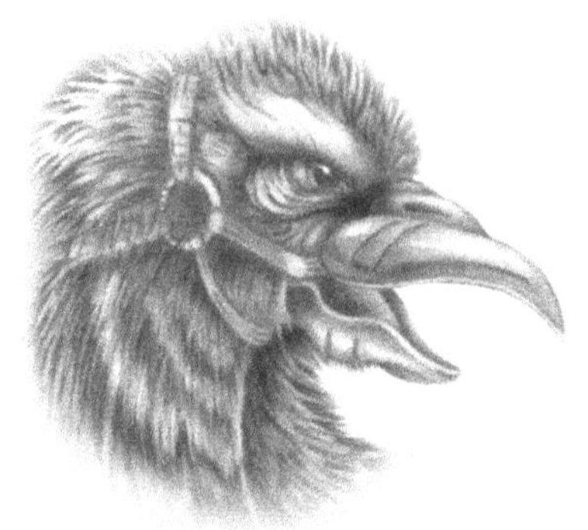

- THE ORAK -

I envisioned a larger ostrich that could carry two humans.

But this animal needed to be swift and agile. After studying the movement of ostriches, I decided they did not fit with what I needed, so I created the orak with a thicker, shorter neck, smaller wings, and a more robust body.

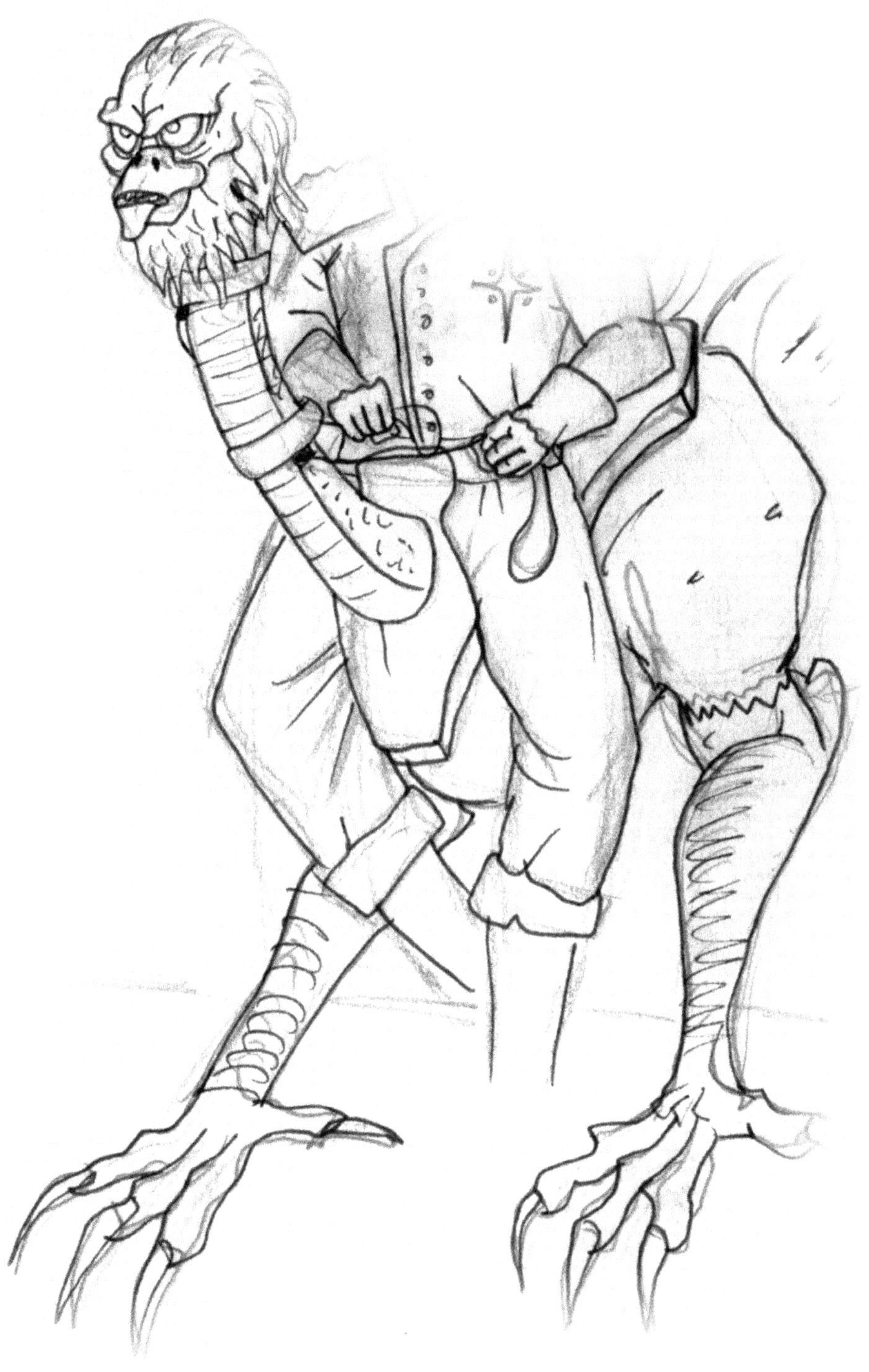

Design: 2018

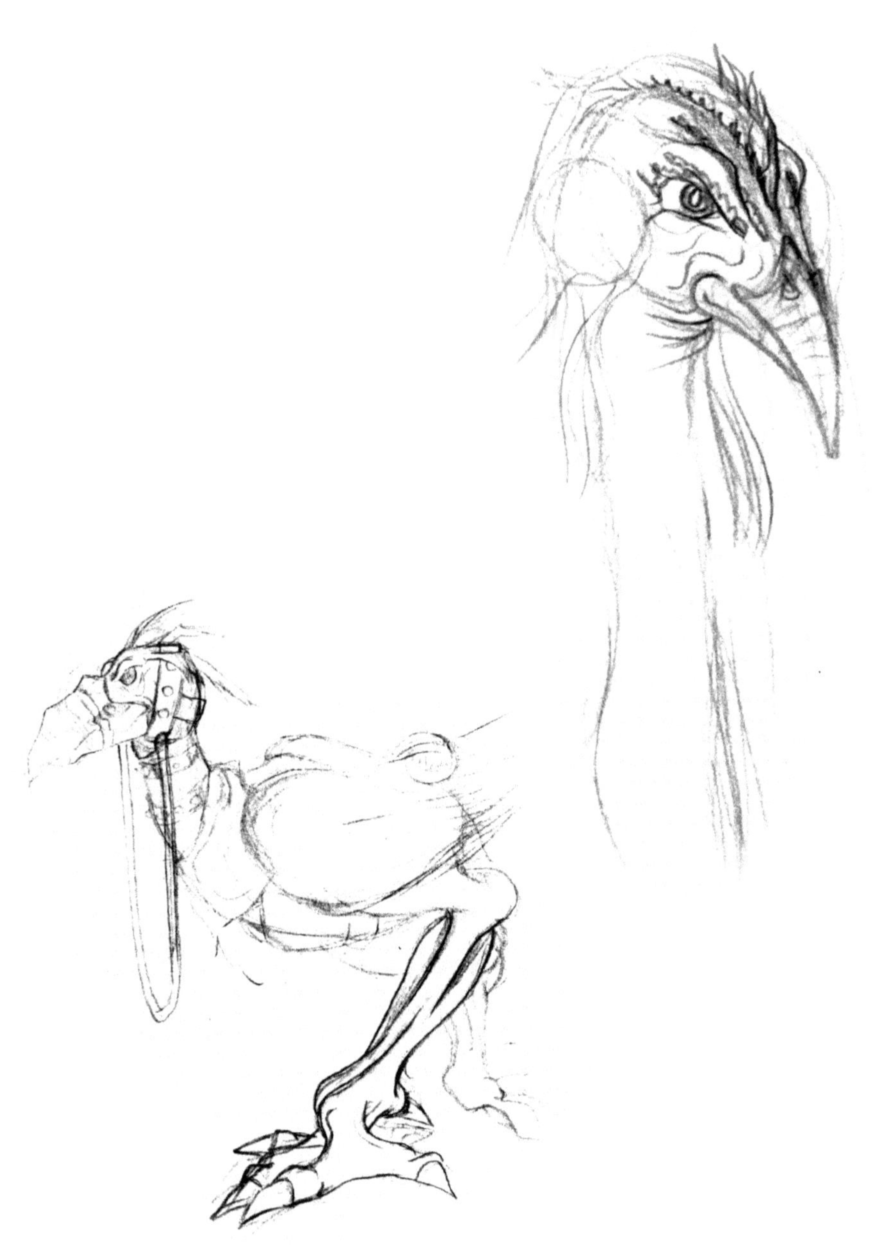

Design: 2021, 2024

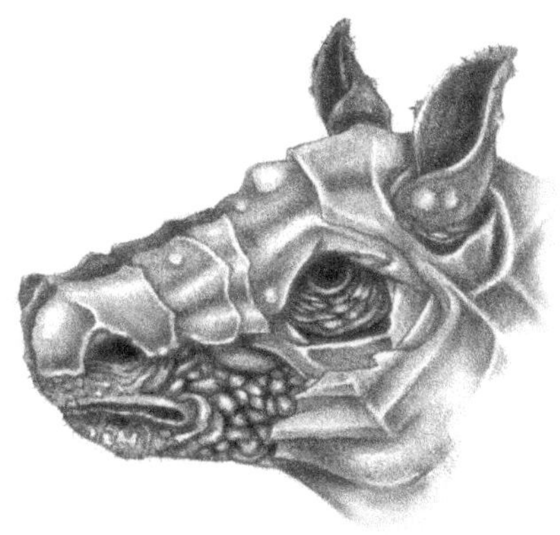

- THE AMSAR -

This creature had more hair and horns than in the way I imagined it. While spending time in Austria when I began writing *Favors Within Ashes*, I had a lot of cows around me (in the countryside), and their robustness inspired me. Not being able to fully decide on the design, I scrapped the amsar, until 2019.

I did not get to draw this animal as often as I did the others because it was a late addition to the story. When writing chapters that now are part of book three, I had one of the characters travel on an animal that was not a rulek or an orak. So I decided to make the amsar a robust and durable animal, and I introduced it throughout the story.

I planned for the amsars to only be found in Admorion, used by Kilean and his loyalists, but they seemed useful in the high-intensity lifestyle of Radiant Star.

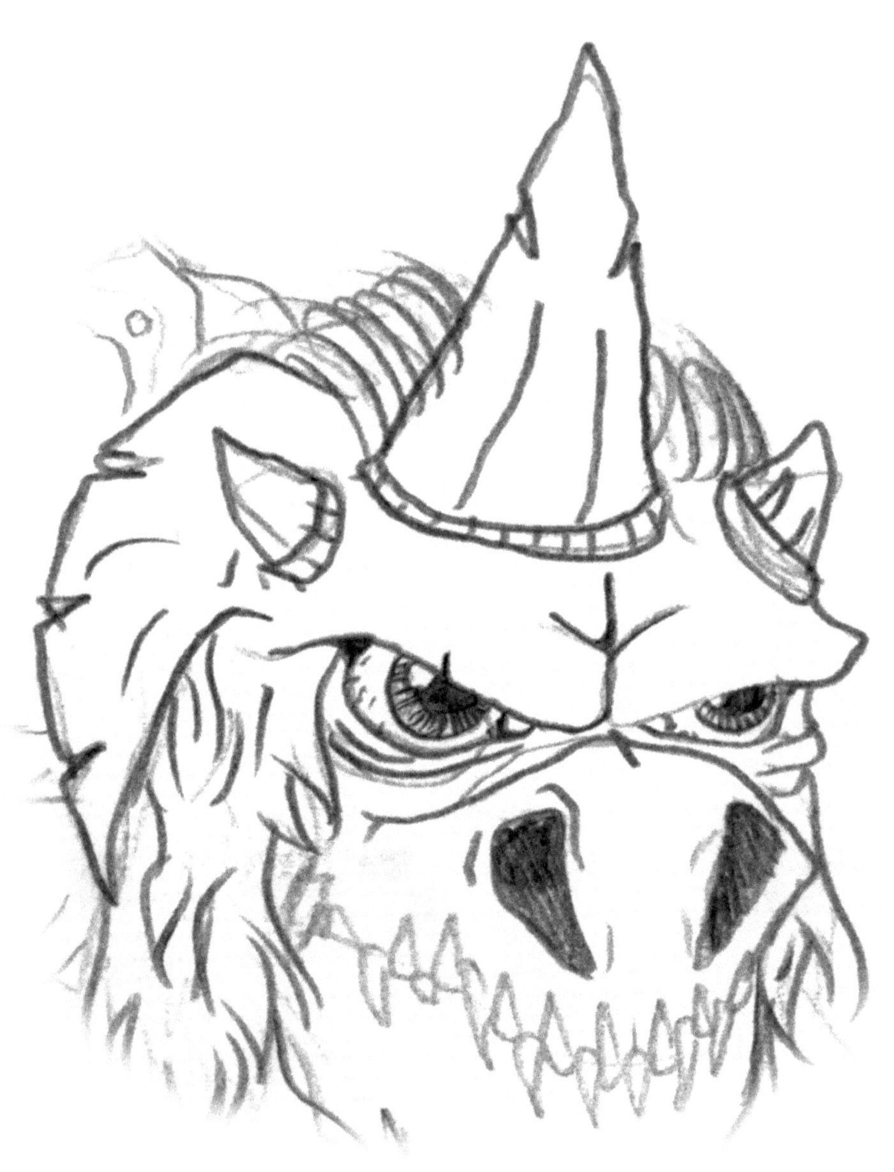

Design: 2020

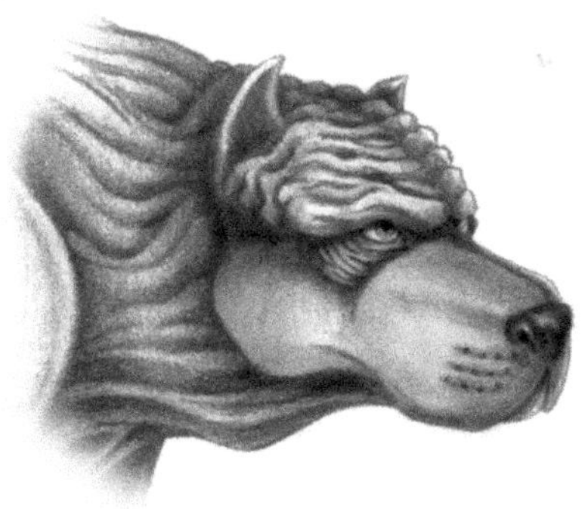

- THE HOUNDS -

My early concepts of the hounds were of larger wolf-like creatures with long hair, not too different from average fighting or guard dogs. I felt as if the long hair would be a disadvantage in battle and opted for shorter hair.

The more they appeared within the story, the more I felt they lost their appearance, which resembled dogs from the real world.

I made the design in August of 2024, and it represents an efficient and obedient killing machine. Nothing more.

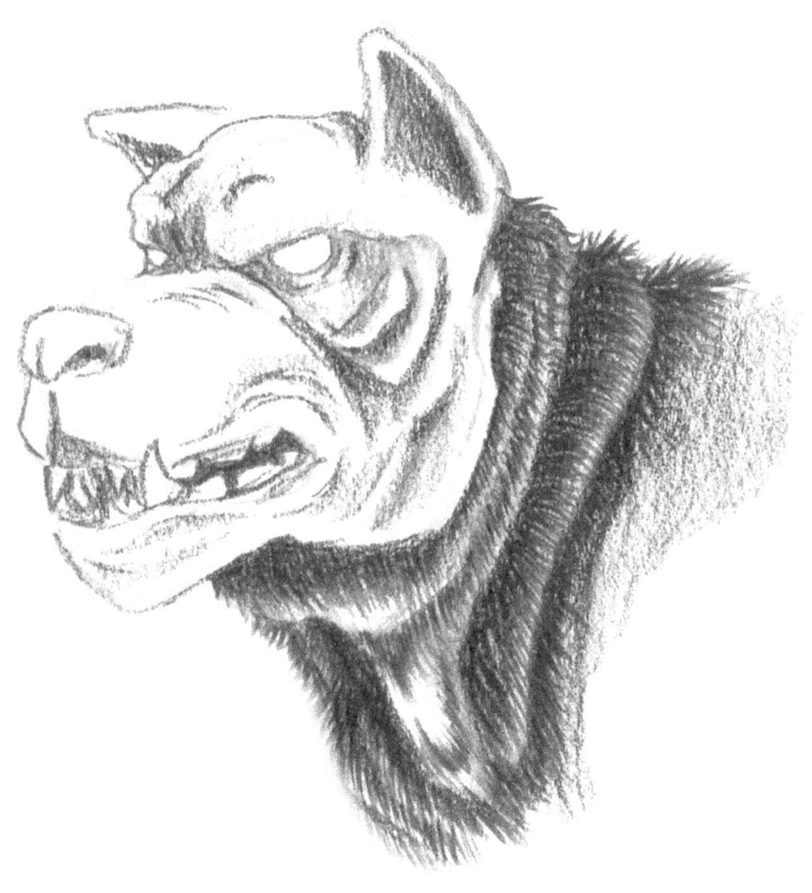

Design: 2024

Bonus: - The Heretics -

The Assassins from my first designs were not that much thought out. I imagined them sneaking under the cover of darkness.

But none could have sneaked inside the temple wearing that attire, so I decided to present them with worker uniforms.

I created more of them in the first drafts of the "Only One" chapter, but gradually through the years, their number was reduced, remaining just two, as it served the plot.

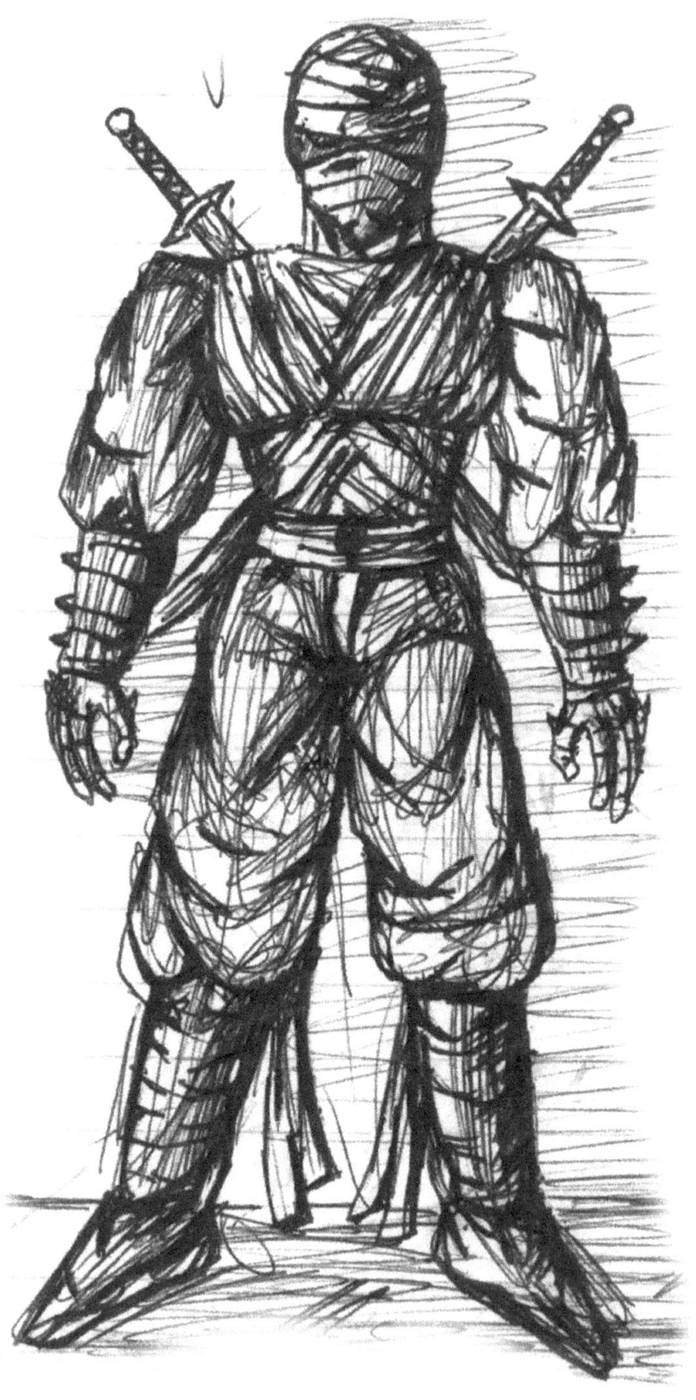

Design: 2005

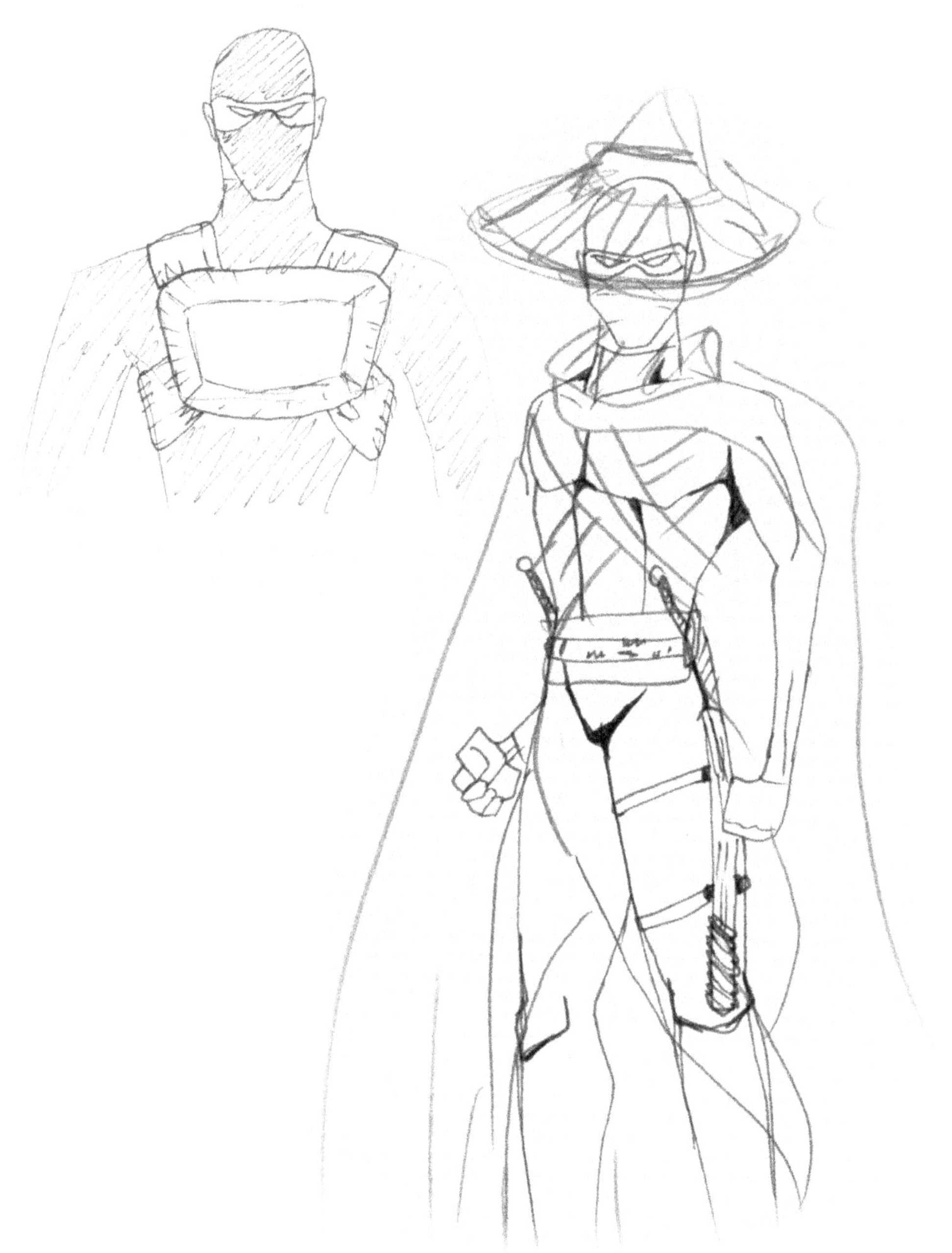

Design: 2018

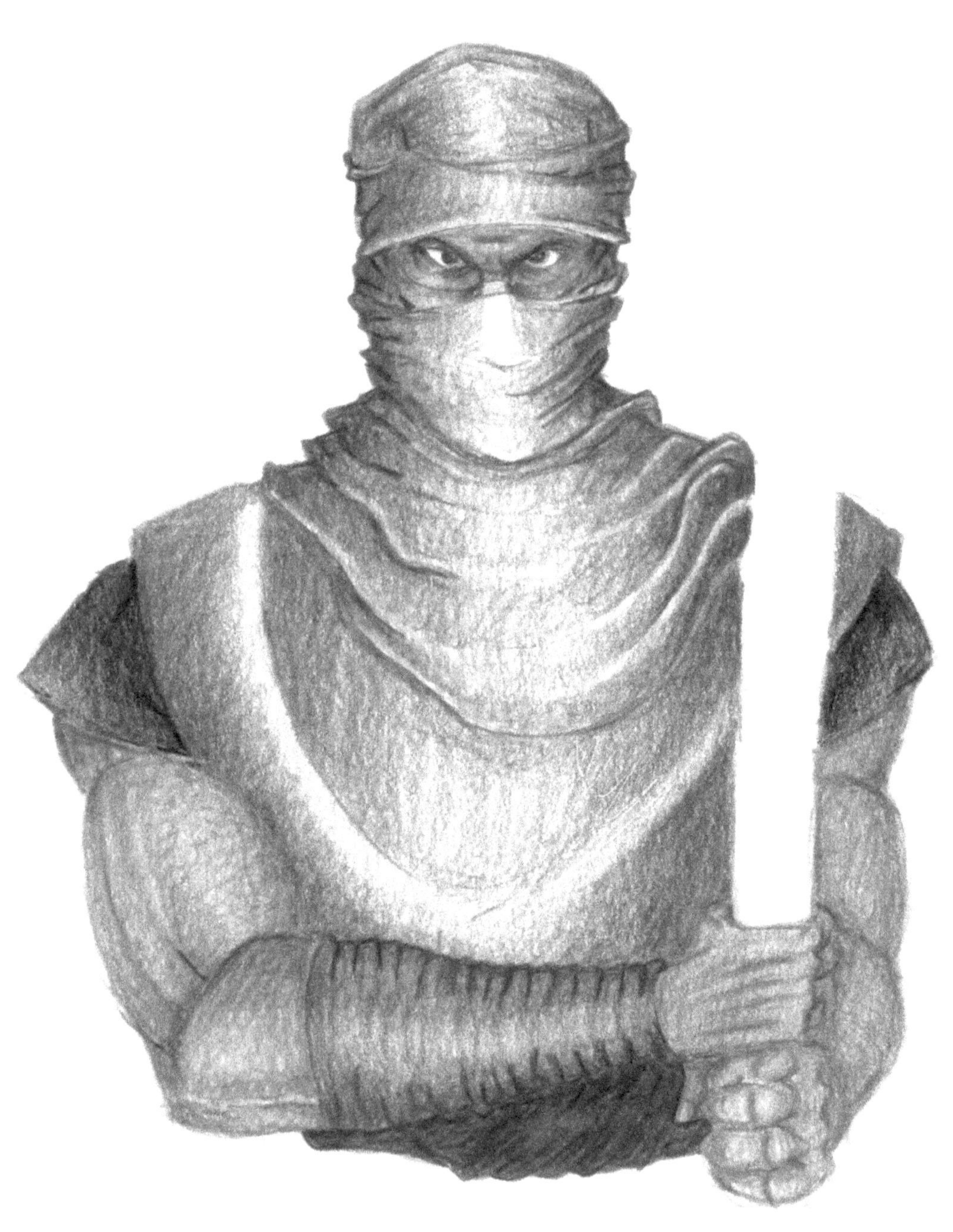

Design: 2021

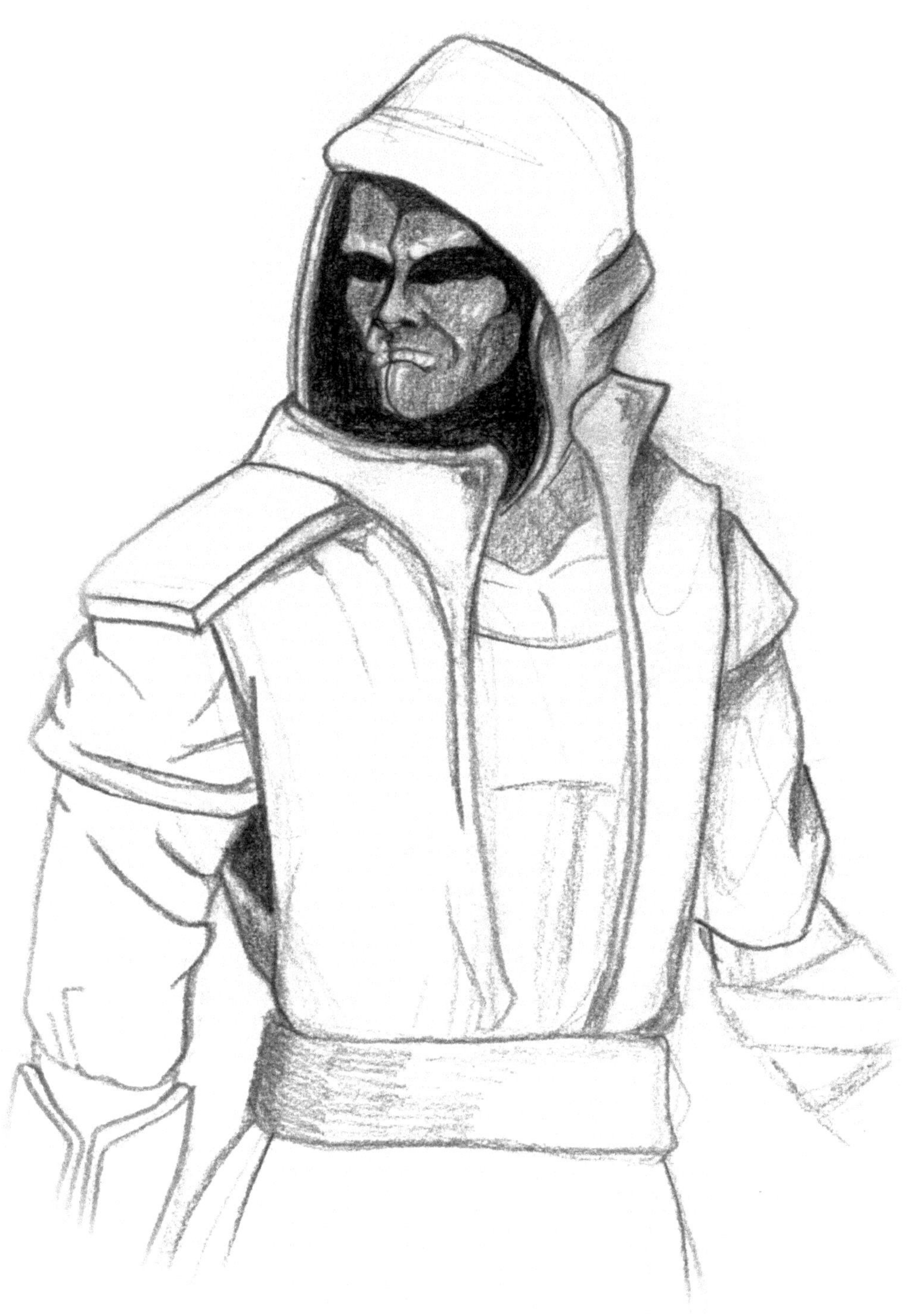

Design: 2021

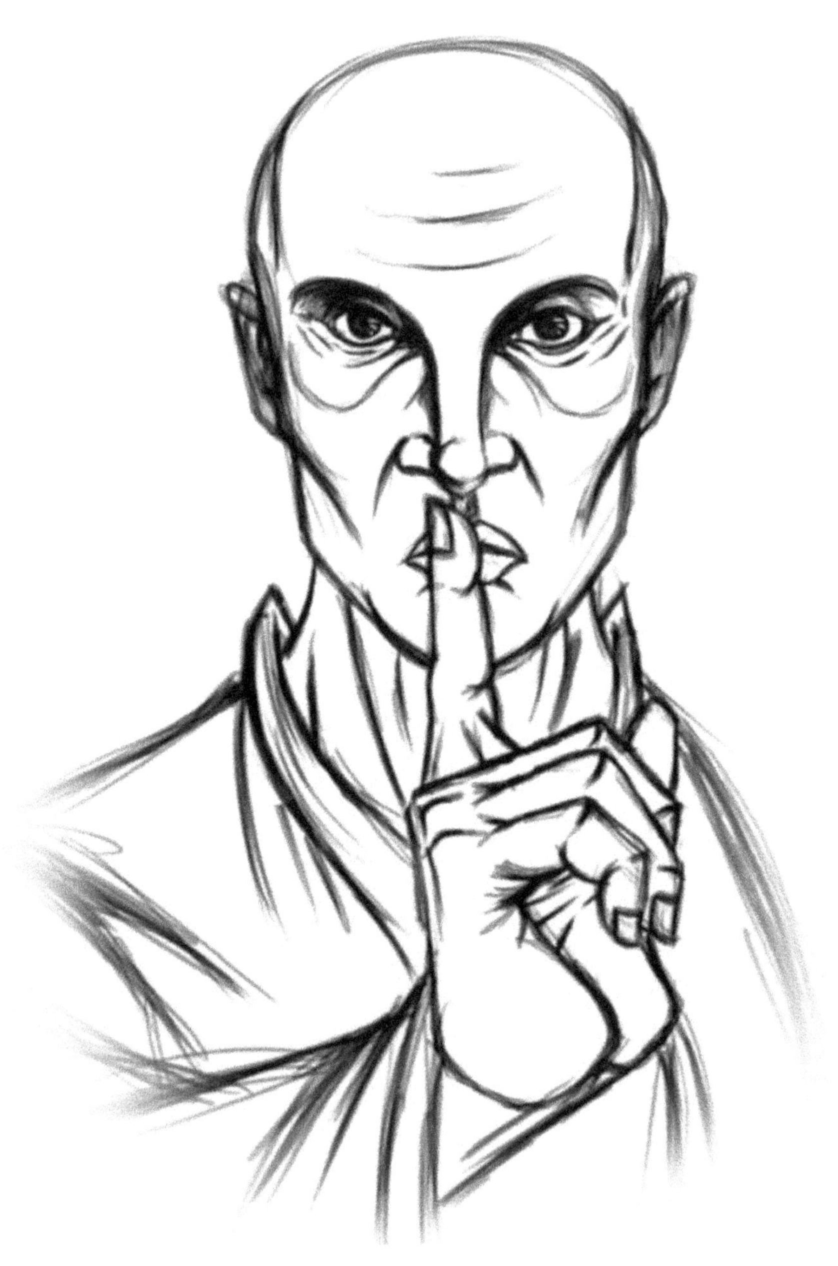

Digital Design: 2022

Bonus: - Book Cover -

The cover design was a difficult process for me. Out of my stubbornness, I wanted to create a cover of my own. Early on, at the sketching and test stages, I knew I wanted to have a movie poster for a book cover. All the POV characters clumped up together, resembling all the blockbuster superhero movies being released in theaters between 2010 and 2022.

The first sketch had me worried. I believed so many characters would look good on an A1 poster, but not that well on a five-by-eight-inch book cover, so I knew I had to redirect my design toward a more simple image, easy to read, understand, and remember.

I wanted to keep it simple and direct. I used to spend a lot of time in the bookstores from the cities I lived in or visited between 2023 and 2024, doing my best to understand what would attract the buyer. One thing that seemed strange was a large part of the bookshelves were all with dark colors and golden elements. I then knew it had to be a white cover. Black and red would work great as a contrast, and I began sketching the Fountain. Many statues of her are scattered throughout Radiant Star and Canoria. The Pillar would have been a little too boring, and I decided just to leave the representation of the Fountain.

Once none of these versions convinced me, I contacted a professional cover designer. After multiple attempts, I found Rafido, and I am forever grateful I got to work with him. Sending my sketches to him, along with a detailed written version of what I was looking for, allowed him to create a cover I was very happy with.

The back side underwent more changes than the front.

The initial blurb was the festivities announcement that can now be read in the "Brother. Son." chapter. Rafido created the illustration of a messenger atop a horse, announcing the event.

I decided including the horse would not fit that well, and I asked Rafido to do an update.

Because I felt the original blurb was not compelling enough and too vague in comparison to the events inside the book, I changed it to its final version, and thus, the back side was modified for a third time.

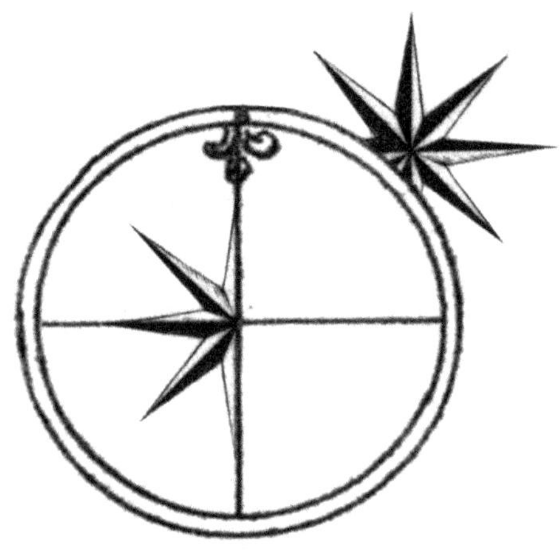

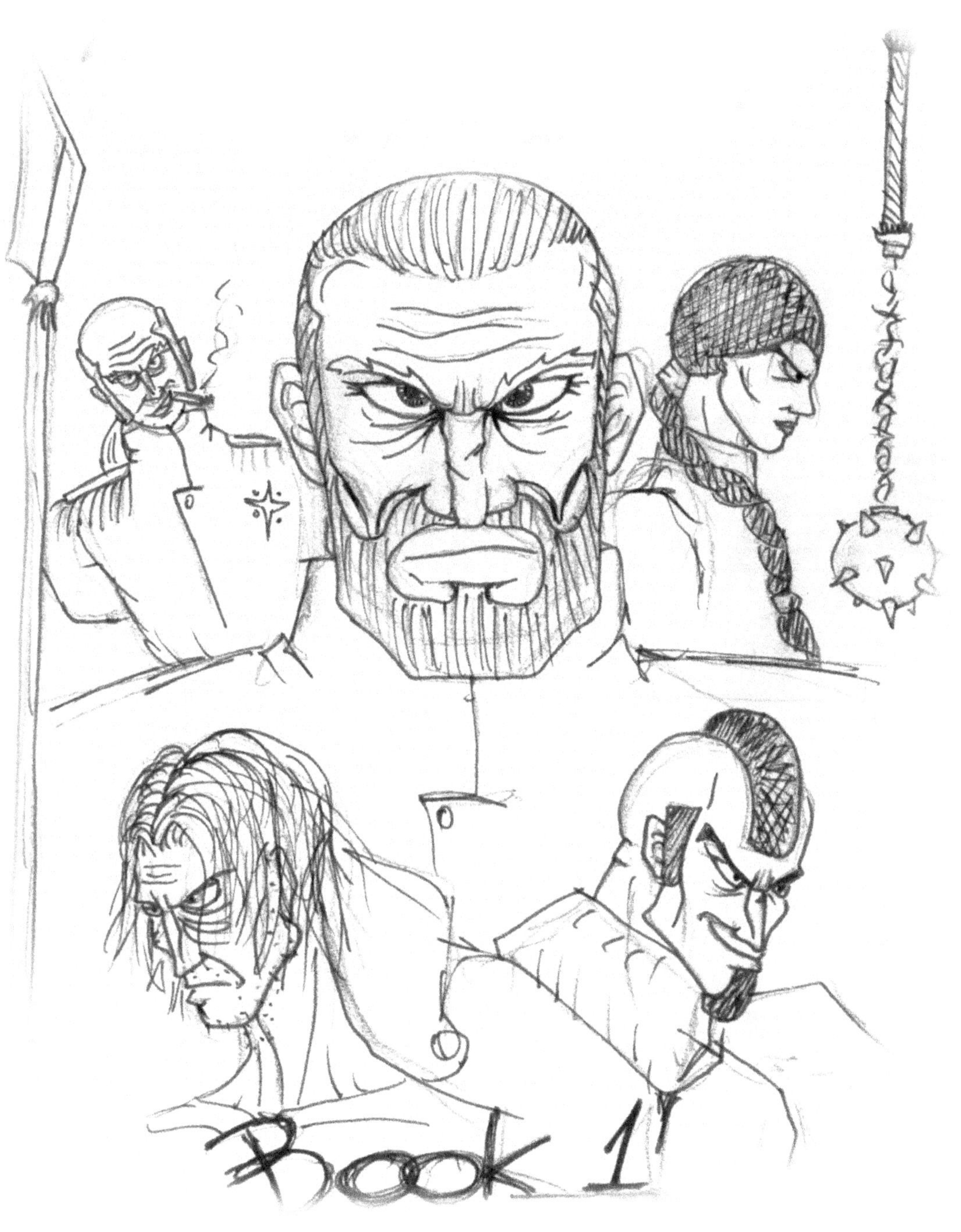

Design: 2019

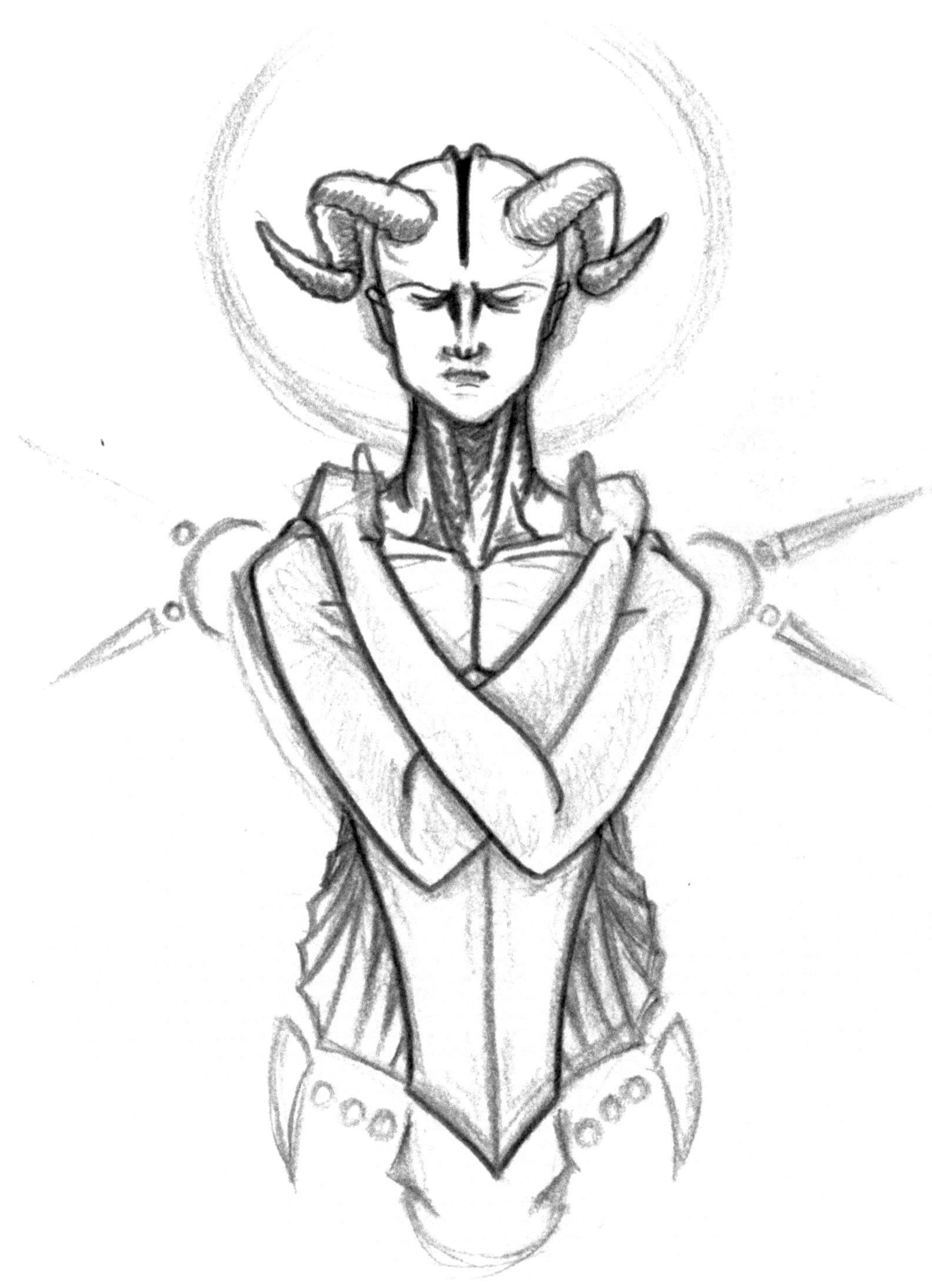

Design: 2021

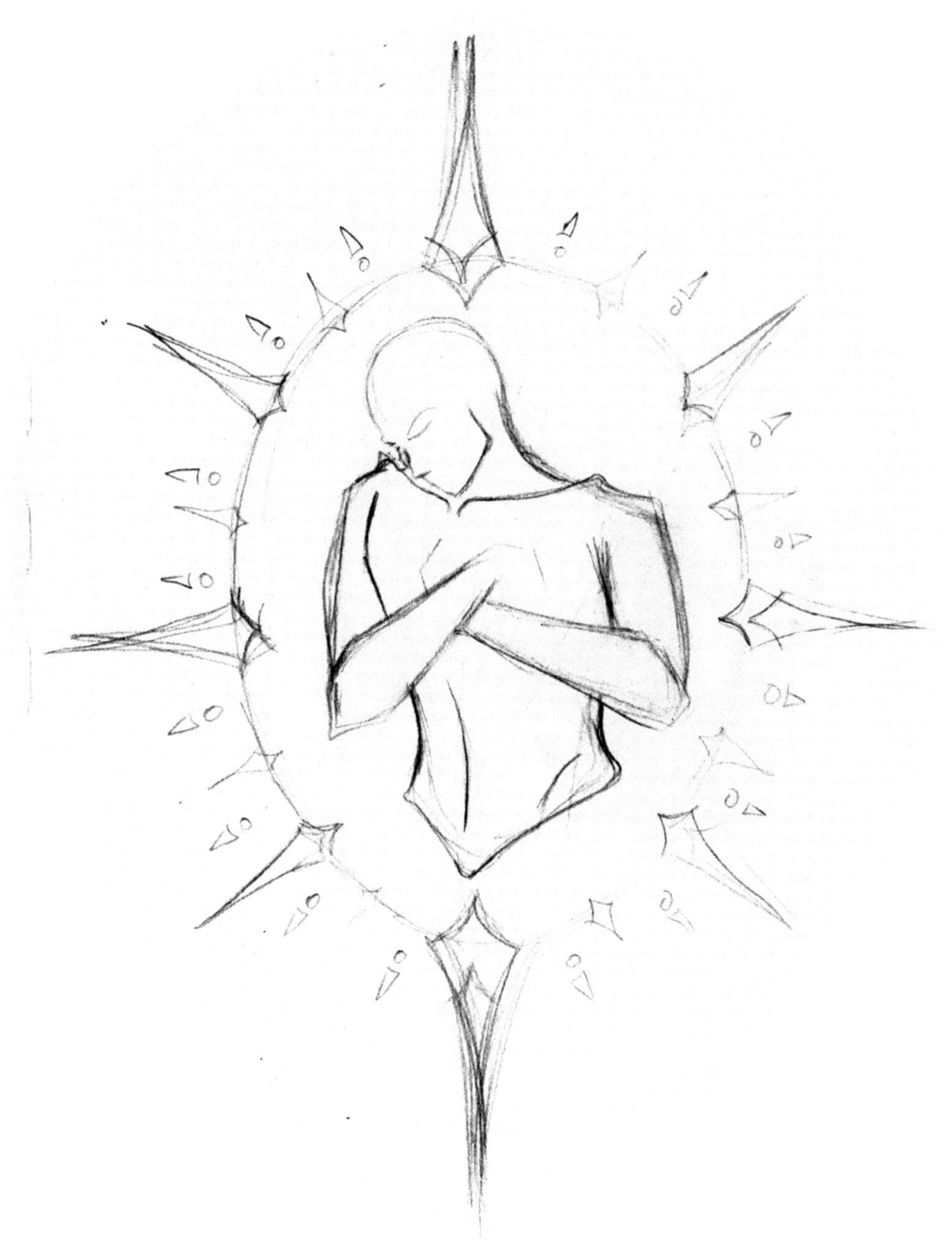

Design: 2022

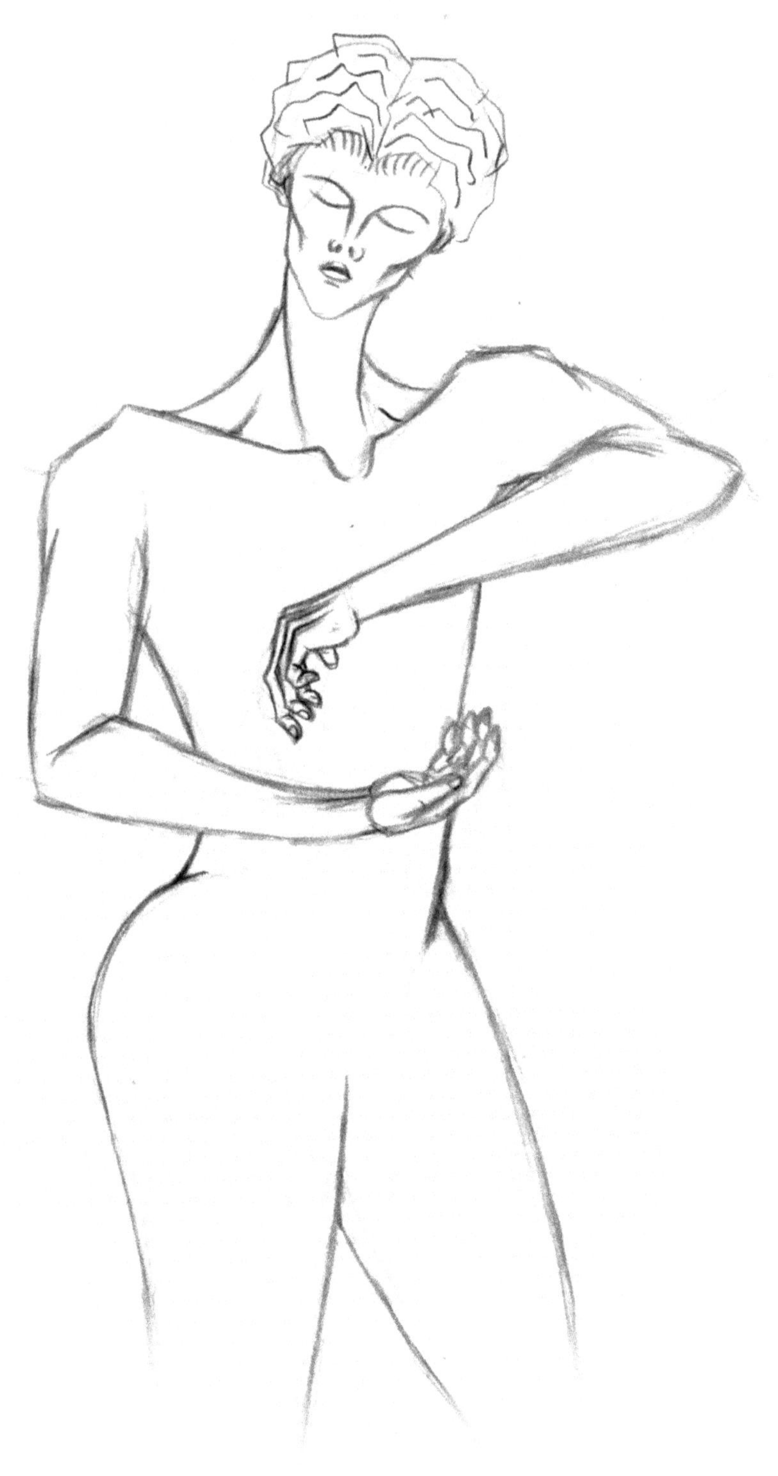

Design: 2022

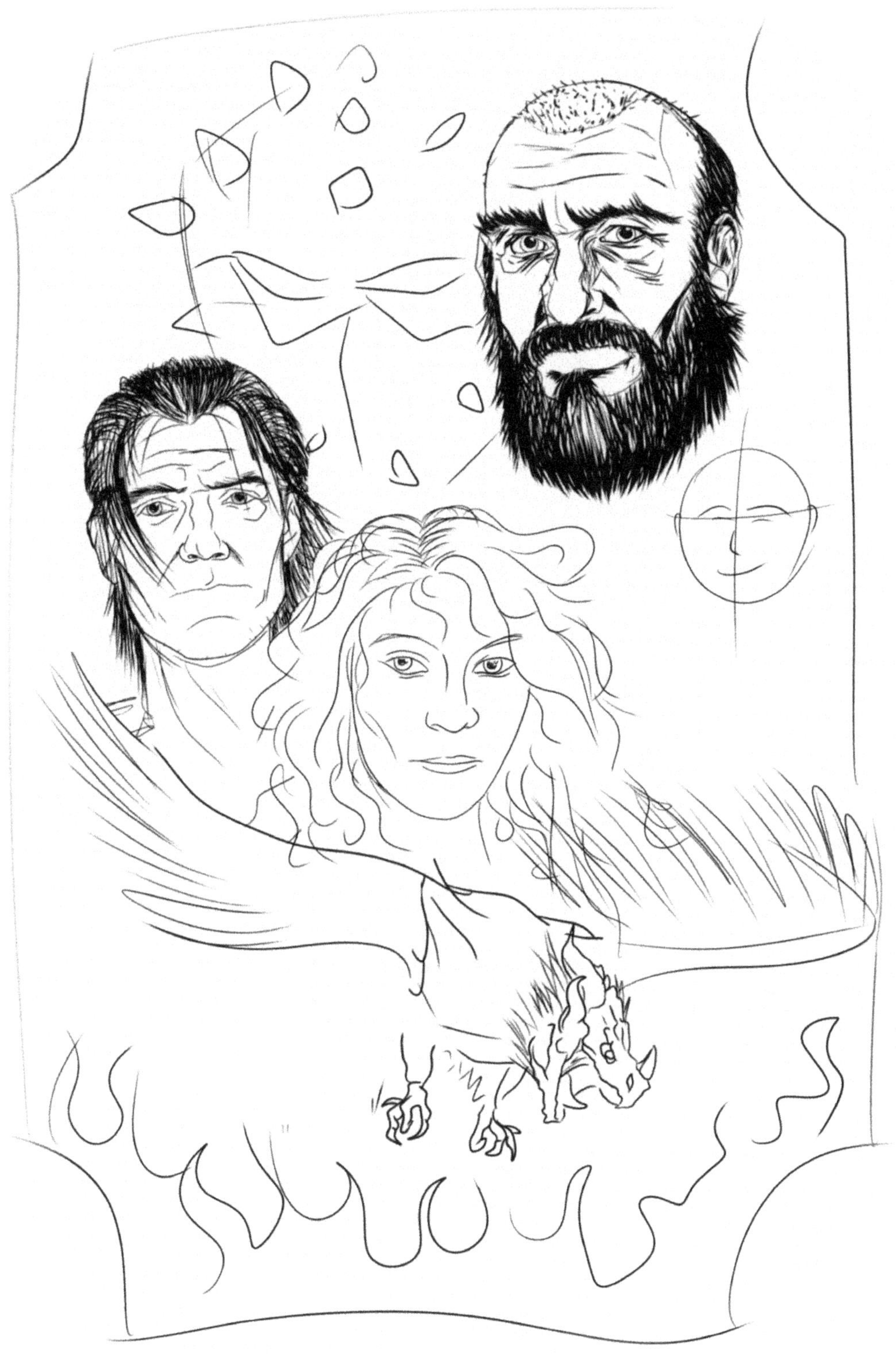

Design: 2024

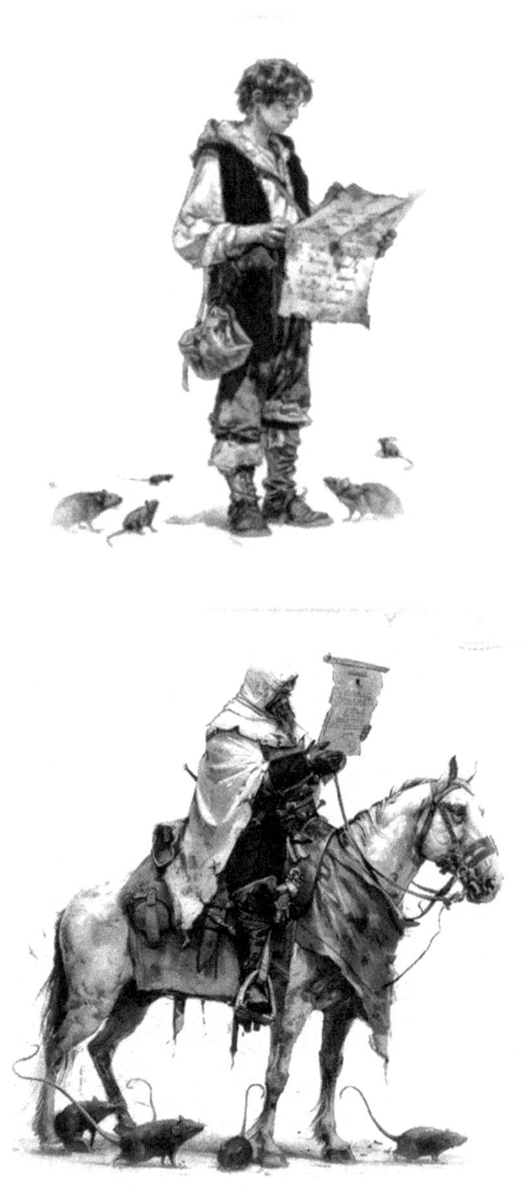

Digital Designs: 2024 (Not hand drawn, made by Rafido)

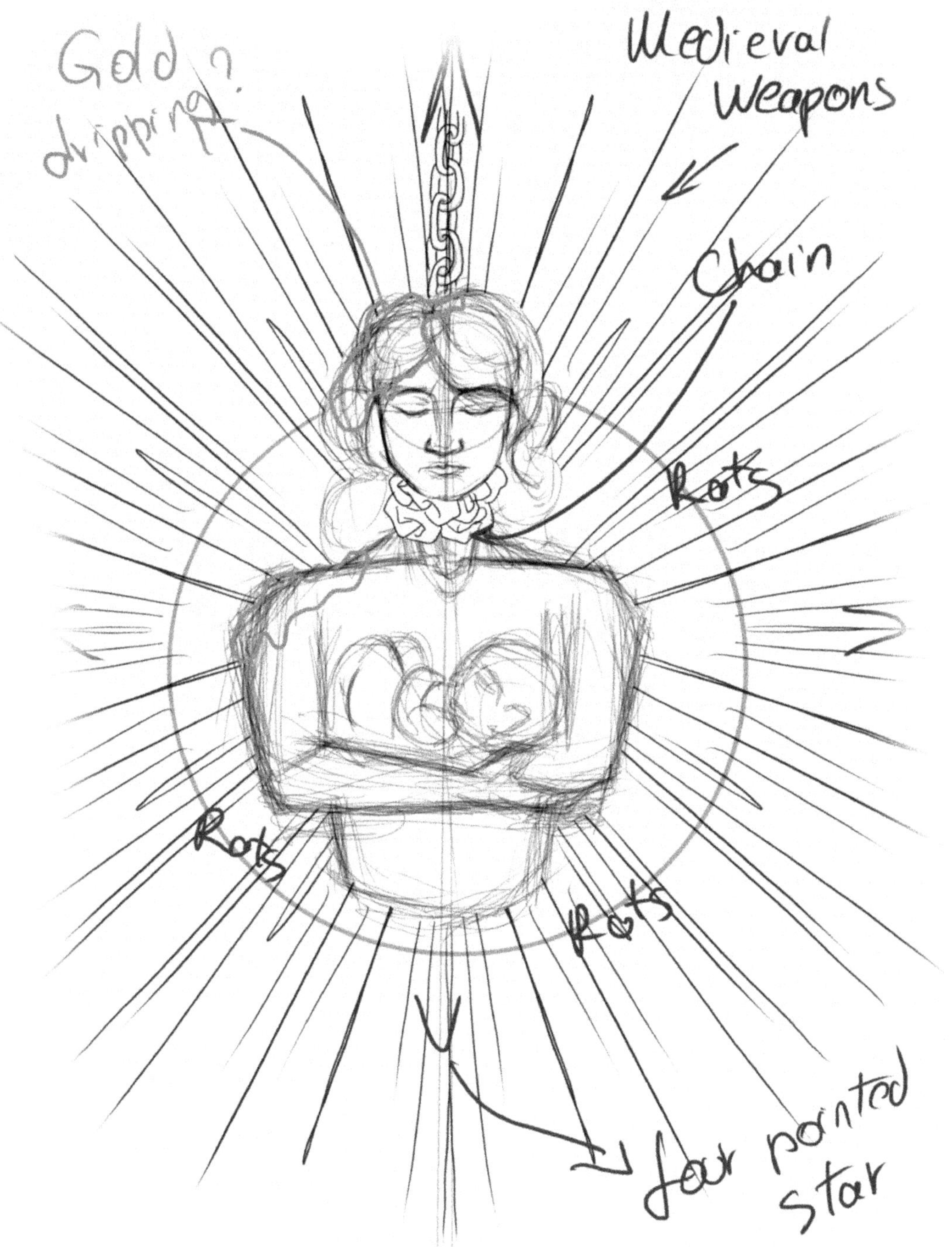

First digital sketch I did for Rafido

Design: 2024

Bonus: - Maps -

2019 was the year I began drawing the first sketches of Dautrinias. I knew roughly I wanted it to be in a vertical position in order to cover more climates.

The map design itself was not a priority from 2019 to 2023. Thus I only sketched basic shapes and sizes, focusing more on location placements and borders.

I found it more difficult to design maps than I'd thought, so I contacted a few cartographers online. None of what they had to offer pleased me, so I decided to just design them myself to the best of my abilities.

After finishing the first rough draft of Radiant Star, I enjoyed the process of working on the map so much that I continued to work on creating maps for Dautrinias, Canoria, Vorandan, and Admorion.

I decided to only have three maps in the first book to avoid confusion and too much information.

The original name of the northern land was called "The Frozen Empire." I changed it in 2024 because I felt the term was used too much in the media I consumed.

The original name of Canoria was Coronia. I had used that word since 2015 because "Coroană" means "crown" in Romanian, so it deviated from that meaning. But after 2020, I changed it to Canoria, for obvious reasons.

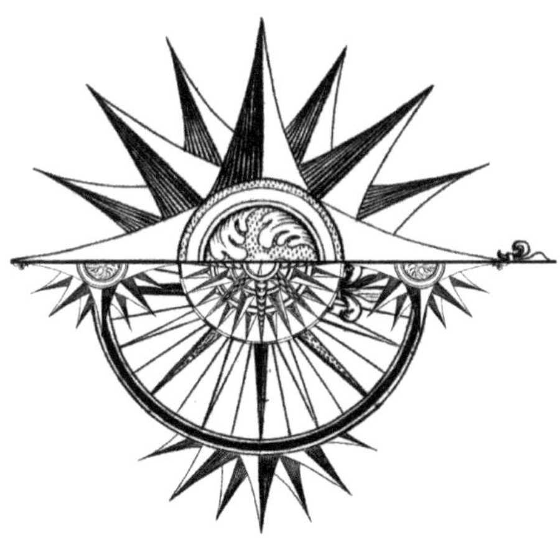

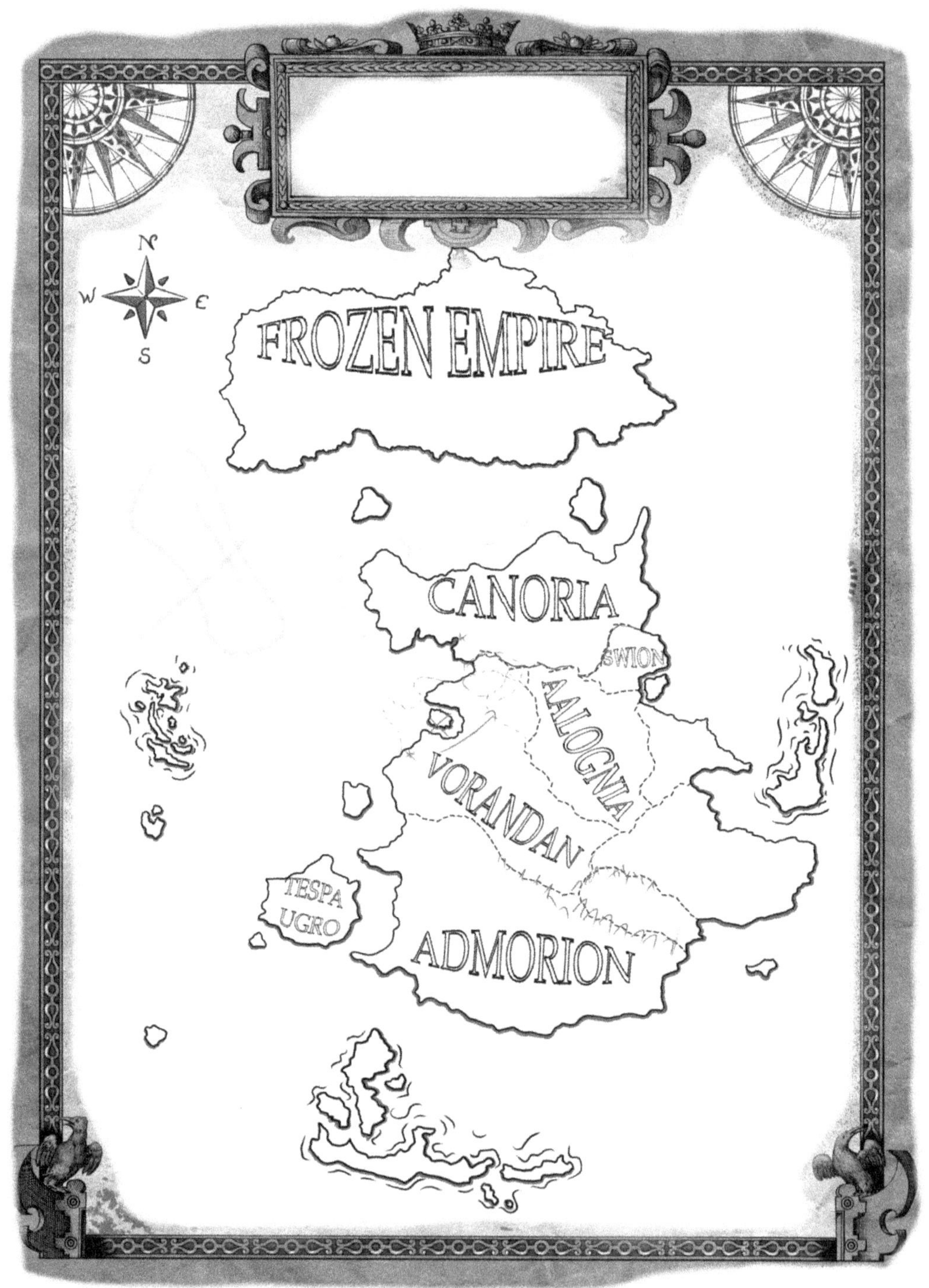

Map Design: 2022   Frame Design: 2023

Bonus: - The Seed of Dreams -

Turia Koar was created in a very strange but special way.

I decided to write the prologue in 2019 regarding a meeting of the Rat Hut inhabitants. At that time, I had undergone surgery in Germany. It was nothing important or life-threatening, but I was stuck in the hospital for a few days, and I thought that would be the right time to write it. I was well into the ending part of what was at that time book two (now, it is in the middle of book three) and wanted a refresher, jumping back to the very beginning.

In the first version of the prologue, the inhabitants of the Rat Huts had a "secret meeting" where Banor Koar would gather his loyal followers for his cause. I felt it was forced, and I did not want to start the book in that way. I wanted something other than that but did not know what.

The second version of the prologue started with a rough and shorter draft of what now is the "Stone" chapter. It was in Marco's POV, not Mara's.

It still didn't feel right.

I returned to the first version, re-reading it. In it, Banor had a speech where he boasted about what he did with the acquired silver and his intentions about raiding the Western Barracks. I told myself, "You take pride in the way you got the silver, but what would your followers think of you if they knew of the method you used?"

And then I thought, what about his wife? She would be devastated. Even if she didn't know what he did, her children were gone.

I kept thinking of Turia's scene throughout my stay in the hospital and the following month after returning home. In January of 2020, I drew the scene of Turia.

I was still sketching for fun and did not invest too much time in the quality of my drawings. I didn't even plan to have illustrations inside the novels. I just had that vision of Turia, and I believed it to be very sad, grounded, and real. I still do. That drawing depicted the world of Dautrinias in a better way than any of the other attempts would.

A few days after, I hung the drawing above my desk monitors at home and wrote the third and final version of the prologue.

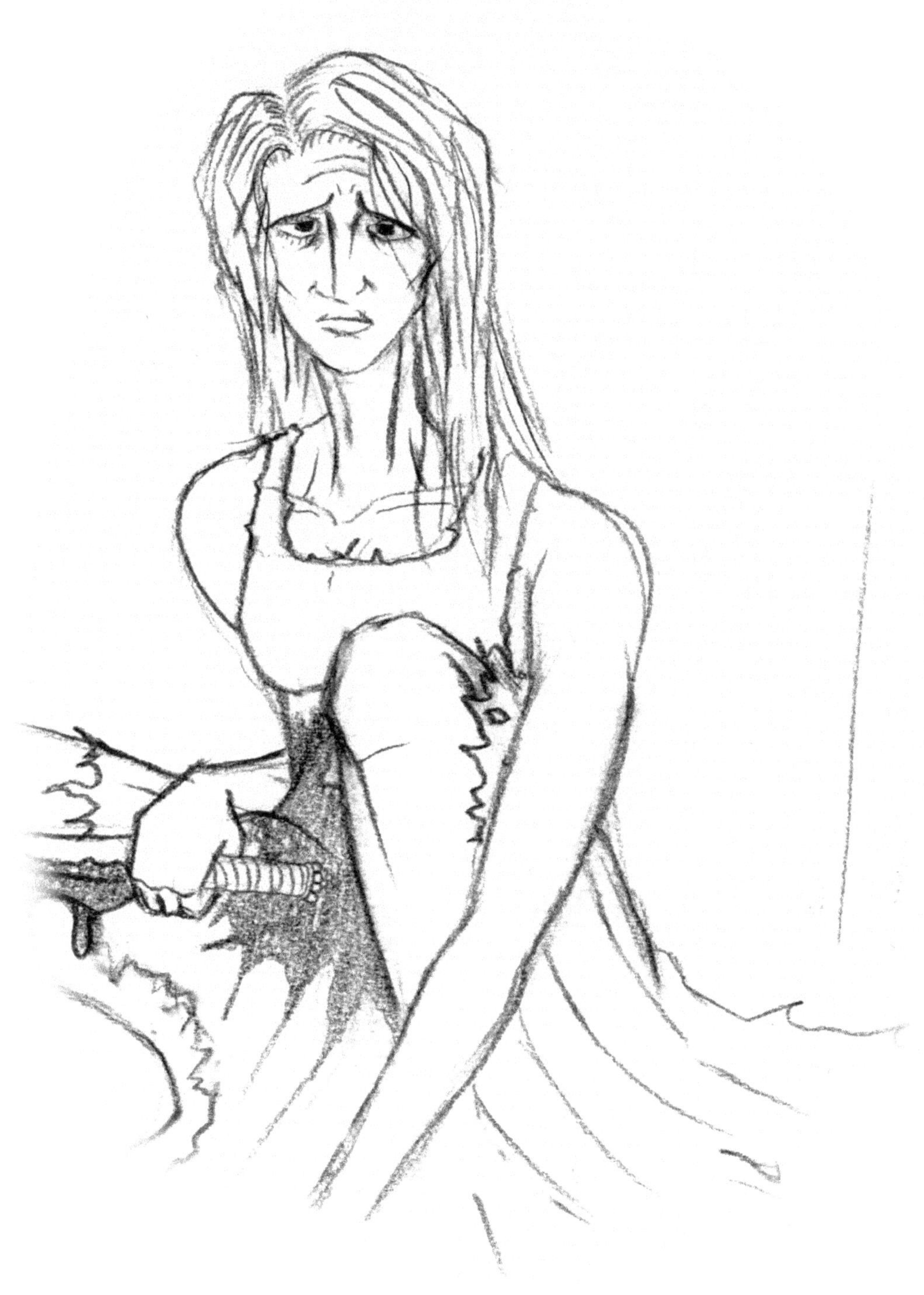

Design: 2020

About the Author

John D. Escu is a Romanian-born tattoo artist and musician living in Germany.

Raised in a military family, John was fascinated as a child with his parents' stories regarding events occurring throughout Medieval Europe, WW1, WW2 and the Romanian Revolution of 1989.

Where his father would focus on warfare and military conquests, his mother would terrify him and his sister with tales and legends of Romanian folklore. Vampires and *Strigois* rising from their graves, roaming the streets under the full moon, gave them both sleepless nights, as they both feared what could be lurking outside their windows.

Fascinated with comic books, Saturday morning cartoons, and early '90s anime, John began drawing and developing his own stories at an early age, creating characters, places, and events that later on could only be presented through the form of novels.

When he is not writing, tattooing, recording music or drawing, John can be found mountain biking in the wilderness of Franconia in Germany.